WAYS OF FORGETTING,
WAYS OF REMEMBERING

WAYS OF FORGETTING, WAYS OF REMEMBERING

JAPAN IN THE MODERN WORLD

JOHN W. DOWER

Requests for permission to reproduce selections from this book should be mailed to:
Permissions Department, The New Press, 38 Greene Street, New York, NY 10013.

Published in the United States by The New Press, New York, 2012
Distributed by Perseus Distribution

LIBRARY OF CONGRESS CATALOGING-IN-PUBLICATION DATA

Dower, John W.
   Ways of forgetting, ways of remembering: Japan in the modern world / John W.
Dower.
      p. cm.
   Includes bibliographical references and index.
   ISBN 978-1-59558-618-6 (hardcover : alk. paper) 1. Japan--History--1945- 2.
Japan--History--1945---Historiography. 3. World War, 1939-1945--Japan. 4. World
War, 1939-1945--Japan--Historiography. 5. World War, 1939-1945--Social aspects--
Japan. 6. World War, 1939-1945--Influence. 7. Collective memory--Japan--History
--20th century. 8. Social change--Japan--History--20th century. 9. Japan--Politics
and government--1945- 10. Japan--Social conditions--1945- I. Title.
   DS889.15.D69 2012
   940.53'52072--dc23
                              2011033861

Now in its twentieth year, The New Press publishes books that promote and enrich
public discussion and understanding of the issues vital to our democracy and to a more
equitable world. These books are made possible by the enthusiasm of our readers; the
support of a committed group of donors, large and small; the collaboration of our
many partners in the independent media and the not-for-profit sector; booksellers,
who often hand-sell New Press books; librarians; and above all by our authors.

www.thenewpress.com

Book design and composition by Bookbright
This book was set in Janson Text

Printed in the United States of America

10 9 8 7 6 5 4 3 2 1

CONTENTS

PREFACE

The eleven essays in this volume, with one exception, were originally published between 1993 and 2005. They follow upon a
previous collection published by The New Press in 1993 under the
title *Japan in War and Peace*.

The one exception is the first entry, an excerpt from a long essay
titled "E.H. Norman, Japan, and the Uses of History" that I wrote
as an introduction to an edited book of Norman's historical writings on Japan published in 1975. Several considerations prompted
including this here. The essay was controversial. It was an early
attempt to wrestle in a case-study way with how the questions historians ask usually reflect what E.H. Carr called the "buzzing" of
their own times.* Reprinting this thus offers a practical starting
point for calling attention to the mottled history of writing about
modern Japan in English between 1940 (when Norman published
the first great scholarly study of the Meiji era and its legacies) and
the late 1960s and early 1970s (when I was a graduate student and
entry-level academic).

---

* E.H. Carr's little book of essays titled *What Is History?*, based on
lectures delivered at Cambridge University and published in 1961, challenged the conceit of historical objectivity and was a provocative contribution to the historiographical debates of the 1960s.

None of the texts have been edited or amended, apart from a few editorial changes and notations, and none of the essay titles have been changed. The "uses of history" phrase in the opening entry is apt in this regard, for it echoes the thematic "ways of forgetting, ways of remembering" title that covers this collection. We use history in many ways: consciously and subjectively, idealistically and perversely, to educate and to indoctrinate. This is addressed through various linguistic portals in today's academic parlance: memory; constructing or reconstructing the past; inventing and reinventing traditions; commemoration and sanitization or historical amnesia; what have you. I rely mostly on plain language here—memory, uses and abuses, how the focused gaze is simultaneously an averted gaze—and, both directly and indirectly, try to convey the complexities of forgetting and remembering through topical treatments of Japan in the modern world.

Most of the selections address Japan at war and after 1945. As such, they also have a great deal to say about the United States—not only about the intense intewrpenetration of the two nations over these many decades, but also about how the Japanese experience is used and misused in English-language commentaries. What is new in this volume are the introductions to each entry, in which I look back on my own compositions "as history" and reflect on the milieu in which they were composed.

January 2012

WAYS OF FORGETTING,
WAYS OF REMEMBERING

1

E.H. NORMAN, JAPAN, AND THE USES OF HISTORY

E.H. Norman, appointed Canadian ambassador to Egypt in 1956, committed suicide in Cairo on April 4, 1957, after being accused in Senate hearings in the United States of being untrustworthy and possibly a Communist spy. He was forty-seven years old, and had been deeply involved in addressing the crisis that erupted in 1956 when the United Kingdom, France, and Israel invaded Egypt after the Egyptian president Gambal Nassar nationalized the Suez Canal. Norman's mentor and staunch supporter, the Canadian diplomat and later prime minister Lester Pearson, was awarded the 1957 Nobel Peace Prize for his leading role in creating the United Nations emergency force that defused the crisis and became the prototype for later UN peacekeeping activities.

The McCarthyist accusations against Norman referred back to the mid-1930s, when Norman became involved in left-wing and Communist activities while a student at Cambridge University's Trinity College, where he was awarded a B.A. in classics in 1935. Born and raised in Japan in a missionary family, and fluent in Japanese, in 1933 Norman had completed an earlier B.A. in classics at the University of Toronto's Victoria College. In 1936, he became a graduate student at Harvard, where he earned a doctorate in Japanese history in 1940. His dissertation was published that same year by the International Secretariat of the Institute of Pacific Relations, under the title Japan's Emergence as a Modern State: Political and Economic Problems of the Meiji

Period. *Stylistically eloquent, and intellectually enriched by Norman's deep familiarity with Western history and historiography,* Japan's Emergence *drew on a range of Japanese sources including scholarship by Marxist historians who until the 1930s—when the imperial state succeeded in suppressing the "dangerous thoughts" of the academic and political left—had engaged in rigorous debates about state formation, authoritarianism, capitalism, and "incomplete revolution" in the decades that followed the Meiji Restoration of 1868.*

Between 1940 and 1949, despite now being embarked on a diplomatic career, Norman wrote a number of incisive long essays on late feudal and early modern Japan. On the one hand, he devoted close attention to the "feudal background" of post-Restoration Japanese politics. At the same time, however, he took care to introduce vivid case studies of grassroots protest and agitation. One of these treatments dealt with millennial movements ("mass hysteria"); another with an iconoclastic eighteenth-century physician and scholar (Andō Shōeki) outraged by the social injustice of his times; another with peasant protest and the post-Restoration introduction of military conscription in a society hitherto dominated by a samurai caste; yet another with one of the earliest radical right-wing societies of the modern era (the Genyōsha). The "freedom and people's rights" (jiyū minken) *movement of the 1870s and 1880s that the Meiji oligarchs effectively stifled by creating a Prussian-inspired constitutional monarchy under the emperor was a major example, in Norman's telling, of an indigenous tradition of liberal political protest.*

Following Japan's defeat in 1945, Norman was posted to Tokyo as the Canadian representative to the U.S.-led Allied occupation that lasted until 1952. There, his personal counsel coupled with his historical writings—especially Japan's Emergence—*were regarded with enormous respect. In the critical early years of the occupation, Norman's pioneer study of 1940 became a bible of sorts to many reformist American planners and administrators who found themselves engaged in attempting to "democratize" Japan. This was an exceptional moment indeed: where an authoritarian and aggressively expansionist state had been shattered; where the conquerors held unprecedented authority; where progressive political idealism prevailed for a while; and where pragmatic thinking about the future as well as the here and now demanded keen analysis of the nation's recent and more distant past.*

Norman's writings spoke to this challenging moment in several compelling ways. His argument that the Meiji state had imposed "revolution from above," and in the process snuffed out a more thoroughgoing revolution from below, encouraged postwar reformers who saw the occupation as an opportunity to complete this thwarted revolution by doing away with the undemocratic institutional legacies of the Meiji state. Simultaneously, his documentation of popular protests dating back to feudal times gave substance to the argument that promoting democracy, pluralism, and greater egalitarianism in the form of civil and human rights in defeated Japan was not an ethnocentric exercise in trying to impose alien "Western" beliefs and values on an incorrigibly backward and inherently hierarchical society. Far more than most of his missionary, diplomatic, and academic peers, Norman conveyed genuine respect for the aspirations and capabilities of ordinary Japanese. His Japanese acquaintances, many of them scholars, spoke and wrote movingly about him after his death. In the words of one of these mourners, a good part of Norman's writings on Japan had been "in praise of lesser names."

My interest in Norman was kindled in the late 1960s, and the excerpt that follows here is taken from a long rumination—almost one hundred pages overall—by a newly minted historian just embarking on an academic career. In the small world of Japanese studies, this essay was regarded as mildly incendiary. It was, in any case, impolitic; and now, decades later, it may seem to be little more than a musty sample of historiographic debates of a bygone time. Still, I have titled this collection Ways of Forgetting, Ways of Remembering, *and this early piece marks a moment shortly after I had turned to history from an original concentration on literature— the moment, more or less, when I began asking myself what doing history really entails as a discipline, and how fixing on a subject simultaneously involves neglecting other subjects and lines of inquiry. In Japanese academic parlance, which I was absorbing at the time, this is called* mondai ishiki, *"problem consciousness." Remembering—or constructing or reconstructing the past, as we would say these days—inevitably involves neglecting and forgetting. The focused gaze and averted gaze go hand in hand.*

The interest in Norman, in any case, came unexpectedly and from divergent directions. For by the late 1960s, Norman himself was for all practical purposes forgotten in U.S. academic circles. Japan's Emergence *was out of print. Neither this nor any of Norman's other writings were assigned or discussed in the graduate history classes I attended at Harvard; I do not recall them even being recommended. There were ostensibly plausible reasons for this virtual blackout, of course: a fair number of historians, political scientists, and economists writing in English had entered the Japan field since Norman's pioneer work was published, and they tapped into a range of new primary and secondary Japanese resources that Norman himself, with his catholic eclecticism, would surely have found fascinating. At the same time (as I would discover), the thrust of this postwar and post-occupation scholarship was fundamentally hostile to Norman's critique of the authoritarian legacies of the Meiji state.*

It is possible to name and quite precisely date the problem consciousness that ruled the day during my years as a neophyte student of Japanese history. The methodological gospel was "modernization theory," and six international conferences beginning in 1960 were devoted to applying this to Japan; this is where the bulk of funding for historical research lay. In the essay from which the excerpt that follows here was taken, I spelled out my reservations about modernization theory by bringing Norman back into the picture—by "remembering" him, as it were; and more particularly, by calling attention to the kind of questions he posed, which had negligible place in a "modernization of Japan" paradigm that emphasized the positive accomplishments of the prewar state rather than its calamitous descent into repression, militarism, and war. The full essay appeared as the introduction to a volume of Norman's writings I edited and published in 1975 under the title Origins of the Modern Japanese State: Selected Writings of E.H. Norman, *in which* Japan's Emergence *in its entirety was brought back into print.*

As it happened, this lengthy introduction was not what I originally envisioned, and turned out to be a learning experience in how putting words to history may lead in unanticipated directions. Using Norman to critique modernization theory was not a simple polemical tactic, that is, for I was not initially drawn to his writing with this in mind. On the con-

trary, I first encountered Japan's Emergence *serendipitously after deciding to conduct research that included the occupation of Japan. This opened my eyes to Norman's influence in the 1940s, which in turn introduced me in the most concrete way imaginable to the "uses of history"—a phrase and practice that oddly did not get much explicit attention in our classes. Reprinting this monograph, I thought, would be a useful contribution to future understanding of U.S. policymaking in the early occupation. This was the almost humdrum beginning that ultimately culminated in the long disquisition about the uses of history not only in Norman's time, but in my own. I began writing what the publisher and I anticipated would be a short preface during winter break in 1973 (the year following completion of my dissertation)—and finished writing during spring recess, albeit over a full year later.*

Part of this unexpectedly prolonged labor involved finding and reading everything Norman had written as a historian, including talks he had given in Japan. Part, obviously, involved rethinking the uses of Japanese history in my own Cold War times, a quarter century after Norman's heyday. It is entertaining to recall now how passionately modernization theory was proselytized as "empirical" and "value-free" scholarship in those years, but to challenge this then was heresy. The most unsettling historical byway that demanded exploration, however, was how McCarthyism had crippled the field of Asian studies (as well as Asia policy overall) in the United States. Norman's suicide in 1957 gave a tragic human face to this witch hunt, but the broader inquisition began several years earlier in the hysterical U.S. response to the "loss of China" to Communism in 1949. This devastating assault on the Asia field included Senate hearings in 1952 that targeted the several decades of wide-ranging critical scholarship and commentary on Asia conducted by the prestigious Institute of Pacific Relations, under whose auspices Japan's Emergence *had been published. (The attack on Norman that precipitated his suicide came in a later round of Senate hearings.)*

This bitter history also was never mentioned in our graduate classes. It was understandably painful to senior scholars. It also was awkward to acknowledge—for, at least as I came to see it, this helped explain why modernization theory fit so nicely with Cold War policy, and how it helped bring the funding that McCarthyism had cut off back into the field of Asian studies. Norman and his cohort in the 1940s had been riveted by the disastrous outcome of imperial Japan's modernization and Westernization—as well as by the misery, corruption, and chaos in China that paved the way for the Communist success. The modernization theorists, by contrast, were fixated on repudiating Marxist theory and simultaneously delineating Japan's fundamentally positive accomplishments ever since the Meiji era—thus, ipso facto, valorizing Japan as a non-Western capitalist counter-model to China. Where Japan was concerned, Norman and his generation asked: what went wrong? The modernization theorists essentially focused on asking: what went right? It all depends, in the end, on the questions.

Norman is now largely forgotten again in the United States.* So is the impact of McCarthyism on the field of English-language Asian studies, and so is the modernization-theory vogue that seemed to be the be-all and end-all of scholarly inquiry when I was entering the field. Indeed, the turbulent 1960s in which my generation of American academics came of age—roiled by the Vietnam War, civil rights movement, and feminist movement—has been pretty much consigned to the memory hole where doing history, certainly Asian history, is concerned. But the uses and abuses of history, the inescapable politics of scholarship, the need to constantly ask what is not being asked—these never go away. That, at least, is what I concluded when discovering E.H. Norman's writings led me to inquire how we forget, and how we remember, the past.

*　　*　　*

---

* He is not forgotten in Canada, where his scholarship draws more attention and his tragic death elevated him, in some circles, to the status of a national hero victimized by American political hysteria. In 2000, twenty-five years after I brought *Japan's Emergence* back into print, the University of British Columbia Press published a "60th Anniversary Edition" of this pioneer text, edited by Lawrence T. Woods and including as an epilogue ten short reflections on Norman and his work "then and now." I contributed one of these essays.

The publication of *Japan's Emergence as a Modern State* in 1940 established E.H. Norman, then thirty-one years old, as the preeminent Western scholar of modern Japan. For more than a decade this work remained perhaps the greatest single influence upon English-language interpretations of the transition from Tokugawa feudalism through the Meiji period. Drawing to a considerable extent upon the research of Japanese scholars, some of whom worked within the Marxist tradition, *Japan's Emergence* was translated into Japanese in 1947 and had a reciprocal influence upon postwar Japanese historiography. Norman, one can assume, must have been gratified by this, for he had a gift, and indeed a passion, for intellectual sharing.

In 1943 Norman published a small study, *Soldier and Peasant in Japan: The Origins of Conscription*, which received lesser attention in the West but is regarded by some Japanese scholars as perhaps even more original than *Japan's Emergence*; the Japanese translation appeared in 1948. In 1944 he prepared a lengthy draft manuscript, *Feudal Background of Japanese Politics*, for presentation at the January 1945 Hot Springs conference of the Institute of Pacific Relations. Sections of this were appended to the Japanese edition of *Japan's Emergence*, and two articles in English ("Mass Hysteria in Japan" and "The Genyōsha: A Study in the Origins of Japanese Imperialism") derived from this manuscript. The entire work was never made generally available in English, however, and its unpublished chapters are reproduced in this present volume for the first time. In 1949 Norman published a study of a virtually unknown, iconoclastic eighteenth-century intellectual, *Andō Shōeki and the Anatomy of Japanese Feudalism*; he was attracted to Andō because he found him "a bold and original mind," a man who had endeavored to construct "a philosophy vindicating resistance to unbridled authority and oppression." *Andō* has been relatively ignored in the West, being seen as the portrait of a man of little influence; in Japan, where the translation appeared almost simultaneously, it has been read differently and, like *Soldier and Peasant*, treated as a work of considerable originality and import. During the early 1950s, Norman published several general historical essays in Japanese scholarly journals, and in 1956 these appeared in a popular edition under the title *Kurio no Kao* (The Face of Clio). The essays are virtually unknown in the West, and one, the preface to the Japanese edition, is reproduced here; the original English manuscripts of several of these pieces have been utilized in the discussion which follows. Although these works represent Norman's major written legacy, he also prepared a number of reviews, lectures, and reports which are generally neglected or inaccessible, but also illuminate his qualities as an historian and as a man. During this entire period, Norman served as a diplomat for the Canadian government, reaching the peak of his career as Ambassador to Egypt during the Suez crisis of 1956–57. He died in 1957, in Cairo, by suicide, after a period of recurrent pressure emanating from the United States because of his early leftist views and associations.

Norman's death and the subsequent neglect of his work in the West provide a saddening chapter on both the politics of the postwar era and the politics of postwar American scholarship on Japan. These, however, seem better left for later discussion, for they are negative concerns and what is memorable about Norman, what makes this present reissue of some of his major writings especially welcome, is his positive contribution to an understanding of Japan and of the tasks of the historian. In his own words, Norman was "addicted to history," and the brief tribute to Clio with which this present volume begins suggests the devotion with which he pursued this avocation and the intimate link which he perceived as existing between historical consciousness and man's fate. Although Japan was his field of specialization, it can be said of Norman as of few other recent Western scholars of Japan that the whole of man's historical experience was his province. Although he did his doctoral work in Japanese history at Harvard (with a period of research at Columbia), his prior training was in the classical British tradition, at Victoria College in Toronto and Trinity College in Cambridge, and his earlier academic background lay in ancient and medieval European history. He read in Latin, Greek, French, and

German, and used also Italian and Chinese. His parents were missionaries in Nagano prefecture, and his solid command of Japanese derived from having lived in Japan from birth until his mid-teens. Throughout his writings there breathes both an enviable knowledge of the experience of the West as well as East, and a sense of humility before the "delicate tracery" of history and the complexity of historical change. "He was a historian of the world before he was a historian of Japan," Maruyama Masao wrote in a moving tribute after Norman's death, and his profound erudition "was always there under the surface, gleaming like silver through the interstices of his conversation."

*   *   *

In various areas Norman's scholarship called attention to problems which still require further research. On the key issue of whether Japanese aggression after 1931 represented an aberrant departure from prior policy or was the result not merely of earlier policies but of the very nature of the Japanese state, his argument was strongly weighted toward the latter view. He implicitly criticized the Tokyo tribunal, which established the assassination of Chang Tso-lin in 1928 as the cutoff point in assessing culpability for Japanese war crimes, arguing that the roots lay deeper. And indeed, it is the very heart of his analysis of modern Japan that the problem originated in the incomplete nature of the Meiji settlement and the militarist policies and authoritarian structure it bequeathed to later generations. This remains a live issue today, although the question of pernicious roots has been greatly qualified by the modernization theorists. This is suggested in a recent volume of essays deriving from the one conference on the modernization of Japan devoted to "dilemmas of growth," particularly in the introductory and concluding essays by James Morley and Edwin Reischauer respectively.[1] Morley spoke of the modernization theorists' belated recognition of the need for a "pathology of growth," but indicated that for Japan this entailed understanding why good beginnings had faltered, and not how flawed beginnings had come to an impasse.

> The Conference had inevitably become impressed with the extraordinary overall success of various phases of the modernization effort in Japan and therefore had devoted considerable effort to trying to explain why things had gone so well.
>
> On the other hand, the discussion of favorable trends frequently lapsed when reference was made to the 1920s and 1930s, everyone recognizing that, for reasons of which they were not sure and in ways they found difficult to define, something in that period had gone wrong.

Such a view reveals more about those who share it than it does about the Japanese experience itself, for the notion that the tragedy of modern Japan was largely a dilemma of the interwar period—an aberration, as it were, after a half century of healthy growth—is one that could certainly never be shared by a Chinese or Formosan or Korean nationalist, or by the great majority of Japanese who belonged to the labor or agrarian classes during the earlier period when "things had gone so well." This attitude points directly to the bias of modernization theory: it reflects, essentially, the position of the state and of the international order as defined and stabilized by the concert of the Great Powers. In this system, growth becomes "pathological" only when it upsets the process of gradual change within the status quo, both domestically and abroad. Thus in the case of internal Japanese policy, to cite an obvious example, the death or abuse of female and child labor during the key period of early industrialization is not regarded as a "dilemma of growth" because this in no way threatened the evolving state structure; on the contrary, it facilitated growth. Similarly, the dual structure which brought hardship to the rural and urban poor begins to be treated as a serious problem only when, some four generations after the Restoration, it posed a specter of social unrest which abetted radicalism and threw the established government off balance; the "dilemma" here is not the misery itself, which was integral to Japanese industrialization or "growth," but the fact that it was allowed to get out of control. Comparable standards are applied to external relations. Japan's acquisition of colonies and a continental foothold through war, its manipulation of international law for purposes of foreign exploitation, its intervention in the affairs of other countries, and its colonial acquisitions are treated as examples of realistic and astute statesmanship, part of the "extraordinary overall success of various phases of the modernization effort," *so long as they succeeded*. Had Japan, implausibly, succeeded also in continuing to cooperate with the Western imperialist order in Asia and in *controlling* the Chinese revolution, the greater part of what is now adduced as evidence of a "pathology of growth" would be eliminated.

Just as "modernization theory" as a whole is essentially a counter-theory, so also do the various parts of the modernization formula have their own implicit targets within the radical tradition. Thus, emphasis upon the "concept of progress" can be seen as a groping attempt to offer an idealistic antithesis to "historical materialism" or "dialectical materialism" (phrases, incidentally, that Marx himself never used).[2] Similarly, the narrow conceptualization of a "dilemma of growth" or "pathology of growth" is also a fundamentally conservative one, clearly intended as a riposte to the radical formulation of "contradictions of capitalism." It is not, however, entirely antithetical to Norman's own approach. He would undoubtedly have agreed with Morley's observation that the breakdown of the interwar period was not yet fully understood, but it is more problematic to suggest how he would have responded to the argument that this occurred in inconsiderable part because Japan's leaders faced a succession of crises at a time when their country "could be called only partially modern." Negative legacies of the Meiji settlement, in this view, did not lead Japan into the dark valley of the interwar era, but rather remained as abscesses in the body politic which erupted only when agitated by other, contemporary problems. Both Morley and Reischauer dismissed the

Marxist emphasis on social structures as being of little use in analyzing this development ("history without people," a "monocausal explanation") and strongly suggested that the heart of the problem lay in the realm of political decision-making, the misperception of proper priorities. Reischauer characterized this departure from the norm as a "malaise," one which permitted "the powerful *re-emergence* [italics added] of ideas and values that belonged to an earlier stage in Japan's history." He acknowledged that the imbalances of the post–World War I era derived in part from the artificially forced growth of Meiji, but the problem lay, not in institutions, but rather in the fact that institutional growth had outpaced social, emotional, and intellectual attitudes. In effect, he indicated that nothing in the past twenty-five years of Western scholarship on Japan suggested the need for fundamental revision of the position he had taken in *Japan Past and Present*, for "the key thing that 'went wrong' was the usurpation of power by the military rather than any broader economic or social breakdown."

Norman's response to the military-takeover argument need not be surmised. The problem, however, carries beyond this, for to a certain extent, aspects of Norman's work (as well as of much Japanese Marxist analysis), notably the focus upon the *Japanese* context of Japan's experience, have been carried to an extreme by many of his successors. Although the modernization theorists have described their endeavors as an attempt to create a more universally applicable mode of analysis, their interpretations have in practice often emphasized the unique aspects of the Japanese experience when it comes to explaining such problems as Japanese aggression. Thus, in addressing the problems of the 1920s and 1930s, Norman's concept of a "feudal legacy" has been refurbished by some to provide an almost self-sufficient explanation, exemplified in the statement by Ronald Dore and Ōuchi Tsutomu (also in the Morley book) that aggression derived primarily from "the ideological framework within which Japanese politics were conducted," that is, the collectivist ethic and cult of familism as opposed to individualism. The popularity of Maruyama Masao's theories among

Western scholars has enhanced this focus upon the uniqueness of the Japanese experience by placing Japanese imperialism largely in the context of Japan's peculiar *kokutai* ("national polity") ideology. The "uniqueness" concept is reinforced (or replaced) by a second line of analysis which is present in the work of both Norman and his successors, namely, that the crisis of late Taishō and early Shōwa can be explained in large part by the dislocations or incompleteness of Japan's late and rapid modernization. Norman's famous "timing thesis" certainly points in this direction; and the modernization theorists have found such an argument essentially compatible with their basic overall emphasis upon the "success story." Thus while the problem may be defined as one of "pathology," it can actually be treated more as a matter of dermatology: Japan's dilemma becomes an unfortunate problem of growth, much like acne in adolescence, which might have been avoided if a few salves had been applied before the unsightly condition erupted. The thrust of such preoccupations has been extremely significant in shaping many recent interpretations of Japanese external behavior, for it turns attention away from the *similarity* of this behavior to that of countries which (1) lacked Japan's peculiar cultural heritage, (2) were early and "gradual" modernizers, and (3) presumedly did attain a higher level of bureaucratic rationalization, bourgeois democracy, and "individualism" than Japan. Problems of indigenous values and of timing are obviously essential to an understanding of Japanese actions and this has in fact been complemented by straightforward descriptions of decision-making in terms of strategic planning and *Realpolitik.* What has not been seriously examined, however, is the extent to which the Japanese experience was similar to that of theoretically more advanced capitalist countries, which also engaged in domestic repression and external aggression, and still do. This will entail a broader perspective than the prevailing framework of particularistic values or isolated "crises" of policymaking, and once again suggests the need to reexamine not only the problem of "substructures" in the classic Marxist sense but also, perhaps, the problem of man himself.

Norman did not carry the argument this far, but his work does offer other suggestions in the general area of foreign relations. Consistent with his axiom that it is the effect rather than the motive which should be of primary concern to the historian, in some of his shorter pieces he called attention to the nature of Japanese behavior abroad: atrocities, military corruption, and disobedience (as opposed to the prevailing image of fanatical discipline), organized prostitution in subject areas, and the crucial role of the narcotics trade in Japanese activities in China, which was used to both finance aggression and, it was hoped, debilitate Chinese resistance. Such observations are of particular interest in the light of recent revisionism by both American scholars such as James Crowley and conservative Japanese scholars such as Tsunoda Jun, who directed the eight-volume *Taiheiyō Sensō e no Michi* (Road to the Pacific War; now being translated into English); their position, in brief, is that Japan's leaders in the 1930s were "honorable and loyal" men.[3] This sense of honor reflects a willingness to judge men by their own time and situation and values, which superficially would seem consistent with some of Norman's more "liberal" statements. But at the same time it reveals a tolerance of, almost indifference to, mass slaughter and brutalization which was obviously beyond Norman's capacity. Passions tempered by time, it would appear, can reemerge not merely as tempered evaluation, as Morley argues, but also as calloused amorality. Norman, admittedly writing at the time, was more acid and outraged in his appraisal of the deeds and words of Japan's honorable and loyal public servants, with their "verbose, redundant and shamelessly hypocritical official Japanese apologies for naked aggression ('We are being surrounded by the ABCD powers'); for wholesale plunder (The Greater East Asia Co-Prosperity Sphere); and for two-faced diplomacy ('The Tripartite Alliance is to preserve peace in the Pacific')." Whether emanating from the Foreign Ministry or the Ministry of War, he commented in a review of Otto Tolischus, such lofty rhetoric was nothing more than "the *ipsissima verba* of Japanese militarists and their civilian fuglemen." He himself supported the validity of the war-crimes trials, and in the early stages of the occupation was in fact attached to SCAP and assigned the task of preparing preliminary reports on such accused war criminals as Konoe and Kido. That he apparently saw no contradiction in holding men of power responsible for the consequences of their actions, while at the same time recognizing the historical and contemporary pressures upon them, reflects the position expressed in the opening pages of *Japan's Emergence*: that leaders must work with the materials on hand, but that at the same time they draw designs; they are architects. Recent Western scholarship has been more sympathetic to those condemned in the Tokyo trials, more concerned with their motives (while paradoxically condemning the support which the Japanese populace gave to radical terrorists in the interwar period because of their "sincerity" of intent). The question is a profound one which will never be answered to the satisfaction of all. Certainly it remains open for the student of Japan, and challenges the individual to clarify his own position on an issue of such basic import.

This question carries, perhaps, philosophical implications. In more conventional areas of scholarship on Japanese actions abroad, many tasks remain to be undertaken. As yet, for example, there are virtually no comprehensive studies in English of the nature of colonial rule in Korea and Formosa; of neocolonial rule in Manchuria prior to 1931 (or even case studies of the Kwantung Army, Kwantung Civil government, South Manchurian Railway Company, Japanese consulates, joint public and private "national policy" companies, or private entrepreneurs); of Manchukuo, which has fascinating implications concerning the problem of "right radicalism," national socialism or state monopoly control, and the relationship between domestic and external policy; of political and economic involvement in China; or of military and "pacification" activities in all of these areas. On other occasions, Norman did warn against the danger of approaching Japanese foreign policy as if it were a one-way street. The historian, he said in his article on the war-crimes trials, must take care to recognize that "Japan was not only *acting* upon others but in some fashion *being acted upon.*" He raised this point in connection with the specific problem of Sino-Japanese relations in the 1930s, but it obviously extends beyond this and implies, for the later period, reevaluation of the entire historiography of the China and Pacific wars. Such revisionism, which has precedents in the Charles Beard school immediately after World War II, has recently been readdressed. Carried to its extreme limit, it presents the curious situation in which radical Western revisionists (outside the Japan field), by assessing Japan's behavior in Asia after the world depression primarily in the context of reaction to immense global U.S. and British economic coercion, have shifted the primary onus of responsibility for Japanese aggression and war from Japan itself to the Western imperialist powers; their conclusion thus in places is close to official Japanese rationalizations at the time, and in contemporary Japan coincides with the Pacific War revisionism of ultraconservative writers such as Hayashi Fusao. Future historians must inevitably confront this dilemma of understanding "Japan's case" without absolving Japan's actions, and once again it does not seem possible to do this rigorously without also taking cognizance of the more classically radical formulation of the problem—that is, by addressing the question of contradictions among the imperialist powers and testing the thesis that the Pacific War was not simply a clash of nation-states or of "democratic" and "fascist" camps, but also a crisis of capitalism— a crisis, moreover, inseparable from the problems of class conflict and counterrevolution. Such an analysis may be labeled "Marxist," but to see it as only this is to ignore the extraordinary prevalence of such concerns among the conservative leaders of both the Axis and the Allied powers at the time.

A further general direction suggested by Norman's writings lies in the area of comparative studies. One of his greatest gifts was certainly the breadth of his comprehension of Western history. This invigorated his studies of feudal Japan and grasp of Japanese intellectual history. It permitted him not only to refine and qualify but also to generalize and to use broad concepts, such as feudalism and authoritarianism, without tedious apology. The vision was exceptional. As Maruyama commented in his tribute written after learning of Norman's death, Western students of Japan who seek out Japanese scholars are usually boring, asking much and offering little. But Norman was different; he gave in return. Few contemporary Western scholars can match that background, but this does not negate the importance of seeing Japan in a context larger than Japan, although not necessarily within the modernization-theory framework. The comparative perspective which Norman brought to feudal and early modern Japan is necessary also in other areas of Japanese history, and can be developed by beginning on very specific problems: by placing the Bakumatsu-Restoration period, for example, in the context of the great revolutions and civil wars which were simultaneously sweeping China, Europe, and the United States; by setting Japanese actions in its colonies and mainland Asia against concurrent American activity in Latin America and the Philippines, or the European powers in Asia and Africa; or by comparing the fear of the left in Japan with simultaneous repression of the left in the United States (Tanaka's Peace Preservation Law and the Sacco-Vanzetti case, for instance). Such examples obviously return to the question posed previously: to what extent can Japan's experience shed light on the actions of *more* developed nations, and conversely, how can the experience of such nations help place Japan in broader perspective, particularly insofar as problems of war, exploitation, and repression are concerned? The answers are not likely to be found in styles of questioning that pose a kind of ladder effect, in which the "lessons" of Japan are seen as relevant primarily to countries lower down on the scale of "modernization." If, like Norman, one is concerned not only with the uses of power but also its abuses, and with issues of human values rather than "value-free" examination of diversification and decision-making, then a logical comparative study is suggested by some of the striking apparent similarities between Japan's experience prior to 1945 and American actions in the postwar period, particularly in Indochina. Certainly the Vietnam War provides a basis for completely re-evaluating standard interpretations of the

China and Pacific wars, but the question can also be turned about to ask what insight the Japanese experience prior to 1945 provides concerning the nature of the postwar American state. Out of such a comparative study, which should of course be broadened beyond these specific periods and countries, it might indeed be possible to refine and develop theories of the modern state itself which would advance the goals of both scholarly understanding and humane concern.

In the case of postwar American aggression and that of Japan between World War I and 1945, to pursue this matter briefly, the areas in which comparative analysis might be undertaken exist on many levels. The discrepancy between rhetoric and reality is blatantly apparent in both cases; indeed, postwar American policymakers have used essentially the same slogans of liberation, self-determination, and co-prosperity for Asia under which the Japanese launched their earlier aggression, while if anything enlarging those "crimes against humanity" of which they had only recently accused the Japanese. Japan in China, like the United States in Indochina, grossly misperceived the limits of technology when confronted with the concerted will of nationalistic resistance. Both countries were trapped in a logic of escalation: of rhetoric and commitment; of inevitable military expansion as "lines of defense" were redefined and in turn created new "buffers" (or dominos) to defend; of increasing political and economic intervention abroad as military involvement made imperative expanded control of strategic resources. Tactically, the actions of both countries bear striking parallels in their reliance upon puppet regimes, use of military "incidents" as a pretext for accelerated aggression, use of "negotiations" as an umbrella for escalation, and official sanction of war crimes (scorched earth, bombing of civilians, biological warfare, abuse and killing of prisoners, "pacification" and strategic hamlets were all resorted to by the Japanese). Both also sought to promote national interests through a neocolonial "regional integration."

The manner in which both Japan and the United States brought misfortune upon themselves and tragedy to the peoples of Asia can be described in terms of a crisis which occurred when the goals of national policy exceeded the means for achieving those defined interests. It is of little value to say that the goals were misperceived and ill-defined, for this simply preempts more fundamental questions concerning the structure, ideology, and locus of power through which those national interests were formulated. The heart of the problem lies in analyzing and comparing the dynamics of this interrelationship in both countries—the manner in which economic structure, growth, and diversification were related to military technology, for example, and the manner in which economic and strategic concerns meshed in the formulation of policies requiring expansion and increasing involvement abroad. Both countries were concerned with control of raw materials (and indeed, to a large extent the same resources: those of Southeast Asia) as well as markets. Both acted under the basic and unquestioned assumption that their national power could be protected and enhanced only by a certain level of political and economic domination abroad, and a secure military deployment outside their own borders. In each case this quest for hegemony was challenged by indigenous nationalistic and revolutionary movements—the Chinese revolution for Japan; and for the United States, whose quest was global, not only the Indochinese revolution but indeed radical movements throughout the less-developed world. Counterrevolution thus became fundamental to each country's definition of its foreign-policy objectives, a fact obvious for the United States but also central to prewar Japanese policy. Anti-Communism, both in the larger strategic sense of opposition to the Soviet Union (and the necessity for creating external "buffers" against it) and in the more particularized concern with indigenous radical movements, is hardly a phenomenon of the Cold War. The foreign policy of prewar Japan cannot be understood without taking this into consideration, and after 1945 the United States in fact took upon itself the task of completing Japan's unfinished campaigns against revolution in China and Indochina (and in Korea as well, in a somewhat different context).

Moreover, if one turns from the definition and dynamic of "national interest" to ask who formulated and interpreted this, it is apparent that the question "Who ruled Japan?" is in certain fundamental respects not greatly different from that of "Who rules America?" The problem is certainly complex, but the answer, just as certainly, excludes the vast majority of people. In both cases one is confronted with an interlocking of civilian and military agencies; with situations where it becomes obvious that real decision-making power lies in the hands of superagencies which circumvent the de jure channels of authority; and with *an essential lack of fundamental opposition to the basic definition of national interests from any significant part of the country's various influential elites.* Indeed, it can be argued that for Japan prior to 1945 as well as the United States in the postwar era, policies and pursuit of national goals which culminated in open aggression were formulated by men whose technical skills were excellent, whose access to relevant information was extensive, whose political views were in many cases reformist, whose policies prior to obvious disaster were endorsed and often initiated by advisers of "liberal" inclinations (a fascinating comparison could be made between the intellectuals who made up Konoe's informal advisory group, the Shōwa Kenkyūkai and John F. Kennedy's advisers, or even the modernization theorists themselves), and whose decisions for war were made after long and "rational" consideration of the basic requirements of national interest and national pride. It is fatuous to describe Japan's first unprofitable war as a lapse into collective irrationality on the part of the country's leaders. One of the more interesting observations that can be made concerning Japanese documents from this period is the extent to which they are similar in tone and thrust to comparable American policy papers such as those exposed in the Pentagon Papers. The concept of irrationality can easily be applied to any country which commits itself to a losing war, but this contributes little to an understanding of why such wars recur, and it also draws attention away from the problem of *successful* repression abroad short of war. In addition to a "pathology of growth," it is perhaps necessary to comprehend the pathology of "realism" as defined by the mandarins of the contemporary state.

The differences between the situation of prewar Japan and American actions in the postwar era are obvious: a vastly different international configuration both economically and militarily; a world war as opposed to a limited war (although paradoxically Japan's aims in Asia were limited, while America's involvement in Indochina was conceived of in terms of global policy); and in the case of the United States, a level of mechanization, rationalization, and secular thought which is highly "modern" by all prevailing standards. That is, compared with Japan in the 1920s and 1930s, postwar America is economically and technologically at an entirely different level, it is theoretically more pluralistic and predominantly middle class, its value system is "individualistic" rather than "collectivist," its electoral and representative system has remained intact, its titular head is not an absolute monarch but an elected executive, power is theoretically defined and balanced by the Constitution, there is no military capable of autonomous action through devices comparable to the "right of supreme command," and through television and other media its citizens have been immeasurably more informed than the prewar Japanese populace. The lack of such characteristics, according to the modernization theorists, goes a long way toward explaining Japan's crisis in the interwar period. Yet these characteristics obviously did not prevent the American crisis of the 1960s, and although the United States did experience a more vigorous antiwar movement than Japan, in practical terms it proved impossible to mount *effective and lasting* opposition to the government in either country. It is perhaps not too much to say that a real understanding of the pathology of growth will begin to emerge only when scholars forsake infatuation with "rationalization, mechanization, and belief in progress" per se, and undertake to examine the nature of the modern state on this broad and critical comparative level.

Scholarly projects such as those suggested above are clearly immense, but life is short and the field is small. Until such problems are addressed, it will be difficult to regard the field of Western studies of Japan as having come of age, and this cannot be accomplished in a situation where scholarship coalesces with the ideology of the American state and reinforces its international policies (such as "nation-building"), and certain lines of inquiry are discouraged. A more practical problem lies in the difficulty of formulating broad problems while maintaining the standards of disciplined research. Here Norman offers encouragement by example. Neither the thoroughness of his research nor, as the very titles of his major works convey, the breadth of his historical perspective and concern can be seriously questioned. It is virtually inconceivable to think of a proposal for a doctoral dissertation on "Japan's Emergence as a Modern State" being approved in an American university today. Yet *Japan's Emergence* was in fact written as a dissertation, and even the least sympathetic of Norman's critics concede that he was able to make optimum use of the major sources then available on this subject. Such resources are far more numerous now, but it is a serious question whether the present emphasis on narrow but "deep" vertical research is more challenging intellectually or more appropriate to creation of a fuller comprehension of Japanese history.

To return again to Norman's own vocabulary, it does not seem premature now to step back and ask this: whether in the field of English studies of Japan there is yet the beginning of an edifice, or merely a proliferation of extended footnotes, a scattering of monographic bricks; whether there are any painters among the photographers; whether in the histories of Japan since Norman's time there breathes a sense of human values, a truly civilizing, humanizing spirit. Norman himself must surely be evaluated against these, his own standards. So must his successors—or if they reject these standards, it must be asked if they have offered a better sense, or better use, of history in return.

PERSUADE OR PERISH: NORMAN'S DEATH

The defense of a free flow of ideas was of course more than an academic concern to Norman. In 1948 he was invited to address an anniversary celebration at Keiō University in Tokyo, and titled his lecture "Persuasion or Force: The Problem of Free Speech in Modern Society." He began by observing that "the course of the history of freedom is never along a direct and straight path. Rather is its course torturous, leading sometimes into a cul-de-sac from which painful detours have to be made." Freedom "has to be consciously won and jealously guarded. It can be lost through negligence or apathy in countries where it has reigned for many years." He argued that "no political party, no religious creed, no social class can claim a monopoly in the service of freedom," but at the same time, and characteristically, he placed the final decisive hope for this cause in "the army of anonymous and less-known humble folk who have provided the rank and file in the battalions of freedom," and emphasized "how steadfast and decent are the people in their desires and hopes."

I am not one of those who regard the people in the mass, when they are not put under the stress and strains of oppressive rule, as prone to behave stupidly or capriciously. When given access to the relevant facts in a situation the people make the sensible and decent choice; I believe the record of history upholds this view of mine. Especially is this true of people in their natural desire to have friendly and peaceful relations with neighboring peoples. I can recall no instance of a people who, without first being subjected to an intense and protracted war propaganda, have spontaneously demanded to make aggressive war on another people. It is precisely those rulers who are determined to exploit their people's blood for aggressive wars who are most concerned first to clamp down controls upon the people and to inflame them with jingoism so that their minds are filled with hate and fear of their neighbors. There is nothing such rulers fear so much as a clear and untrammeled expression of the popular desire for peace. I am sure in the light of the tragic history of Japan in the years before the war you would bear me out in this assertion.

His definition of freedom was in fact close to traditional liberalism, couched in the concept of "self-government," which he described as "a most reasonable, common-sense, and civilized way of life for any modern society whether it call itself republican, a constitutional monarchy, socialist or capitalist, or a mixture of these last two as most societies are today." He did not attack capitalism per se, and on this crucial point his position was quite clearly at variance with radical thought. To a certain extent it can be argued that Norman's political premises were in line with the attitude prevalent among most Western spokesmen at the end of World War II and exemplified in the initial reform policies in occupied Japan, namely, that "democracies" do not initiate war. Thus in the concluding paragraph of the first chapter of *Feudal Background*, he describes prewar Japanese absolutism in familiar liberal terms as the absence of "a genuinely democratic mass movement . . . some concept of popular sovereignty . . . freedom of speech, press and public assembly." But there is this difference in Norman: if he did not attack capitalism as a system, neither did he attack socialism, or see bourgeois society as necessarily the best possible vessel of democracy, or regard the cause of freedom as being embodied in the policies of any one particular state. The concern was not the label or the path, but the creation of *genuine* democracy.

By its very nature, he explained in "Persuasion or Force," self-government "means that the people look upon government officials as their servants or as their deputies and not as their masters. It is the very opposite of that old concept, *kanson mimpi*." And it does *not* mean freedom from control: "To keep within bounds of a self-governing society one may use only persuasion and not force. And by force I mean not necessarily riotous behavior but even the passive refusal to comply with such laws as conscription, taxation, etc." This dictum may come as a surprise to many who thought they knew their Norman, and some Japanese intellectuals have interpreted the expression of such views by Norman in his later years as reflecting a recantation, or *tenkō*, from his earlier position. In fact, the problem of gradual and revolutionary change, of law and resistance, which was clearly central also to his concerns as a historian, remains one of the most complex aspects of Norman's view. He touched on this later, in "On the Modesty of Clio," in these more qualified terms:

> Thus as a tentative axiom one might say that while men can by violence destroy peaceful and prosperous civilizations the corollary would seem to be that the slow and painful progress toward either a material prosperity or a higher culture is not achieved by any such bloody and dramatic acts. This is not to say that a cruelly oppressed nation or people may not on some occasions have found a forceful breaking of their bonds a necessary prerequisite for further progress. But such an act is usually nothing more than the climax of a long and arduous period of social and psychological development, as de Toqueville so convincingly argued was the case with the French Revolution. A spontaneous act of mob violence can never achieve a basic change in the social and political structure of a great nation.

And, as has been noted, he did suggest earlier that the world might have been spared the ordeal of Japanese aggression had more blood been shed in the early Meiji and the Japanese people thereby won for themselves a truer freedom. In "Persuasion or Force," he endeavored to illustrate this dilemma by citing the position of Socrates in Plato's dialogues *The Apology of Socrates* and *Crito*: Socrates would neither compromise his *right* of disobedience nor deny the state its duly constituted right to punish. That this was a paradox Norman himself acknowledged, and he said he did not propose to pursue it beyond stressing two lessons: "First, how delicate and intricate a problem is involved in the relation between freedom and self-government, and secondly, by abridging free speech, a self-governing society will no longer find itself self-governing in the true sense of that word." But he also added this significant point: "Let me remind you here that Socrates is speaking of the civic obligation of obedience in a society of which he felt himself to be an intimate and integral part. We cannot assume from this what his attitude might be had he been living in an oppressive society repugnant to him." Rather than suggest that Norman was inconsistent, or later retreated from an earlier position, it seems more just to suggest that throughout his thought there exists the inherent tension of commitment to the basic values of human life and civilized behavior and the confrontation with situations in which violence, the antithesis of these values, may appear to be the only recourse remaining to destroy a system which represses freedom, sacrifices life, and retards the creation of true self-government. In his work he held back somewhat from this problem. In his life he could not avoid it. And in his death, like Socrates, the paradox remained.

Norman concluded his speech at Keiō with these words:

Once liberty is dead, people must lose their self-respect; despair, envy, deceit and malice will grow apace like weeds in a deserted garden. We have seen in the past generation how a nation can lose its freedom and yet wage a terrible war; but no people who have lost their freedom can bequeath any lasting benefit to succeeding ages. They will leave behind no inspiration or generous work to which their descendants can look with pride and gratitude. This was well expressed by J.S. Mill a century ago when he wrote: "A state which dwarfs its men in order that they may be more docile instruments in its hands even for beneficial purposes, will find that with small men no great thing can really be accomplished."

. . . The world is tired of war and of force. Not only as between different classes in a nation but as between nations themselves force must give way to persuasion and reason if the world is not to retrogress fatally. Force is terribly easy to use, especially against some unpopular minority in the community. It is possible in this way to silence the voice of those whom an impatient government is irked to hear. But by so doing the community carries within it an embittered and disaffected member. The same is true today of relations between great and small nations.

Persuasion is not only the way of reason and humanity, it is now the sole path of self-preservation. Thus we are, all of us, whatever our nation or status, faced with the stern alternative: PERSUADE OR PERISH.

2

RACE, LANGUAGE, AND WAR
IN TWO CULTURES:
WORLD WAR II IN ASIA

In a 1986 monograph titled War Without Mercy: Race and Power in the Pacific War, *I attempted to meld the official or quasi-official documents I was trained to focus on as a researcher in history with a range of unofficial "texts" such as cartoons, films, songs, slogans, and rough colloquial rhetoric. I was, in a word, trying to integrate polished formal and elite resources with the more visceral expressions and dynamics of our human experience. This sort of popular cultural history was coming into its own in scholarship on Europe and the United States in those days. It had not yet made much of a mark on the Asia field, however; and it was rarely if ever used to draw the sort of even-keel comparisons between Anglo-Americans and Japanese that I ended up drawing.*

Rather like the Norman essay excerpted in chapter 1, War Without Mercy *started out as something different than the book it ended up being. It began as a sentence in the opening pages of a manuscript that was going to be about postwar Japan—a passing comment about how remarkable it was that the vicious racial hatreds of the Pacific War, especially between Americans and Japanese, dissipated so quickly after the fighting ended. This sentence needed expanding, I thought; and the sentence became a paragraph that became a chapter that ended up becoming a book.*

While racial thinking made both national solidarity and killing eas-

ier on all sides in the war in Asia, it is not my argument that racism is the key factor to understanding the cause or conduct of this conflict. Rather, the Anglo and Japanese antagonists, each in their own way, pumped up racial identity to both boost morale and abet war conduct; their racism was embedded in language at every level from the formal to the vulgar; such blinders impeded war conduct (such as intelligence evaluations) as much as they fired up the killing machines; and, as it turned out once Japan had been defeated, they could be turned off, or almost off, like a spigot. Racism is always with us, but its idioms and uses prove to be remarkably malleable.

The essay reproduced here recapitulates some of the themes introduced in War Without Mercy *and appeared in a collection of articles on "the war in American culture" published in 1996. Essentially the same text was included in my 1993 volume of essays* Japan in War and Peace, *but this present version incorporates samples of the visual materials that now seem indispensable to any serious attempt to recapture the clamorous ambiance of our modern times.*

* * *

For most Americans, World War II always has involved selective consciousness. The hypocrisy of fighting with a segregated army and navy under the banner of freedom, democracy, and justice never was frankly acknowledged and now is all but forgotten. In Asia, Japan was castigated for subjugating the native peoples of the Dutch East Indies (Indonesia), British Hong Kong, Malaya, Burma, the American Philippines, and French Indochina—and neither then nor later did the anomaly of such condemnation sink in. Consciousness and memory have been deceptive in other ways as well. If one asks Americans today in what ways World War II was atrocious and racist, they will point overwhelmingly to the Nazi genocide of the Jews. When the war was being fought, however, the enemy Americans perceived as most atrocious was not the Germans but the Japanese; and the racial issues that provoked their greatest emotion were associated with the war in Asia.

With few exceptions, Americans were obsessed with the uniquely evil nature of the Japanese. Allan Nevins, who twice won the Pulitzer Prize in history, observed immediately after the war that "probably in all our history, no foe has been so detested as were the Japanese." Ernie Pyle, the most admired of American war correspondents, conveyed the same sentiment unapologetically. In February 1945, a few weeks after being posted to the Pacific following years of covering the war in Europe, Pyle told his millions of readers that "in Europe we felt that our enemies, horrible and deadly as they were, were still people. But out here I soon gathered that the Japanese were looked upon as something subhuman and repulsive, the way some people feel about cockroaches or mice." Pyle went on to describe his response on seeing Japanese prisoners for the first time. "They were wrestling and laughing and talking just like normal human beings," he wrote. "And yet they gave me the creeps, and I wanted a mental bath after looking at them." Sober magazines like *Science Digest* ran articles titled "Why Americans Hate Japs More Than Nazis." By incarcerating Japanese Americans, but not German Americans or Italian Americans, the United States government—eventually with Supreme Court backing—gave its official imprimatur to the designation of the Japanese as a racial enemy. It did so, of course, in the most formal and judicious language.

It is not really surprising that the Japanese, rather than the Germans and their decimation of the Jews, dominated American racial thinking. In the United States, as well as Britain and most of Europe, anti-Semitism was strong and—as David Wyman among others has documented so well—the Holocaust was wittingly neglected or a matter of indifference. Japan's aggression, on the other hand, stirred the deepest recesses of white supremacism and provoked a response bordering on the apocalyptic. As the Hearst papers took care to editorialize, the war in Europe, however terrible, was still a "family fight" that did not threaten the very essence of occidental civilization. One Hearst paper bluntly identified the war in the Pacific as "the War of Oriental Races against Occidental Races for the Domination of the World."

There was almost visceral agreement on this. Thus Hollywood formulaically introduced good Germans as well as Nazis but almost never showed a "good Japanese." In depicting the Axis triumvirate, political cartoonists routinely gave the German enemy Hitler's face and the Italian enemy Mussolini's, but they rendered the Japanese as plain, homogeneous "Japanese" caricatures: short, round-faced, bucktoothed, slant-eyed, frequently myopic behind horn-rimmed glasses. In a similar way, phrasemakers fell unreflectively into the idiom seen in the *Science Digest* headline: Nazis and Japs. Indeed, whereas the German enemy was conflated to bad Germans (Nazis), the Japanese enemy was inflated to a supra-Japanese foe—not just the Japanese militarists, not just all the Japanese people, not just ethnic Japanese everywhere, but the Japanese as Orientals. Tin Pan Alley, as so often, immediately placed its finger on the American pulse. One of the many popular songs inspired by Pearl Harbor was titled "There'll Be No Adolph [sic] Hitler nor Yellow Japs to Fear." Pearl Harbor and the stunning Japanese victories over the colonial powers that followed so quickly in Southeast Asia seemed to confirm the worst Yellow Peril nightmares.

World War II in Asia was, of course, not simply or even primarily a race war. Alliances cut across race on both the Allied and Axis sides, and fundamental issues of power and ideology were at stake. Where the Japanese and the Anglo-American antagonists were concerned, however, an almost Manichaean racial cast overlay these other issues of contention. This was true on both sides. The Japanese were racist too—toward the white enemy, and in conspicuously different ways toward the other Asians who fell within their "Co-Prosperity Sphere." Thus the war in Asia offers an unusually vivid case study through which to examine the tangled skein of race, language, and violence from a comparative perspective—not only with the luxury of retrospect, moreover, but also at a time when U.S.-Japan relations are very different and yet still riven with racial tension.

The war exposed core patterns of racist perception in many forms: formulaic expressions, code words, everyday metaphors, visual stereotypes. Such ways of thinking, speaking, and seeing were often vulgar, but their crudeness was by no means peculiar to any social class, educational level, political ideology, or place or circumstance (such as the battlefield as opposed to the home front as opposed to the corridors of power and policymaking). On the other hand, in many instances the racist patterns of perception and expression were just the opposite: subtle, nuanced, garbed in the language of empiricism and intellectuality. This too was typical. Ostensibly objective observations often are laced with prejudice.

That racist perceptions shape behavior may seem obvious, but the war experience calls attention to how subtly this occurs, and at how many different levels. Myths, in this case race myths, almost always override conclusions drawn from sober, rational, empirical observation—until cataclysmic events occur to dispel or discredit them. It took Pearl Harbor and Singapore to destroy the myth cherished by Caucasians that the Japanese were poor navigators and inept pilots and unimaginative strategists, for example, and it required a long, murderous struggle to rid the Japanese of their conceit that the Anglo-Americans were too degenerate and individualistic to gird for a long battle against a faraway foe. We have become so mesmerized by the contemporary cult of military intelligence gathering that we often fail to recognize how extensively unadulterated prejudice colors intelligence estimates, causing both overestimation and underestimation of the other side. Beyond this, in its most extreme form racism sanctions extermination—the genocide of the Jews, of course, but also the plain but patterned rhetoric of exterminating beasts, vermin, or demons that unquestionably helped raise tolerance for slaughter in Asia.

Five categories subsume the racist perceptions of the Japanese that dominated Anglo-American thinking during World War II. The Japanese were subhuman. They were little men, inferior to white Westerners in every physical, moral, and intellectual way. They were collectively primitive, childish, and mad—overlapping

Fig. 2-1. As this popular song title reveals, Americans routinely regarded the German enemy as but one part of the German populace ("Hitler," "the Nazis"), while at the same time identifying the "Japs" as a whole with an even larger Yellow Peril. © Galerie Bilderwelt/Hulton Archive/Getty Images.

concepts that could be crudely expressed but also received "empirical" endorsement from social scientists and old Japan hands. At the same time, the Japanese also were portrayed as supermen. This was particularly true in the aftermath of their stunning early

Fig. 2-2. The notion that "the only good Jap is a dead Jap" was an American cliché during the entire course of the war. Undiluted rage at the surprise attack on Pearl Harbor greatly reinforced this sentiment, as seen in this graphic that appeared in a monthly magazine for Marines. From *Leatherneck*, March 1942.

victories, and it is characteristic of this thinking that the despised enemy could be little men and supermen simultaneously. Finally, the Japanese in World War II became the nightmare come true of the Yellow Peril. This apocalyptic image embraced all others and made unmistakably clear that race hates, and not merely war hates or responses to Japanese behavior alone, were at issue.

Dehumanization of the enemy is desirable among men in combat. It eliminates scruples and hesitation from killing, the reasoning goes, and this contributes to self-preservation; the enemy, after all, is simultaneously dehumanizing and trying to kill you. Among

Allied fighting men in the Pacific, this attitude emerged naturally in the ubiquitous metaphor of the hunt. Fighting Japanese in the jungle was like going after "small game in the woods back home" or tracking down a predatory animal. Killing them was compared to shooting down running quail, picking off rabbits, bringing a rabid and desperate beast to bay and finishing it off. The former sportsman was now simply "getting *bigger* game." One put the crosshairs on the crouching Jap, just as in deer hunting back home.

The kill did not remain confined to the combat zones, however, nor did the metaphors of dehumanization remain fixed at this general, almost casual level. In the United States, signs appeared in store windows declaring "Open Season on Japs," and "Jap hunting licenses" were distributed amid the hysteria that accompanied the incarceration of Japanese Americans. The psychology of the hunt became indistinguishable from a broader psychology of extermination that came to mean not merely taking no prisoners on the battlefield, but also having no qualms about extending the kill to the civilian population in Japan. Here the more precise language and imagery of the race war became apparent. The Japanese were vermin. More pervasive yet, they were apes, monkeys, "jaundiced baboons." The war in Asia popularized these dehumanizing epithets to a degree that still can be shocking in retrospect, but the war did not spawn them. These were classic tropes of racist denigration, deeply embedded in European and American consciousness. War simply pried them loose.

Vermin was the archetypal metaphor Nazis attached to the Jews, and the appalling consequences of that dehumanization have obscured the currency of this imagery in the war in Asia. On Iwo Jima, the press found amusement in noting that some marines went into battle with "Rodent Exterminator" stenciled on their helmets. Incinerating Japanese in caves with flame-throwers was referred to as "clearing out a rats' nest." Soon after Pearl Harbor, the prospect of exterminating the Japanese vermin in their nest at home was widely applauded. The most popular float in a daylong victory parade in New York in mid-1942 was titled "Tokyo: We Are Coming," and depicted bombs falling on a frantic pack of yellow rats. A cartoon in the March 1945 issue of *Leatherneck*, the monthly magazine for Marines, portrayed the insect "Louseous Japanicas" and explained that though this epidemic of lice was being exterminated in the Pacific, "before a complete cure may be effected the origin of the plague, the breeding grounds around the Tokyo area, must be completely annihilated." "Louseous Japanicas" appeared almost simultaneously with initiation of the policy of systematically firebombing Japanese cities and accurately reflected a detached tolerance for annihilationist and exterminationist rhetoric at all levels of United States society. As the British embassy in Washington noted in a weekly report, Americans perceived the Japanese as "a nameless mass of vermin."

Perception of the Japanese as apes and monkeys similarly was not confined to any particular group or place. Even before Pearl Harbor, Sir Alexander Cadogan, the permanent undersecretary of the British Foreign Office, routinely referred to the Japanese as "beastly little monkeys" and the like in his diary. Following Japan's capitulation, United States General Robert Eichelberger, alluding to the Japanese mission en route to the Philippines to arrange the surrender procedures, wrote to his wife that "first, monkeys will come to Manila." Among Western political cartoonists, the simian figure was surely the most popular caricature for the Japanese. David Low, the brilliant antifascist cartoonist working out of London, was fond of this. The *New York Times* routinely reproduced such graphics in its Sunday edition, at one point adding its own commentary that it might be more accurate to identify the Japanese as the "missing link." On the eve of the British debacle at Singapore, the British humor magazine *Punch* depicted Japanese soldiers in full-page splendor as chimpanzees with helmets and guns swinging from tree to tree. *Time* used the same image on its cover for January 26, 1942, contrasting the monkey invaders with the dignified Dutch military in Indonesia. The urbane *New Yorker* magazine also found the monkeymen-in-trees conceit witty. The *Washington Post* compared Japanese atrocities in the Philippines and German atrocities in Czechoslovakia in a 1942 cartoon pairing a gorilla labeled "Japs" and a Hitler figure labeled simply "Hitler." In well-received Hollywood combat films such as *Bataan* and *Guadalcanal Diary*, GIs routinely referred to the Japanese as monkeys.

The ubiquitous simian idiom of dehumanization came out of a rich tradition of bigoted Western iconography and graphically revealed the ease with which demeaning racist stereotypes could be floated from one target of prejudice to another. Only a short while before they put the Japanese in trees, for example, *Punch's* artists had been rendering the Irish as apes. Generations of white cartoonists also had previously refined the simian caricature in their depictions of Negroes and various Central American and Caribbean peoples. The popular illustrators, in turn, were merely replicating a basic tenet in the pseudoscience of white supremacism—the argument that the "Mongoloid" and "Negroid" races (and for Englishmen, the Irish) represented a lower stage of evolution. Nineteenth-century Western scientists and social scientists had offered almost unanimous support to this thesis, and such ideas persisted into the mid-twentieth century. President Franklin D. Roosevelt, for example, was informed by a physical anthropologist at the Smithsonian Institution that Japanese skulls were "some 2,000 years less developed than ours."

In the world outside the monkey house, the Japanese commonly were referred to as "the little men." Their relatively short stature contributed to this, but again the phrase was essentially metaphorical. The Japanese, it was argued, were small in accomplishments compared with Westerners. No great "universal" achievements were to be found in their traditional civilization; they were latecomers to the modern challenges of science and technology, imitators rather than innovators, ritualists rather than rationalists. Again, the cartoonists provided a good gauge of this conceit. More often than not, in any ensemble of nationalities the Japanese figures were dwarfish.

THE MONKEY FOLK
"Always pecking at new things are the bandar-log. This time, if I
have any eyesight, they have pecked down trouble for themselves."
—The Jungle Book

Fig. 2-3. Taking its caption from Rudyard Kipling's *Jungle Book*, this full-
page illustration appeared in the British humor magazine *Punch* on January
14, 1942, as Japanese forces were advancing down the Malayan Peninsular.
On January 31, the British abandoned Malaya, leaving close to 40,000
prisoners in Japanese hands. Two weeks later, on February 15, Britain's
"impregnable fortress" at Singapore surrendered unconditionally to a much
smaller Japanese army numbering roughly 30,000 men, and an additional
80,000 Commonwealth forces (British, Indian, and Australian) became
prisoners of the Japanese. Reproduced with permission of Punch Limited.

Fig. 2-4. The popular Anglo-American rendering of the war in Asia as
a conflict between Japanese "monkeymen" and civilized Caucasians was
conveyed to a national audience in *Time* magazine's cover for January 26, 1942,
which portrayed the commander of the Royal Dutch East Indies Army and a
simian soldier dangling from a tree. Japanese forces invaded the Dutch East
Indies (present-day Indonesia) in mid-January, and the Dutch surrendered
in Java on March 8—consigning over 40,000 Dutch military and civilians to
internment camps and paving the way for a Japanese occupation regime that
brutalized the native population. "Major General Poorten" © 1942 Time Inc.
Used under license.

Fig. 2-5. In this famous photograph from the May 22, 1944, issue of *Life* magazine, a young woman sweetly contemplates a "Jap skull" sent by her boyfriend. Although it was well known that American fighting men collected such grisly battlefield trophies in the Pacific theater, such practices would have caused an uproar had they involved desecration of the German and Italian war dead. © Ralph Crane/TIME & LIFE Images/Getty Images.

Such contempt led, among other things, to a pervasive underestimation of Japanese intentions and capabilities by British and American observers at even the highest levels. Before Pearl Harbor, it was common wisdom among Westerners that the Japanese could not shoot, sail, or fly very well. Nor could they think imaginatively; as a British intelligence report carefully explained, this was because the enormous energy required to memorize the ideographic writing system dulled their brains and killed the spark of creativity. There can be few better examples of the power of myth and stereotype over the weight of objective analysis than the unpreparedness of the Westerners when Japan attacked. Almost everything was a shock: the audacity of the Pearl Harbor attack and the ability of the Japanese to bring it off, the effectiveness of the Zero aircraft (which had been in operation in China for over a year), the superb skills of the Japanese pilots, the esprit and discipline of the Japanese ground forces, the lightning multipronged assault against the European and American colonial enclaves. Equally shocking, of course, was the Western side of the coin: the unpreparedness in Hawaii, the debacle at Singapore, the humiliation in the Philippines. In the long view, despite Japan's eventual defeat, the events of 1941–42 exposed the dry rot of the old empires and irreparably shattered the mystique of white superiority among the native peoples of Asia.

These Japanese victories—coupled with the spectacle of Japanese brutality and atrocity—set whole new worlds of racial thinking in motion. The little men suddenly became supermen; and at the same time more elaborate versions of the little-men thesis were developed. A remarkable intelligence report circulated by psychological warfare experts within General Douglas MacArthur's command in mid-1944, for example, masticated the old thesis with excruciating thoroughness:

> And yet in every sense of the word the Japanese are *little people*. Some observers claim there would have been no Pearl Harbor had the Japanese been three inches taller. The archipelago itself is a land of diminutive distances. Japanese houses are artistic but flimsy and cramped. The people, tiny in stature, seem to play at living. To a Westerner they and their country possess the strange charm of toyland. Centuries of isolation have accentuated the restrictive characteristics of their outlook on life.

Being *little people*, the Japanese dreamed of power and glory, but lacked a realistic concept of the material requirements for a successful world war. Moreover, they were totally unable to envisage the massive scale of operations in which the United States is now able to indulge.[1]

At the same time, the little-men thesis also was elaborated on in ways that shed harsh light on racist bias in the academic disciplines by revealing how Western social sciences could be used to support popular prejudices. The war years witnessed the emergence of anthropologists, sociologists, psychologists, and psychiatrists as the new mandarins of theories of "national character," and on the whole they performed a valuable service in repudiating the old theories of biological determinism. What the social scientists did not dispel, however, were the racial stereotypes that had been associated with biological determinism. On the contrary, they essentially reaffirmed these stereotypes by offering new cultural or sociopsychological explanations for them.

This is seen most clearly in three of the most influential themes that American and British social scientists introduced to explain Japanese behavior. The Japanese, they argued, were still essentially a primitive or tribal people, governed by ritualistic and particularistic values. The influence of cultural anthropologists was particularly apparent here. Furthermore, it was emphasized that Japanese behavior could be analyzed effectively using Western theories of child or adolescent behavior. Here the Anglo-American intellectuals turned to Freudian-influenced theories concerning toilet training and psychic blockage at various stages of immaturity (the British social anthropologist Geoffrey Gorer was extremely influential on this theme) and also extolled the value of applying insights gained from American studies "of individual adolescent psychology and of the behavior of adolescents in gangs in our society, as a systematic approach to better understanding of the Japanese" (the quotation is from the minutes of a large 1944 symposium involving, among others, Margaret Mead and Talcott

Parsons). Finally, in the third great preoccupation of the new intellectual mandarins, it was argued that the Japanese as a collectivity were mentally and emotionally unstable—neurotic, schizophrenic, psychotic, or simply hysterical.

In the final analysis, the "national character" studies amounted to a new way of explaining what the presumedly discredited biological determinists had concluded long ago: the Japanese as a people displayed arrested development. Although this was not inherent in their genes, it was the inevitable consequence of their peculiar history and culture. All this was expressed with considerable erudition, and many of the insights of wartime social scientists concerning societal pressures and situational ethics remain influential today. For the proverbial man from Mars given access only to such wartime writings, however, it would be reasonable to conclude that imperialism, war, and atrocity had been invented in Asia during the twentieth century by developmentally retarded Japanese. They were unique, sui generis, and very peculiar indeed.

When all was said and done, however, these designations of Japanese peculiarity possessed a universal quality. They were formulaic and rested in considerable part on code words that transcended Japan and even transcended racial and cultural discourse in general. In suggestive ways, these code words also overlapped with vocabularies associated with discrimination based on gender and class. The central image of arrested growth, or "childishness," for example, was and remains one of the most basic constructs used by white Euro-Americans to characterize nonwhite peoples. This could be buttressed with pseudoscientific explanations (nonwhites being lower on the evolutionary scale, and thus biologically equivalent to children or adolescents vis-à-vis the "mature" Caucasian races) or meretricious social scientific equations (the "less developed" peoples of "less developed" nations, for example, or peoples alleged to be collectively blocked at a primitive or immature state psychologically by indigenous cultural practices or mores). In the milieu of war, the image of the Japanese as children conveyed utter contempt (as in *Newsweek*'s wartime reference to "the child mind of the Jap conscript"), but in less harsh circumstances it also was capable of evoking a condescending paternalism (as reflected in the depiction of Japanese after the surrender as "MacArthur's children" or as the beneficiaries of a student-teacher relationship with Americans). This same metaphor also is integral to the rationale of male domination and rule by elites. Thus, to describe women as childish or childlike is one of the most familiar ways men traditionally have signified both the inherent inferiority of women and their own obligation to protect or at least humor them. Similarly, dominant social and political classes commonly affirm their privileged status and inherent right to rule by dismissing the masses as irrational, irresponsible, and immature. In its softer guise, the elite sense of noblesse oblige masks class inequalities with a paradigm of parent-to-child obligations.

The resonances of this broader conceptual world also help clarify how Japan's attack on the West revitalized other fantasies. It is characteristic of the paranoia of self-designated master groups that even while dismissing others as inferior and "less developed," they attribute special powers to them. The lower classes may be immature to the elites, but they also are seen as possessing a fearsome potential for violence. Women may be irrational in male eyes, but they also are said to have special intuitive powers and the Jezebel potential of becoming castrators. Where Western perceptions of the Japanese and Asians in general are concerned, there is in fact a provocative congruence between the female and Oriental mystiques as expressed by white male elites. Thus, even in the war years, the "femininity" of Japanese culture was indirectly if not directly emphasized. Traits attributed to the Japanese often were almost identical to those assigned to women in general: childishness, irrationality, emotional instability, and "hysteria"—and also intuition, a sixth sense, and a talent for nondiscursive communication. It even was said that the Japanese, like women generally, possessed an exceptional capacity to endure suffering. Put negatively, these latter intuitive and emotional qualities could be equated with nonrationality and simply integrated into the argument of arrested development.

Positively framed, they became suprarational powers—impossible to explain, but all the more alarming to contemplate.

Because nothing in the "rational" mind-set of Western leaders prepared them for either the audacity and skill of Japan's attack or the debacle of British, Dutch, and American capitulations to numerically inferior Japanese forces that followed in Southeast Asia, it was natural to look to nonrational explanations. Scapegoating helped obfuscate the situation—the United States commanders at Pearl Harbor were cashiered, and the West Coast Japanese Americans were locked up—but this was not enough. It also became useful to think of the Japanese as supermen. Graphic artists now drew the Japanese as giants on the horizon. Rhetorically, the new image usually emerged in a more serpentine or backhanded fashion. Thus the United States print media from 1941 to the end of the war featured a veritable "between the lines" subgenre debunking the new myth of the supermen. Battle A proved they could be beaten at sea, battle B that they could be beaten in the jungle, battle C that they were not unbeatable at night fighting, battle D that the myth of the "invincibility of the Zero" was finally being destroyed. The *New York Times Magazine* took it upon itself to address the issue head-on with a feature article titled "Japanese Superman: That Too Is a Fallacy." Admiral William Halsey, the most blatantly racist officer in the United States high command, later claimed that he deliberately belittled the Japanese as "monkeymen" and the like in order to discredit "the new myth of Japanese invincibility" and boost the morale of his men.

The myth of the superman was never completely dispelled. To the end of the war—even after most of the Japanese navy and merchant marine had been sunk; after Japanese soldiers in the field, cut off from support, had begun starving to death and were being killed by the tens and hundreds of thousands; after the urban centers of the home islands had come under regular bombardment—Allied planners continued to overestimate the will and capacity of the Japanese to keep fighting. There are surely many explanations for this, but prominent among them is a plainly racial consideration:

the superman image was especially compelling because it meshed with the greatest of all the racist bogeys of the white men—the specter of the Yellow Peril.

Hatred toward the Japanese derived not simply from the reports of Japanese atrocities, but also from the deeper wellsprings of anti-orientalism. *Time* magazine's coverage of the American response to Pearl Harbor, for example, opened on this very note. What did Americans say when they heard of the attack, *Time* asked rhetorically. And the answer it quoted approvingly as representative was, "Why, the yellow bastards!" *Time*'s cover portrait for December 22, 1941, depicting Admiral Yamamoto Isoroku, who planned the Pearl Harbor attack, was colored a single shade: bright yellow. At one time or another almost every mainstream newspaper and magazine fell into the color idiom, and yellow was by far the dominant color in anti-Japanese propaganda art. Among the music makers, we already have encountered Tin Pan Alley's revealing counterpoint of Hitler and the "Yellow Japs." Other song titles included "We're Gonna Find a Fellow Who Is Yellow and Beat Him Red, White, and Blue" and "Oh, You Little Son of an Oriental." In some American pronouncements, the Japanese were simply dismissed as "LYBs," a well-comprehended acronym for the double entendre "little yellow bellies."

Spokesmen for Asian Allies such as China were aghast at such insensitivity, and the war years as a whole became an agonizing revelation of the breadth and depth of anti-Asian prejudice in the United States. In the very midst of the war these revelations prompted a yearlong congressional hearing to consider revision of the notorious "Oriental Exclusion Laws"—the capstone of formal discrimination against all people of Asian origin. What the Japanese attack brought to the surface, however, was something more elusive and interesting than the formal structures of discrimination: the concrete fears that underlay the perception of a menacing Orient.

Since the late nineteenth century, when the Yellow Peril idea was first expressed in the West, white people had been unnerved by a triple apprehension—recognition that the "hordes" of Asia outnumbered the population of the West, fear that these alien masses might gain possession of the science and technology that made Western domination possible, and the belief that Orientals possessed occult powers unfathomable to Western rationalists. By trumpeting the cause of Pan-Asianism and proclaiming the creation of a Greater East Asia Co-Prosperity Sphere, Japan raised the prospect that the Asian hordes might at last become united. With their Zero planes and big battleships and carriers, the Japanese gave notice that the technological and scientific gap had narrowed dramatically. And with the aura of invincibility that blossomed in the heat of the early victories, the Japanese "supermen" evoked the old fantasies of occult oriental powers. All this would be smashed in August 1945, when Japan capitulated. And it would all resurface three decades later when Japan burst on the scene as an economic superpower and other Asian countries began to emulate this "miracle."

Racism also shaped the Japanese perception of self and other—again in patterned ways, but patterns different from those of the West. History accounts for much of this difference. Over centuries, Japan had borrowed extensively from India, China, and more recently from the West, and had been greatly enriched; and it acknowledged these debts. And over the course of the preceding century, the Japanese had felt the sting of Western condescension. Even when applauded by the Europeans and Americans for their accomplishments in industrializing and "Westernizing," the Japanese were painfully aware that they were still regarded as immature and unimaginative and unstable—good in the small things, as the saying went among the old Japan hands, and small in the great things.

Thus Japanese racial thinking was riven by an ambivalence that had no clear counterpart in white supremacist thinking. Like the white Westerners, they assumed a hierarchical world; but unlike the Westerners, they lacked the unambiguous power that would enable them to place themselves unequivocally at the top of the racial hierarchy. Toward Europeans and Americans, and the science and civilization they exemplified, the national response was one of admiration as well as fear, mistrust, and hatred. Toward all others—that is, toward nonwhites including Asians other than themselves—their attitude was less complicated. By the twentieth century Japan's success in resisting Western colonialism or neo-colonialism and emerging as one of the so-called Great Powers had instilled among the Japanese an attitude toward weaker peoples and nations that was as arrogant and contemptuous as the racism of the Westerners. The Koreans and Chinese began to learn this in the 1890s and early 1900s; the peoples of Southeast Asia learned it quickly after December 7, 1941.

For Japan, the crisis of identity came to a head in the 1930s and early 1940s, taking several dramatic forms. Behind the joy and fury of the initial attacks in 1941–42, and indeed behind many of the atrocities against white men and women in Asia, was an unmistakable sense of racial revenge. At the same time, the Japanese began to emphasize their own destiny as a "leading race" (*shidō minzoku*). If one were to venture a single broad observation concerning the difference between the preoccupations of white supremacism and Japanese racism, it might be this: that whereas white racism devoted inordinate energy to the denigration of the other, Japanese racial thinking concentrated on elevating the self. In Japanese war films produced between 1937 and 1945, for example, the enemy was rarely depicted. Frequently it was not even made clear who the antagonist was. The films concentrated almost exclusively on the admirable "Japanese" qualities of the protagonists. The focus of the broader gamut of propaganda for domestic consumption was similar. In its language and imagery, Japanese prejudice thus appeared to be more benign than its white counterpart—by comparison, a soft racism—but this was mis-leading. The insularity of such introversion tended to deperson-alize and, in its own peculiar way, dehumanize all non-Japanese "outsiders." In practice, such intense fixation on the self contributed to a wartime record of extremely callous and brutal behavior toward non-Japanese.

The central concept in this racial thinking was that most tantalizing of cultural fixations: the notion of purity. In Japan as elsewhere, this has a deep history not merely in religious ritual, but also in social practice and the delineation of insider and outsider (pure and impure) groups. By turning purity into a racial ideology for modern times, the Japanese were in effect nationalizing a concept traditionally associated with differentiation within their society. Purity was Japanized and made the signifier of homogeneity, of "one hundred million hearts beating as one," of a unique "Yamato soul" (*Yamato damashii*, from the ancient capital of the legendary first emperor). Non-Japanese became by definition impure. Whether powerful or relatively powerless, all were beyond the pale.

The ambiguity of the concept enhanced its effectiveness as a vehicle for promoting internal cohesion. At a superficial level, this fixation on the special purity or "sincerity" of the Japanese resembles the mystique of American "innocence." Whereas the latter is a subtheme in the American myth, however, the former was cultivated as the very essence of a powerful racial ideology. Like esoteric mantras, a variety of evocative (and often archaic) words and phrases were introduced to convey the special racial and moral qualities of the Japanese; and like esoteric mandalas, certain visual images (sun, sword, cherry blossom, snowcapped Mount Fuji, an abstract "brightness") and auspicious colors (white and red) were elevated as particularistic symbols of the purity of the Japanese spirit.

Where Westerners had turned eventually to pseudoscience and dubious social science to bolster theories of the inherent inferiority of nonwhite and non-Western peoples, the Japanese turned to mythohistory, where they found the origins of their superiority in the divine descent of their sovereign and the racial and cultural homogeneity of the sovereign's loyal subjects. Deity, monarch, and populace were made one, and no words captured this more effectively than the transcendent old phrase resurrected to supersede plain reference to "the Japanese": *Yamato minzoku*, the "Yamato race." "Yamato"—the name of the place where Jimmu, grandson of the grandson of the sun goddess, was alleged to have founded the imperial line in 660 B.C.—was redolent with the archaic mystique of celestial genetics that made Japan the divine land and the Japanese the chosen people. In *Yamato minzoku*, the association became explicitly racial and exclusionary. The race had no identity apart from the throne and the traditions that had grown up around it, and no outsider could hope to penetrate this community. This was blood nationalism of an exceptionally potent sort.

Many of these themes were elaborated in the ideological writings of the 1930s and early 1940s, and the cause of blood nationalism was elevated when 1940 became the occasion for massive ceremony and festivity in celebration of the 2,600-year anniversary of the "national foundation day." At the same time, the racial ideologues took care to emphasize that purity was not merely an original state, but also an ongoing process for each Japanese. Purity entailed virtues that needed to be cultivated, and preeminent among these were two moral ideals originally brought to Japan from China: loyalty and filial piety (*chūkō*). Why these became a higher expression of morality in Japan than elsewhere, higher even than in China, was explained by their ultimate focus in the divine sovereign. Purity lay in transcendence of ego and identification with a greater truth or cause; and in the crisis years of the 1930s and early 1940s this greater truth was equated with the militarized imperial state. War itself, with all the sacrifice it demanded, became an act of purification. And death in war, the ultimate expression of selflessness, became the supreme attainment of this innate Japanese purity. We know now that most Japanese fighting men who died slowly did not pass away with the emperor's name on their lips, as propaganda claimed they did. Most often they called (as GIs did also) for their mothers. Still, they fought and died with fervor and bravery, enveloped in the propaganda of being the divine soldiers of the divine land, and this contributed to the aura of a people possessed of special powers.

Both the Western myth of the superman and the bogey of the Yellow Peril had their analogue in this emphasis the Japanese themselves placed on their unique suprarational spiritual qualities. In Western eyes, however, this same spectacle of fanatical mass behavior also reinforced the image of the little men, of the Japanese as a homogeneous, undifferentiated mass. There is no small irony in this, for what we see here is the coalescence of Japanese indoctrination with the grossest anti-Japanese stereotypes of the Westerners. In the crudest of Anglo-American colloquialisms, it was argued that "a Jap is a Jap" (the famous quotation of General John DeWitt, who directed the incarceration of the Japanese Americans). In the 1945 propaganda film *Know Your Enemy—Japan*, produced by Frank Capra for the United States Army, the Japanese were similarly described as "photographic prints off the same negative"—a line now frequently cited as the classic expression of racist American contempt for the Japanese. Yet in essence this "seen one seen them all" attitude was not greatly different from the "one hundred million hearts beating as one" indoctrination that the Japanese leaders themselves promoted. Homogeneity and separateness *were* essential parts of what the Japanese ideologues said about themselves. In their idiom, this was integral to the superiority of the Yamato race. To non-Japanese, it was further cause for derision.

The rhetoric of the pure self also calls attention to the potency of implicit as opposed to explicit denigration. In proclaiming their own purity, the Japanese cast others as inferior because they did not, and could not, share in the grace of the divine land. Non-Japanese were, by the very logic of the ideology, impure, foul, polluted. Such sentiments usually flowed like an underground stream beneath the ornate paeans to the "pure and cloudless heart" of the Japanese, but occasionally they burst to the surface with extraordinary vehemence. Thus, in a book of war reportage titled *Bataan*, Hino Ashihei, one of the best-known Japanese wartime writers, described American POWs as "people whose arrogant nation once tried to unlawfully treat our motherland with contempt." "As I watch large numbers of the surrendered soldiers," he continued, "I feel like I am watching filthy water running from the sewage of a nation which derives from impure origins and has lost its pride of race. Japanese soldiers look particularly beautiful, and I feel exceedingly proud of being Japanese."[2] These were the American prisoners, of course, whom Japanese soldiers brutalized in the Bataan death march. Hino's contempt for the "impure" American prisoners provides an almost perfect counterpoint to Ernie Pyle's revulsion on seeing his first "subhuman" Japanese POWs.

As a rule, however, the Japanese turned to one particular negative image when referring directly to the Anglo-American enemy: the demon or devil. "Devilish Anglo-Americans" (*kichiku Ei-Bei*) was the most familiar epithet for the white foe. In the graphic arts the most common depiction of Americans or British was a horned Roosevelt or Churchill, drawn exactly like the demons (*oni, akuma*) found in Japanese folklore and folk religion. As a metaphor of dehumanization, the demonic white man was the counterpart of the Japanese monkeyman in Western thinking, but the parallel was by no means exact. The demon was a more impressive and ambiguous figure than the ape, and certainly of a different category entirely from vermin. In Japanese folk renderings, the demon was immensely powerful; it was often intelligent, or at least exceedingly crafty; and it possessed talents and powers beyond those of ordinary Japanese. Not all demons had to be killed; some could be won over and turned from menaces into guardians. Indeed, Japanese soldiers killed in battle often were spoken of as having become "demons protecting the country" (*gokoku no oni*)—easy to imagine when one recalls the statues of ferocious deities that often guard Buddhist temples. Here again, like the flexible Western metaphor of the child, was an intriguingly malleable stereotype—one that would be turned about dramatically after the war, when the Americans became the military "protectors" of Japan.

During the war years, however, this more benign potential of the demonic other was buried. For the Japanese at war, the demon worked as a metaphor for the enemy in ways that plain subhuman or bestial images could not. It conveyed a sense of the adversary's great power and special abilities, and in this respect it captured some of the ambivalence that had always marked Japan's modern relationship with the West. At the same time, the demonic other played to deep feelings of insecurity by evoking the image of an ever-present outside threat. Unlike apes or vermin, the demon did not signify a random presence. In Japanese folklore, these figures always lurked just beyond the boundaries of the community or the borders of the country—in forests and mountains outside the village, on islands off the coast. In origin, they exemplified not a racial fear, but a far more basic fear of outsiders in general.

Contrary to the myth of being homogeneous, Japanese society was honeycombed with groups suspicious of one another, and the blue-eyed barbarians from across the seas became absorbed into patterns of thinking that had emerged centuries earlier as a response to these tense and threatening insider/outsider relationships. The Westerners who suddenly appeared on Japan's horizon in the mid-nineteenth century were the most formidable of all outsiders, and the response to them mobilized nationalist and racist sentiments in unprecedented ways. Symbolically the demonic other was already present to be racialized. There was, moreover, a further dimension to this complicated play of symbolic representation, for it was but a short step from the perception of an ever-present threat to the consciousness of being an eternal victim. This too is a sentiment that recurs frequently in the Japanese tradition, and in the modern world this "victim consciousness" (*higaisha ishiki*) became inextricably entangled with the perception of foreign threats. From this perspective, modern Japanese racism as exemplified in the demonic other reflected an abiding sense of being always the threatened, the victim, the aggrieved—and never the threat, the victimizer, the giver of grief.

Where images and actions came together most decisively, however, demon, ape, and vermin functioned similarly. All made

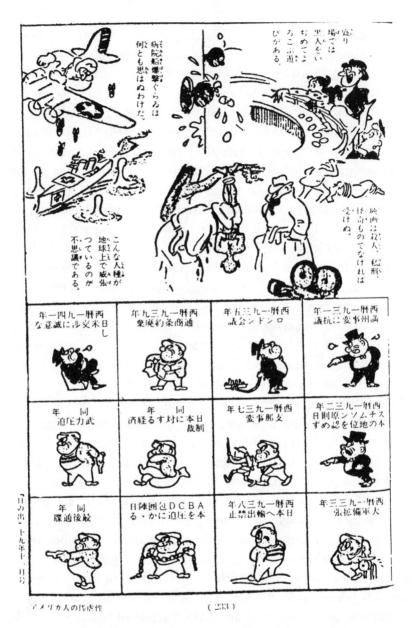

Fig. 2-6. Entitled "The Cruel Nature of Americans," this two-page spread appeared in the November 1944 issue of a popular Japanese magazine. Read from right to left, the top portion illustrates American viciousness with scenes of boxing matches, white people stoning a drowning Negro (a reference to the Detroit race riots), Negroes being humiliated as carnival targets, a black man being lynched, and an American pilot bombing a

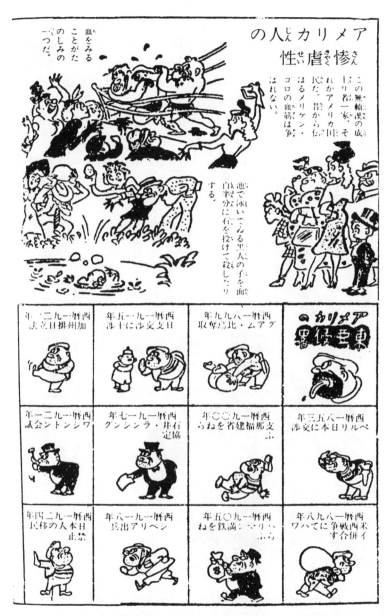

Japanese hospital ship. The bottom panels offer a chronological cartoon history of "American Aggression in East Asia," beginning with the arrival of Commodore Matthew Perry in Japan in 1853 and ending with the encirclement of Japan by the "ABCD" (American, British, Chinese, and Dutch) powers on the eve of Pearl Harbor, and gangster America's final ultimatum to Japan. From *Hinode*, November 1944.

killing easier by dehumanizing the enemy. The rhetoric of "kill the American demons" and "kill the British demons" became commonplace not only in combat, but also on the home front. A popular magazine published in late 1944 conveyed the fury of this rhetoric. Under the title "Devilish Americans and English," the magazine ran a two-page drawing of Roosevelt and Churchill as debauched ogres carousing with fellow demons in sight of Mount Fuji and urged all Japanese, "Beat and kill these animals that have lost their human nature! That is the great mission that Heaven has given to the Yamato race, for the eternal peace of the world!" Another

Fig. 2-7. In the most common Japanese rendering, the Anglo-American enemy was demonized. This illustration, which appeared immediately after Pearl Harbor, accompanied a discussion of the road to war and depicts innocent Japan extending the hand of friendship while the United States and Britain (President Roosevelt and Prime Minister Churchill) feign amity and clandestinely extend their demonic claws (marked "conspiracy") to seize the Orient. From *Osaka Puck*, January 1942.

Fig. 2-8. The Japanese counterpart to the Anglo-American exterminationist imagery of killing beasts entailed annihilating demons. In this poster from 1942, the bayonet of Japanese righteousness skewers the Anglo-American demons. The caption reads, "The death of these wretches will be the birthday of world peace." From *Osaka Puck*, February and December 1942.

magazine, reporting on the decisive battle in the Philippines, declared that the more American beasts and demons "are sent to hell, the cleaner the world will be." Iwo Jima, where United States marines called themselves "rodent exterminators," was described in official Japanese newsreels as "a suitable place to slaughter the American devils."

Demonization was by no means an essential precondition for killing, however. The most numerous victims of Japanese aggression and atrocity were other Asians, who were rarely depicted this way. Toward them the Japanese attitude was a mixture of "Pan-Asian" propaganda for public consumption, elaborate theories of racial hierarchy and Japanese hegemony at official and academic levels, and condescension and contempt in practice. Apart from a small number of idealistic military officers and civilian officials, few Japanese appear to have taken seriously the egalitarian rhetoric of Pan-Asian solidarity and genuine liberation of colonized Asian peoples. Never for a moment did the Japanese consider liberating their own Korean and Formosan colonies, and policy toward Southeast Asia—even when "independence" was granted—was always framed in terms that made Japan's preeminence as the "leading race" absolutely clear. The purity so integral to Japanese thinking was peculiar to the Japanese as a race and culture—not to "oriental" peoples in general—and consequently there emerged no real notion of "Asian supremacism" that could be regarded as a close counterpart to the white supremacism of the Anglo-Americans.

Before the 1930s, the Japanese did not have a clearly articulated position toward other Asians. The rush of events thereafter, including the invasion of China and the decision to push south into Southeast Asia, forced military planners and their academic supporters to codify and clarify existing opinions on these matters. The result was a small outpouring of studies, reports, and pronouncements—many of a confidential nature—that explicitly addressed the characteristics of the various peoples of Asia and the appropriate policy toward them. That these were not casual undertakings was made amply clear in 1981, when a hitherto unknown secret study dating from 1943 was discovered in Tokyo. Prepared by a team of some forty researchers associated with the Population and Race Section of the Research Bureau of the Ministry of Health and Welfare, this work devoted over three thousand pages to analysis of race theory in general and the different races of Asia in particular. The title of the report gives an inkling of its contents: *An Investigation of Global Policy with the Yamato Race as Nucleus.*

The *Investigation* was a serious intelligence report, and its style was academic. In its way it was a counterpart to the "national character" writings of the Anglo-American social scientists who mobilized in support of the Allied war effort. The Japanese researchers called attention to Western theories of race and, while attentive to Nazi ideas, surveyed the gamut of racial thinking beginning with Plato and Aristotle. In the modern world, they noted, racism, nationalism, and capitalist imperialism had become inseparably intertwined. And though modern scholarship had repudiated the notion of biologically pure races, blood still mattered greatly in contributing to psychological unity. In this regard, as Karl Haushofer had observed, Japan was fortunate in having become a uniform racial state (Haushofer, the geopolitician whose writings influenced the Nazis, had done his doctoral work on Japan). At the same time, overseas expansion should be seen as essential not merely for the attainment of military and strategic security, but also for preserving and revitalizing racial consciousness and vigor. On this point the Japanese again quoted Western experts, including not merely the Germans but also the British. Looking ahead, it was predictable that the second and third generations of overseas Japanese might face problems of identity, and thus it was imperative to develop settlement policies that would thwart their assimilation and ensure that they "remain aware of the superiority of the Japanese people and proud of being a member of the leading race."

The focus of this massive report was on Asian rather than Western peoples, and its dry language provides insight into how racial inequality in Asia was rationalized. The central metaphor was the family. The critical phrase was "proper place"—a term that had roots in Confucian prescriptions for domestic relationships but was carefully extended to cover international relations beginning in the late 1930s. The family idiom is another example of the malleable social construct, for it suggests harmony and reciprocity

on the one hand, but clear-cut hierarchy and division of authority and responsibility on the other; and it was the latter that really
mattered to the Japanese. The authors of the *Investigation* were emphatic in condemning false consciousness concerning equality. "To
view those who are in essence unequal as if they were equal is itself
inequitable," they observed. And it followed from this that "to treat
those who are unequal unequally is to realize equality." The family exemplified such equitable inequality, and the Japanese writers
made clear that Japan was not merely the head of the family in Asia,
but also destined to maintain that position "eternally." Whether
the Yamato race also was destined to become the head of the global
family of races and nations was left unanswered, although passing
comments suggested that this was the ultimate goal. The opening
pages of the study flatly declared that the war would continue "until Anglo-American imperialistic democracy has been completely
vanquished and a new world order erected in its place." And as the
Investigation made amply clear, the Japanese-led imperium in Asia
would assume a leading role in this new world order.

Despite their Confucian overtones, the family metaphor and
proper-place philosophy bore close resemblance to Western thinking on issues of race and power. The Japanese took as much pleasure as any white Westerner in categorizing the weaker peoples
of Asia as "children." In their private reports and directives, they
made clear that "proper place" meant a division of labor in Asia in
which the Yamato race would control the economic, financial, and
strategic reins of power within an autarkic bloc and thereby "hold
the key to the very existence of all the races of East Asia." A secret
policy guideline issued in Singapore at the outset of the war was
equally frank. "Japanese subjects shall be afforded opportunities
for development everywhere," it stated, "and after establishing firm
footholds they shall exalt their temperament as the leading race
with the basic doctrine of planning the long-term expansion of the
Yamato race." Despite their detailed country-by-country, race-by-
race summaries, the Japanese were interested in other Asians only
as subordinate members of the family who could be manipulated

to play roles assigned by Japan. For other Asians the real meaning of Japan's racial rhetoric was obvious. "Leading race" meant master race, "proper place" meant inferior place, "family" meant patriarchal oppression.

Given the virulence of the race hate that permeated the Pacific war, at first it seems astonishing that Americans and Japanese were able to move so quickly toward cordial relations after Japan's surrender. Intimate face-to-face contact for purposes other than mutual slaughter enabled each side to rehumanize the other in the highly structured milieu of the Allied Occupation of Japan, which lasted from 1945 to 1952. Although the United States–dominated Occupation was ethnocentric and overbearing in many respects, it also was infused with goodwill and—in its early stages—a commitment to "demilitarization and democratization" that struck a responsive chord among most of the defeated Japanese. Contrary to the wartime stereotypes of propagandists in both the Allied and Japanese camps, most Japanese were sick of regimentation, indoctrination, and militarism. At the same time, the Cold War facilitated a quick diversion of enmity, and anti-Communism became a new crusade uniting the two former antagonists at the state level. Enemies changed, enmity did not.

On both sides, the abrupt metamorphosis from war to peace was cushioned by the malleability of racial, cultural, and ideological stereotypes. With only a small twist, patterns of perception that had abetted mass slaughter now proved conducive to paternalistic patronage on the American side—and to acquiescence to such paternalism by many Japanese. Racism did not disappear from the U.S.-Japan relationship, but it was softened and transmogrified. For the Americans, the vermin disappeared but the monkeymen lingered for a while as charming pets. The September 1945 cover of *Leatherneck*, for example—the first issue of the marine monthly to appear after Japan's capitulation—featured a cheery cartoon of a GI holding a vexed but thoroughly domesticated monkey wearing the cap, shirt, and leggings of the Imperial Army. *Newsweek*, in its feature article on what sort of people the Americans might expect to find in Japan when the Occupation commenced, ran "Curious Simians" as one subheading.

Other racist stereotypes traveled from war to peace in comparable ways. Although defeat temporarily extinguished the superman mystique, it reinforced the perception of the Japanese as little men or lesser men. Stated conversely, victory over Japan reinforced the conceit of inherent white and Western superiority. The more precise associations of Japan's "lesser" stature, however—the primitive social relations and attitudes, the childishness of the populace both psychologically and politically, the collective neurosis—all now provoked a paternalistic response. The American overseers of Occupied Japan thought in terms of a civilizing mission that would eliminate what was primitive, tribal, and ritualistic—an old but idealistic colonial attitude indeed. They would guide an immature people with backward institutions toward maturity. The Japanese "children" now became pupils in General MacArthur's school of democracy, learners and borrowers of advanced United States technology, followers of U.S. Cold War policies. Where the Japanese psyche was tortured, the Americans would be healers.

These were not frivolous attitudes, any more than paternalism itself is necessarily frivolous. At the individual level, moreover, countless Japanese and Americans collaborated equitably in pursuit of common goals. Neither democratization and demilitarization nor—later—economic reconstruction and remilitarization were ethnocentric American goals forced on unwilling Japanese. The overall relationship, however, was inherently unequal and patronizing on the part of the Americans, and it is here that racist attitudes survived. U.S. policymakers at the highest level also were not above cynically manipulating Japanese racism to serve their own purposes. In 1951, when Japan's allegiance in the Cold War was still not entirely certain, for example, John Foster Dulles recommended that the Americans and British take advantage of Japanese feelings of "superiority as against the Asiatic mainland masses" and play up the "social prestige" of being associated with the Western alliance. (In a fine example of a truly free-floating stereotype, Dulles and other American leaders also liked to emphasize that the Soviet menace could be better understood if one remembered that the Russians were an Asiatic people.)

On the Japanese side, defeat was bitter but peace was sweet, and certain attitudes associated with wartime racial thinking also proved adaptable to the postsurrender milieu. Proper-place thinking facilitated acceptance of a subordinate status vis-à-vis the victorious Allies, at least for the time being. In this regard it is helpful to recall that the "leading race" rhetoric of the war years was a relatively new ideology in Japan, and that for most of their modern history the Japanese had played a subordinate role in the world order. The militarism of the 1930s and early 1940s arose out of a desire to alter that insecure status, and it ended in disaster. To seek a new place in new ways after 1945 was in fact the continuation of a familiar quest.

In fascinating ways, the wartime fixation on purity and purification proved adaptable to this commitment to a new path of development. Individuals who had been exhorted to purge self and society of decadent Western influences before the surrender now found themselves exhorted to purge the society of militarism and feudalistic legacies. This sense of "cleansing" Japan of foul and reactionary influences was truly phenomenal in the early postwar years, and while this tapped popular aspirations for liberation, it also politicized the militarists' ideology of the pure self in undreamed-of ways. Universal "democratic" values now became the touchstone of purity. And the guardians at the gates, to cap these astounding transmogrifications, were the erstwhile American demons. The United States assumption of a military role as protector of postwar Japan was a hard-nosed, rational policy, but from the Japanese perspective it had a subtle, almost subconscious logic. The fearsome demons of Japanese folklore, after all, were often won over and put to use by the ostensibly weaker folk.

The transitional adaptations of proper place, purity, and the demon more or less deracialized the wartime fixations. They did not, however, eliminate racial tensions latent in the structure of institutionalized inequality that has characterized postwar U.S.-Japan relations until recently. So long as Japan remained conspicuously inferior to the United States in power and influence, the structure and psychology of what is known in Japan as "subordinate independence" could be maintained. When relations of power and influence changed, neither side could be expected to rethink these fundamental relationships without trauma. The great change came in the 1970s, when it became apparent—abruptly and shockingly for almost everyone concerned—that Japan had become an economic superpower while America was in relative decline. In this situation, war talk became fashionable again: talk of trade wars; ruminations on who really won the Pacific war; doomsday warnings of a new yen bloc, a seriously rearmed Japan, a "financial Pearl Harbor." In American rhetoric, the simian subhumans were resurrected as "predatory economic animals," the old wartime supermen returned as menacing "miraclemen," garbed in Western business suits but practicing sumo capitalism. Japanese, in turn, often in high government positions, decried America's demonic "Japan bashing" and at the same time attributed their country's accomplishments to a "Yamato race" homogeneity and purity that "mongrelized" America could never hope to emulate.[3]

As times change, the malleable idioms of race and culture, power and status, change with them. They never completely disappear.

3

JAPAN'S BEAUTIFUL MODERN WAR

Since 1945 a great deal of international attention has been devoted to imperial Japan's wartime atrocities against the peoples of China and Southeast Asia, against Anglo-American prisoners of war, and against hundreds of thousands of the nation's brutalized Korean colonial subjects. The number of books, articles, films, symposiums, exhibitions, permanent museums, and now websites devoted to one or another aspect of this barbaric conduct is beyond counting. This stain on the nation's reputation is indelible.

It is vastly harder to reconstruct and recall how the Japanese were socialized to see their invasion of China and subsequent attack on the United States and European colonial powers as a just and even holy war (seisen), the very opposite of atrocious. Modern societies are not mobilized for war in the name of committing aggression. Losers do not get to propagate the propaganda that made them willing to fight and die. No one, whether winner or loser, really wants to revisit all the beautiful lies. Indeed, to attempt to do so runs the risk of being regarded as an apologist for, or even denier of, all those grievous war crimes. What becomes lost in this averted gaze is any meaningful understanding of how men, women, and children become harnessed to the war machine.

It can be plausibly argued that no nation in World War II launched a more sophisticated propaganda blitz domestically than the Japanese. Academics assisted the state's rabid ideologues in ransacking the classical literary tradition for ornate tracts and a cascade of evocative slogans. Talented composers and lyricists churned out what may well be the most robust, melodic, and romantic body of war songs of any of the belligerents. Most of Japan's top writers and artists were recruited to contribute to the war effort, as were the most creative young filmmakers. The visual propaganda of the period from 1937 to 1945 was stunning—but has remained largely unseen and forgotten since the war ended.

One example of the visual beautification of the war effort that had no real counterpart elsewhere was the introduction of martial themes into textiles worn in the form of traditional garments. Particularly on festive occasions, boys, men, and even women could literally wrap themselves in aestheticized patriotism. These textiles remained virtually unknown even to present-day Japanese until recently, and were the subject of a pathbreaking exhibition at Bard College in 2005, curated by Jacqueline Atkins. The essay that follows appeared in the lavish catalog to that exhibition as a background piece on the beautification of the war, in which these textiles were but one tiny part.

*   *   *

So much depends on the eye of the beholder. World War II in Asia is a good example. For most Americans, the beginning of that war, like its end, is perfectly clear. Japan's surprise attack on Pearl Harbor on December 7, 1941, marks the beginning. August 14, 1945—when Emperor Hirohito announced Japan's capitulation following the atomic bombing of Hiroshima and Nagasaki— marks the end. The British and their Commonwealth compeers would more or less agree, although the indelible image they usually associate with the onset of all-out war in Asia is the fall of England's colonial enclave Singapore in the wake of the Pearl Harbor attack.

From an Asian perspective, however, the war began much earlier. Indeed, the trial of accused war criminals that was convened by the victorious Allied Powers in Tokyo in 1946 as counterpart to the Nuremberg Trial of German leaders was premised on the prosecution's charge that Japanese policymakers had pursued a "common plan or conspiracy" to wage "wars of aggression" ever since 1928.

No serious scholar today would endorse this simplistic conspiracy thesis, which so blithely ignores imperialist rivalries in Asia and the collapse of the capitalist world order in the Great Depression that began in 1929. At the same time, no one can ignore the fact that the so-called Manchurian Incident of 1931 marked the beginning of a new level of Japanese aggression and expansion on the Asian continent that led, seemingly inexorably, to all-out war with China six years later. From the Asian perspective, the "Pacific War" that began with Pearl Harbor and Singapore and ended with Hiroshima and Nagasaki was simply the final stage in a fifteen-year war.

The 1931 Manchurian Incident itself began with a bogus *casus belli*—a plot by officers in Japan's elite Kwantung Army that involved blowing up a small portion of the Japanese-controlled South Manchurian Railway and attributing the nefarious deed to the Chinese. This led to Japan's takeover of the three Chinese provinces north of the Great Wall collectively known as Manchuria. And this, in turn, led to establishment of a puppet regime ("Manchukuo") under "Emperor" Puyi, scion of the former Manchu ruling dynasty that reigned over China until the early twentieth century.

In 1933 Japan withdrew from the League of Nations after that international body condemned the takeover of Manchuria, and in 1936 the now isolated Japanese, in the name of fighting international Communism, entered into an Anti-Comintern Pact with Nazi Germany. In 1940, three years after plunging into all-out war with China, Imperial Japan joined Germany and fascist Italy in the so-called Tripartite Pact better known to the world as the Axis Alliance.

Just as it was the Soviet Union that suffered the most catastrophic losses on the Western front in World War II, so it was China that endured the greatest suffering and loss of life in the war in Asia. Unlike the conspiratorial incident that precipitated the takeover of Manchuria in 1931, the eruption of all-out war in China in July 1937 did not involve a plot on the Japanese side. Rather, relations had become so volatile by this time that a minor incident involving Chinese and Japanese troops near Peking quickly escalated out of control. War may well have been inevitable; we can never say for sure. Japanese imperialism and Chinese nationalism were on a collision course, but the conflagration that erupted in 1937 was not planned.

For practical reasons, neither China nor Japan formally declared war in 1937. Under American "neutrality" legislation, this would have made both sides ineligible to obtain crucially needed military-related matériel from the United States. Despite such legal nicety—which enabled U.S. business interests to continue to feed the Japanese war machine while their government condemned Japan and extended aid to China—what the Japanese called the China Incident quickly turned ferocious and atrocious. Hard-line militarists predicted victory within six months over the technologically inferior and politically divided Chinese, and the emperor refused to grant an audience to more cautious Army General Staff officers.

Unexpectedly fierce Chinese resistance prompted Japan's civilian prime minister Konoe Fumimaro to observe, early in 1939, that Japan was actually engaged in a "war of annihilation." And indeed it was. When battle-weary and undisciplined Japanese forces finally entered the Chinese capital of Nanking in December 1937, after having fought their way up from Shanghai, they ran amok in the frenzy of rape, murder, and pillage the world knows today as the Rape of Nanking.[1]

In the end China did not fold, although the greater part of it—the whole vast territory along the seacoast, with a population of over 200 million—remained under Japanese occupation from 1937 to 1945. We will never know for certain how many Chinese were killed in Nanking, or in other Japanese atrocities, or in the course of the tenacious eight-year-long Chinese resistance outside the occupied areas. After the war, official estimates put the number of Chinese military dead at around 1.3 million and total fatalities at anywhere between 9 and 15 million, figures that have been substantially (but not necessarily persuasively) enlarged in recent years. The numerology of victimization is itself a form of contemporary nationalism, but the number of Asians who perished as a consequence of Japanese aggression in China, and later in Southeast Asia, was incontestably huge.

Where the Japanese and American war dead are concerned, we can speak with greater certainty. Approximately 2 million Japanese fighting men died between 1937 and the end of the war in 1945, out of a population that originally numbered a little more than 70 million. At least 700,000 civilians also perished, most of these deaths occurring in 1945 and the immediate aftermath of the war—in the American air raids on major Japanese cities, in the devastating Battle of Okinawa, and in the perilous and chaotic withdrawal from Manchuria after Japan's defeat. On the American side, battle fatalities in the Pacific totaled approximately 100,000. Three times that number of American fighting men were killed in the European theater.[2]

Japanese propaganda presented the Manchurian Incident and the China Incident, as well as the war against the Allied Powers that followed, as legitimate and necessary acts of self-defense. While most of the world outside the fascist camp dismissed this as patently fatuous, within Japan such propaganda was enormously persuasive. There were many reasons why this was so, beginning with Japan's "legitimate rights and interests" on the Asian continent. These privileges rested on a web of formal treaties and agreements dating back to the turn of the century, when Japan first emerged as a modern imperialist power by defeating China (in 1895) and Russia (in 1905). From the moment Japan had been forced to abandon its policy of feudal seclusion in the mid-nineteenth century, the country's leaders had turned to the great, expansionist Western powers themselves for lessons about how to survive and prosper in a fiercely competitive world. The key, they concluded, was "wealth and military power" (*fukoku kyōhei*); and the key to wealth and power, in turn, was to be found in the wisdom of Social Darwinism and "survival of the fittest" thinking. *Realpolitik* and *Machtpolitik*—

pragmatic realism and power politics—were the name of the game. This may seem an elemental lesson, but no other non-Western, non-Caucasian, non-Christian country learned it—and practiced it—remotely as well.

More concretely, it became an article of faith among virtually all Japanese that survival and prosperity required both stability in the regions bordering Japan and guaranteed access to the markets and resources of continental Asia. Drawing on the nineteenth-century European and American models of gunboat diplomacy and "unequal treaties," they used their stunning victories over China and Russia to put the screws to beleaguered China in particular. This adroit marriage of military force and legalistic finesse was how Japan established itself militarily and economically in Manchuria and the rest of China in the first place. (Japan's acquisition of Formosa [now Taiwan] and Korea as colonies, in 1895 and 1910, respectively, was part of the spoils from these early wars.)

When propagandists defended blatant aggression in the 1930s in terms of defending Japan's acknowledged rights and interests, they were thus referring to an elaborate web of treaty rights and concessions they had succeeded in extracting from China over the preceding decades. (The Western powers, including the United States, did not completely repudiate their own unequal treaties with China until the 1940s.) This, however, was but the skin of the propaganda appeal. By the 1930s, most Japanese had become persuaded that the nation was imperiled by events and forces more threatening than anything previously imagined.

One such perceived threat was the warlord politics and domestic chaos that roiled China in the wake of the overthrow, in 1911, of the Manchu dynasty that had ruled the country since the seventeenth century. Another was the birth of Chinese nationalism (popularly known as the May Fourth Movement) that erupted in 1919 in response to great-power manipulations disadvantageous to China at the Paris Peace Conference that followed World War I. It is testimony to how successfully Japan had mastered the power politics of the West that it sat as one of the victorious nations at this conference, acknowledged as a "great power" alongside the United States, Great Britain, and France. In the crude realpolitik that ignited Chinese nationalism on this occasion, the Western powers essentially endorsed not only their own privileged positions in China, but also additional onerous "rights and interests" Japan had extracted from China shortly after World War I broke out.

All this was compounded by a new threat that went far beyond China per se: the emergence of international Communism in the wake of the Bolshevik Revolution of 1917. By the mid-1920s, Communism had established roots in China and become a potent ideological weapon for mobilizing popular sentiment against "imperialist" encroachment and exploitation. To the very end of World War II in Asia, evocation of the "red peril" remained a staple of Japanese propaganda. Russia had been replaced by the vastly more threatening Soviet Union; Communism was on the rise in China; "red" thought was even percolating into Japan itself.

The collapse of Wall Street in 1929 and the disastrous global depression that followed naturally deepened the sense of impending crisis, particularly since the United States and European countries attempted to protect their own economies by erecting trade barriers against imports from Japan. In this increasingly unstable milieu, Japanese military and civilian planners became obsessed with the concept of autarky—the vision of an autonomous and self-sufficient strategic and economic "new order" in Asia, led of course by Japan. The Manchurian Incident and China Incident took place in this atmosphere of acute and protracted crisis. Never had the economic "lifeline" of China seemed more critical to Japanese survival.

When the Western powers condemned Japan's aggressive actions and threw their support behind China, they were denounced as hypocrites: the British, French, Dutch, and Americans, after all, all possessed their own colonies and acknowledged spheres of influence. (Drawing on the Monroe Doctrine, under which the United States laid claim to preeminent rights and interests in

Central America and the Caribbean, Japanese in the 1930s some-times referred to their own "Monroe sphere" in Asia.) Beyond this, however, the United States and Europe were now seen to be threat-ening Japan's very ability to survive in a world that seemed to be spiraling into chaos. There was no "world order" any more—only international disorder everywhere one looked.

This was a time, moreover, when "yellow peril" sentiment was on the rise in the West. A signal example of this, in Japanese eyes, was the refusal of the new League of Nations to adopt a proposal by the Japanese delegation to include a "racial equality" clause in its founding principles in 1919. The U.S. Congress added insult to injury a few years later, in 1924, by enacting the now notori-ous "Oriental exclusion" legislation. The Japanese response to such blatant white supremacism was to pump up both antiwhite animus and counterpart paeans to the superiority of the "Yamato race" (a term evoking the mythic divine origins of the Japanese).

Thus, to the Chinese peril of rising anti-Japanese nationalism and the red peril of international Communism, Japanese propa-gandists added the "white peril" of Western racism, imperialism, and power politics. Japan was engaged in a holy war to defend its very survival as a viable nation and culture.

The lofty rhetoric of holy war (seisen) had more than just de-fensive or reactive connotations, however. The Japanese public had no idea that the Manchurian Incident had been a Kwantung Army plot (this did not become widely known until after the war). On the contrary, the seizure of Manchuria was presented as be-ing not merely a legitimate and necessary response to Chinese provocation, but also an opportunity for enormous creativity. Manchukuo would become a buffer against the spread of Soviet power. It would become a fertile new frontier to which poor Japanese farm families could emigrate. It would become a melting pot for bringing about the "harmony of the five races" (Japanese, Chinese, Koreans, Manchurians, and Mongolians). It would be-come a pilot project for "constructing a new Asia" free from the scourge of Chinese warlordism and international Communism and Western imperialism—free, indeed, from the rapacious and unstable kind of capitalism that had brought about the Great Depression.

When this quest for security and autonomy spilled into China proper, and then into Southeast Asia and the Pacific (to gain access to resources essential to continue the struggle for China), the stakes in the holy war were simply raised to the highest imaginable level. This was madness, as is clear in retrospect, and some Japanese did think this at the time; most of them remained silent, and a small number (mostly members of the Japan Communist Party who refused to recant) were imprisoned. To the great majority of Japanese, however, the holy war was a cause worth dying for. There was, indeed, little alternative.

Like any other people at war, the Japanese mourned their dead while ignoring their victims. Early in the China war, it was common to designate certain of the war dead as *gunshin*, "military gods," whose sincerity, strength of character, and abiding patriotism exemplified

Fig. 3-1. Kimono fabric showing Admiral Tōgō Heihachirō. Japan 1934. Printed muslin; 13 ½" × 23". Collection Alan Marcuson & Diane Hall, London. Courtesy of Bard Graduate Center: Decorative Arts, Design History, Material Culture; New York. Photographer: Bruce White.

Many commemorative objects were created after the death in 1934 of Admiral Tōgō Heihachirō, who was revered for his resounding victory over the Russian navy at both the outset and the end of the Russo-Japanese war. The shrine in the background of this textile design indicates the general's status as a *gunshin*, or military god, after his death.

a pure spirit of sacrifice for sovereign and country. Fittingly for a nation obsessed by the recent history of its struggle for security and stature, the prototype *gunshin* was Admiral Tōgō Heihachirō, hero of the victory over Russia in 1905. Although he did not die in combat, Tōgō's image was venerated through the course of Japan's fifteen-year war (Fig. 3-1).

As the China war escalated into the larger "world war" against the Allied Powers, veneration of individual heroes receded before homage to the war dead in general—all of whom were venerated as *eirei*, or departed heroes. Their names were enshrined in Tokyo's imposing Yasukuni Shrine, a modern (late-nineteenth-century) establishment dedicated to men who, beginning in 1853, had died defending the emperor and imperial cause. (The year 1853 was when the feudal government was forced to open Japan's doors to

Fig. 3-2. M. Terauchi, *Paying Homage to the Nation's War Dead*, Yasukuni Shrine. Japan, undated. Oil on canvas. From *Reports of General MacArthur*, vol. 2, part 2. Collection National Archives and Records Administration.

the outside world.) When the emperor's subjects visited Yasukuni, they were mourning and thanking all who had made the supreme sacrifice for sovereign, country, and culture (Fig. 3-2).

"See you at Yasukuni" became the morbidly romantic catchphrase that men prepared to die for the nation were supposed to utter upon taking leave of one another. The cherry blossom—which falls from the bough at the height of its beauty—became appropriated from ancient texts as the supreme symbol of young patriots perishing in modern warfare. Popular songs, poems, and illustrations propagated this imagery, and it was even said that those who died in the war would be reborn as blossoms on the cherry trees that graced Yasukuni Shrine.[3]

As the war drew to its terrible denouement, ideologues and propagandists exhorted the entire populace to fight to the bitter end. "One hundred million hearts beating as one" (*ichioku isshin*), long a favorite slogan for evoking unity, was transformed; the "hundred million," it was now proclaimed, should be prepared to die "like a shattered jewel" (*ichioku gyokusai*). Death in defense of the holy cause became the ultimate form of purification. Pillage, rape, and the slaughter of others had no place in this dreamworld.

These popular images of purity, heroism, and supreme sacrifice took hold, of course, in a partial vacuum. Just as there was no awareness that the Manchurian Incident had been a Japanese plot, so there was little if any recognition that the Japanese themselves bore grave responsibility for escalation of the China Incident. The atrocities committed by the emperor's soldiers and sailors went unreported at home. Official censorship was abetted by voluntary and ardent self-censorship. The holy war was reinforced by rousing slogans along the lines of *hakkō ichiu* (eight corners of the world under one roof), underscoring Japan's avowed objective of liberating Asian lands from Western domination and bringing them together under an overarching pan-Asian identity. Criticism of the war effort—or, as the years passed, any expression of war weariness or defeatism—was denounced as lèse-majesté, treasonous behavior that violated the integrity of the august sovereign himself.

Fig. 3-3. Child's kimono (detail), "Nanking Occupied." Japan 1937. Printed wool muslin; 25" × 28 ⅜". Collection Jacqueline M. and Edward G. Atkins, New York. Courtesy of Bard Graduate Center: Decorative Arts, Design History, Material Culture; New York. Photographer: Bruce White. This celebratory design for a boy's kimono includes a military balloon trailing a banner proclaiming "Nanking Occupied." The capital of Republican China, Nanking was taken by the Japanese in mid-December 1937.

In this patriotic milieu, public figures and the media focused overwhelmingly on the hardships and triumphs of "our troops." The conquest of vast reaches of China, essentially completed by 1938, unfolded as a succession of hard-won battles. The fall of Nanking was portrayed at home as a stunning, sterling victory—not a massacre, certainly not a "rape" (Fig. 3-3). Governance of the vast occupied area of China that followed was carried out through a collaborationist National Government of China ensconced in Nanking under the well-known politician Wang Ching-wei. As the propagandists would have it, Japan was this administration's generous mentor in collaborative nation-building. "Bandits and Communists" led the Chinese resistance that operated out of the hinterlands, where Nationalist forces under Chiang Kai-shek had established a temporary new capital at Chungking while Mao Tse-tung directed Communist guerrilla activity from Yenan.

Similarly, the 1941 attack on Pearl Harbor and the American, British, and Dutch colonial possessions in Southeast Asia was presented as a defensive act against powers that supported the enemy in China and threatened to cut Japan off from essential resources and to thwart its destiny as the leader of a prosperous Asia. "It has been truly unavoidable and far from Our wishes that Our Empire has been brought to cross swords with America and Britain," the emperor declared in his rescript announcing the expanded war to his subjects on December 8 (Japan time). "More than four years have passed," he continued, "since China, failing to comprehend the true intentions of Our Empire, and recklessly courting trouble, disturbed the peace of East Asia and compelled Our Empire to take up arms. Although there has been established the National Government of China, with which Japan had effected neighborly intercourse and cooperation, the regime which has survived at Chungking, relying upon American and British protection, still continues its fratricidal opposition. Eager for the realization of their inordinate ambition to dominate the Orient, both America and Britain, giving support to the Chungking regime, have aggravated the disturbances in East Asia. Moreover these two Powers, inducing other countries to follow suit, increased military preparations on all sides of Our Empire to challenge Us."

After more rhetoric along these lines, the emperor concluded with these words: "The hallowed spirits of Our Imperial Ancestors guarding Us from above, We rely upon the loyalty and courage of Our subjects in Our confident expectation that the task bequeathed by Our forefathers will be carried forward and that the sources of evil will be speedily eradicated and an enduring peace immutably established in East Asia, preserving thereby the glory of Our Empire."

The rescript was reissued for the emperor's subjects to reread on the eighth day of each month until the end of the war.[4]

In retrospect, escalation of the China war into an Asia-Pacific war involving the United States and European colonial powers was an act of desperation if not outright insanity. At the time, however, Japan's leaders deemed this wider war unavoidable if Japan were not to be reduced to the status of a "fourth-class" nation. The Allied powers, it was argued, preoccupied with the Nazi onslaught in Europe, would be inclined to negotiate some sort of settlement

that would enable Japan to retain access to Southeast Asian resources and suppress the tenacious resistance in China.

Japan's ability to bring the Western powers to the negotiating
table, the argument continued, would be strengthened by indigenous Asian support for the noble goal of liberation from colonial
oppression. By the time the emperor delivered his December 1941
declaration of war, the "white" enemy in Asia had been conflated
with the Chinese resistance into a handy alphabetic shorthand.
Japan, it was said, was being strangled by the "ABCD" enemy—the
Americans, British, Chinese resistance, and Dutch. The Americans
and Dutch controlled the Philippines and Indonesia, respectively,
and the British were colonial overlords of Hong Kong, Malaya (including Singapore), Burma, and India. Once Japan stood up firmly
against them, the propagandists promised, other Asians would rise
up in support. Were the Japanese not, after all, liberators? (Fig. 3-4)

They were not, but this pipe dream was not entirely divorced
from plausibility. Two hundred million Chinese, after all, had
submitted to Japanese control. As it turned out, small "independence" armies of Burmese and Indians also bought into the liberation rhetoric and threw their lot in with the Japanese, and the
Philippines and Indonesia did produce their native collaborators.
(The Japanese had already negotiated the takeover of France's colonies in Indochina after the fall of France to Germany in 1940.)
To Japanese fighting men and their families and supporters back
home, the notion that their deeds would bring about the expul-
sion of Western imperialism and the "rise of Asia" clarified and
ennobled the great sacrifices they were being called upon to make.

The Japanese campaign against Western and Communist influences in Asia extended to the domestic scene as well, where the
"thought police" of the Home Ministry devoted great energy to
ferreting out "dangerous thoughts." In the 1920s, so-called Peace
Preservation legislation had targeted Communist organizers and
left-wing intellectuals in particular. By the late 1930s, the definition of dangerous views had been expanded to include "Anglo-
American thought" in general. What this entailed was eventually

Fig. 3-4. Government poster, Japan, c. 1943 (reproduction). Private
Collection, New York. Courtesy of Bard Graduate Center: Decorative
Arts, Design History, Material Culture; New York.

This poster aimed at foreign audiences captures official propaganda
about liberating Asia from American, British, and Dutch ("A," "B," and
"D") oppression and the Chinese ("C") resistance to Japan's "noble"
mission in China.

spelled out in lengthy official tomes such as *Cardinal Principles of the National Polity* (*Kokutai no Hongi*, 1937) and *The Way of the Subject* (*Shinmin no Michi*, 1940). A cartoon published in the officially approved humor magazine *Manga* in May 1942 captured the thrust of "Purging One's Head of Anglo-Americanism" in an unusually graphic manner. It depicted a young woman combing flakes of dandruff from her scalp—the scruff being variously identified as "extravagance," "selfishness," "hedonism," "liberalism," "materialism," "money worship," "individualism," and "Anglo-American ideas."[5]

Such broad-brush attacks on Anglo-American values and character traits served several functions. Portraying the Western enemy as incorrigibly decadent and consumed by egoistic concerns did more than just incite contempt for the foe. It reinforced the wishful belief that the Americans and British would be unwilling and unable to mount a prolonged military response to Japan's escalated aggression in Asia. At the same time, these "national character" polemics laid the ground for trumpeting so-called traditional Japanese virtues. Ideologues and propagandists ransacked the past for usable images and ideas—and came up with the cherry blossom, for example, and the mystique of a unique Yamato spirit (*Yamato damashii*) and a great deal of flowery language about purity. Medieval texts provided highly idealized codes concerning the "way of the warrior" (*bushidō*)—prose easily adaptable to positing spiritual and aesthetic aspects of war that, it was declared, no other people or culture could ever hope to truly understand or emulate.[6]

More potent yet, the old writings provided fodder for high rhetoric about a putative Imperial Way (*Kōdō*) that wedded loyalty and filial piety under the inimitable aegis of a dynasty that traced its lineage back to Amaterasu, the sun goddess. The imperial rescript of December 8, 1941, was redolent with such hot air. When it came to reinventing tradition for practical, contemporary purposes—a concept much beloved by present-day historians—no one surpassed the Japanese.

At the same time, however, the propagandists proved equally adept at dressing their holy war in the most up-to-date, futuristic apparel. And at least initially—when there still seemed to be a real prospect of victory in China, or against the Americans and British who had proven so astonishingly inept in defending Pearl Harbor and Singapore—this positive, forward-looking vision was the real key to mobilizing popular sentiment. The Japanese populace was bombarded with propaganda about creating a new structure at home and a new order abroad; about liberating Asia from the scourge of Western exploitation and creating a "Greater East Asia Co-Prosperity Sphere"; about crushing the menace of Communism and bringing about revolutionary change "under the brocade banner" of the throne. Japan's mission, philosophers associated particularly with Kyoto Imperial University said, was nothing less than to "overthrow the modern" and lead the way to a brave new world. As plainer phrasemakers put it, Japan would be "the Light of Asia"[7] (Fig. 3-5).

This emphasis on Japan's *modernity*—even, as it were, on its destiny to show the way to a postmodern world beyond what the decadent West offered—is often overlooked.[8] Yet the thrust of the country's wartime propaganda cannot be understood without this. Why were the Japanese destined to be the leading race (*shidō minzoku*) of Asia, and perhaps of the whole world? Because, the

Fig. 3-5. Poster, "Develop Asia!" Designed by Tsuruta Gorō and issued by Japan's Ministry of War in celebration of Army Day. Japan, undated. From *Reports of General MacArthur*, vol. 2, part 1. Collection National Archives and Records Administration.

ideologues declared, the Japanese people exemplified values and talents no other people possessed or could ever hope to possess in like manner.

All manner of "evidence" was evoked in support of such ultranationalistic palaver. Imperial Japan had absorbed Confucian ideals—and the cardinal virtue of filial piety in particular—from a China where these values no longer flourished. It had forged a modern nationalism out of elements peculiar to its own history and culture: the loyalty and self-sacrifice ascribed to feudal warriors, coupled with myths of racial purity that could be squeezed out of the indigenous Shinto religion, and all this coupled again with the mystique of a divinely descended dynasty. And, not least, Japan alone of all the non-Caucasian, non-Christian, non-Western peoples and countries of the world had escaped domination by the West. How? By mastering their science and technology. Japan and Japan alone, the propaganda held, had succeeded in hybridizing the very best of East and West.

The *machinery* of modernity—both literal and figurative—was of absorbing interest in 1930s Japan. The rapid technological and industrial change that had enabled Japan to leap from feudal seclusion to a place among the great powers of the world within a mere half century was manifest in more than military prowess. In the wake of World War I and the massive Kanto earthquake of 1923 (which prompted an enormous construction boom along more modern lines in the Tokyo-Yokohama area), Western-style modernism was visible wherever one looked. Tall buildings arose in the cities. Automobiles appeared on the streets. Trains crisscrossed the land. Airplanes dotted the sky. A subway rumbled through the bowels of Tokyo (Fig. 3-6). Western-style fashions—music, clothing, food, movies, even "free love"—captivated a new urban bourgeoisie.

At the same time, it was also indisputable that such creative modernization went hand in hand with technocratic "rationalization" and the mobilization of hitherto unimaginable violence. World War I had taught military planners throughout the world that future victories would depend on the capability of mobilizing

Fig. 3-6. *Nagajuban*, "Modernity" (detail). Japan, ca. 1930. Printed muslin; 13¾" × 19¼". Collection Tanaka Yoku, Tokyo. Courtesy of Bard Graduate Center: Decorative Arts, Design History, Material Culture; New York. Photographer: Nakagawa Tadaaki/Artec Studio.

Reconstruction of the Tokyo-Yokohama area along more modern lines after the devastating Kantō earthquake of 1923 was reflected in everything from department stores and subways to electric and telephone lines crisscrossing city streets.

every aspect of society behind the war effort—not only government, industry, finance, and armies and navies, but the support of
the entire population as well. *Psychological* mobilization, drawing
upon all the resources of modern means of communication, was as
important as weaponry in waging all-out war.

By the mid-1930s, such "total war" planning had become
extremely influential in Japan, invariably framed in terms that
strengthened the role and authority of the state. Former Marxists
joined right-wing ideologues in calling for some form of state socialism or national socialism. Iconoclastic cadres of new bureaucrats (*shin kanryō*) and reform bureaucrats (*kakushin kanryō*) moved
into positions of influence in key ministries. A score or so giant
industrial conglomerates emerged under the generic name "new
combines" (*shinko zaibatsu*), distinguished by their close ties with
the military, by their concentration in military-related enterprises,
and often by their close involvement with the industrial development of Manchukuo. In certain critical sectors, so-called national
policy companies (*kokusakugaisha*) were created to forge a formal
mix of public and private capital and management.

None of this took place without opposition. Factionalism was
intense in military as well as civilian circles, and 1930s Japan reeled
under the impact of assassinations and even (in 1936) a serious attempted coup d'etat led by young Army officers. But ultimately
the hard-nosed militarists and reform bureaucrats had their way.
The Peace-Preservation legislation of the 1920s was enforced with
increasing severity to repress not only the dangerous thoughts of
those deemed too liberal and supportive of Anglo-American ideals,
but also those deemed to have moved too far toward the radical,
terrorist right.

The takeover of Manchuria that began in 1931 became an ideological touchstone and signpost for many of these developments.
While Chinese diplomats denounced Japan's seizure of China's
"three eastern provinces" and the League of Nations formally
condemned this disturbance of the international status quo, the
Japanese public was persuaded that their country had embarked

on a great mission. "Manchukuo as Ideology" became yet one more uplifting catchphrase. In print media, propaganda posters, films, and songs, the new puppet state was presented not merely as a bountiful, almost utopian land to which poor Japanese families could emigrate, but also as a perfect pilot project for the realization of state socialism. In Manchukuo, the new bureaucrats and their reformist military counterparts declared, it would be possible to create a model state free of the exploitation and instability of the

Fig. 3-7. *Haori* with "Mantetsu" *haura*. Japan, early 1930s. *Haori*: black silk; 41 ½" × 51". *Haura*: *yūzen*-dyed silk; 22"× 21 ¾". Collection Tanaka Yoku, Tokyo. Courtesy of Bard Graduate Center: Decorative Arts, Design History, Material Culture; New York. Photographer: Nakagawa Tadaaki/Artec Studio.

The textile rendering of a roaring locomotive was based on posters advertising the South Manchurian Railway, which lay at the heart of Japan's neo-colonial presence north of the Great Wall of China. Such images elicited pride in Japan's technological prowess, as well as heady excitement about the pioneering challenge of developing the new puppet state of Manchukuo.

Fig. 3-8. Nakamura Shūkō, *The Great Victory of Japanese Warships off Haiyang Island*. Japan, 1894. Woodblock print. Photograph © 2011 Collection Museum of Fine Arts, Boston. Anonymous Gift (23.288–90).

In this typically dramatic celebration of Japanese naval prowess in the first Sino-Japanese War, the majestic battleship *Matsushima* sinks a Chinese warship. Intrepid sailors man small craft in the turbulent waves, while other large Japanese vessels loom in the background.

capitalist system that had plunged the world into depression and chaos. Simultaneously, racial harmony would be promoted—so unlike the intolerant world of white, yellow, and red perils.

The raw, expansive beauty of Manchuria enhanced its great appeal. A cadre of distinguished professional photographers sent back memorable, brooding images in the mode of social realism. Travel agencies and the powerful South Manchurian Railway Company churned out colorful posters inviting tourists to ride the great trains across this new frontier. Children's culture was permeated with the same image of an inviting land ripe for development (Fig. 3-7).[9]

Such pictures of Manchukuo as a place of great drama, great opportunity, and great machines were part and parcel of a larger national pride at the remarkable development of the Japanese economy. The turn-of-the-century victories over China and Russia represented the first great demonstration of this transformation from

Fig. 3-9. Migita Toshihide, *Chief Gunner of Our Ship* Fuji *Fights Fiercely in the Naval Battle at the Entrance to Port Authur.* Japan, 1904. Woodblock print. Photograph © 2011 Collection Museum of Fine Arts, Boston. Jean S. and Frederic A. Scharf Collection (2000.75).

This illustration from the Russo-Japanese War recycles the formulaic depiction of disciplined fighting men manning the most up-to-date military technology that first appeared ten years earlier in woodblock prints depicting the Sino-Japanese War.

an agrarian to an industrial society. Manchukuo and the total-war mobilization of the 1930s provided an even more spectacular display, and few adult Japanese could fail to be impressed by the speed and scale of this industrial and technological change. A man or woman fifteen years old when Japan defeated Russia in 1905, for example, would have been only forty-one when the Manchurian Incident occurred—and only fifty-one when, in 1941, Japan took on the world.

Many of the patterns and conventions that characterized war imagery in the 1930s and early 1940s were actually established in the Sino-Japanese War of 1894–95. Although photojournalism was becoming widespread in the United States and Europe by then, in Japan the most dramatic depictions of this earlier war against China took the form of popular woodblock prints. In the course of the ten months this conflict lasted, a small coterie of woodblock artists churned out an estimated three thousand brightly colored battle scenes. Many of these stylized images of heroic struggle were recycled in the war against Russia ten years later, even as the woodblock medium was fading away before the advent of photography and other forms of illustration in Japan. And they returned, transmogrified, in the fifteen-year war. The warships were stupendous. The artillery was huge. The emperor's fighting men were not merely stalwart and resolute, but tall and square-jawed and almost perfectly Western in their dress and facial hair—clearly much closer to the Russians than to the pumpkin-headed, pigtailed, grotesquely garbed Chinese (Figs. 3-8 and 3-9).

Modern economic growth made these turn-of-the-century victories possible (plus large loans from New York and London where fighting the Russians was concerned). And, indeed, that earliest stage of industrialization had been deliberately skewed to promote heavy state involvement in strategic military-related industries. Nonetheless, the early-twentieth-century economy remained fundamentally concentrated in textiles and light industry, with female workers constituting more than half the factory workforce. Japanese capitalism was still at a relatively rudimentary stage.

Beginning a mere decade after the Russo-Japanese War, World War I sparked a war boom in Japan that saw great advances in factory production and the expansion of a male urban working class, as well as the consolidation of the huge "old" *zaibatsu* oligopolies (Mitsui, Mitsubishi, Sumitomo, and Yasuda). It was not until the 1930s, however, that Japan actually experienced what economists refer to as its "second industrial revolution," marked by rapid and autonomous development in heavy and chemical industries. Mobilization for total war not only helped pull Japan out of the depression. It propelled the nation to entirely new levels of technological accomplishment.[10]

In a context of actual war, these developments were spectacular to behold. All modern nations take pride in flexing their industrial muscle; and at a time when photography and then cinema were becoming accessible to mass audiences, a peculiar fascination was reserved for images of assembly lines and heavy machinery and remarkable vehicles. Add to this the furniture of modern war—machine guns and heavy artillery, battleships, submarines, fighter planes, tanks—and the impact could easily become mesmerizing.

This love affair with the machinery of war was as conspicuous in Japan as it was in wartime America. In retrospect, it is easy and natural to dismiss Japan's war against China and the Allied Powers as hubristic and atrocious. Certainly the attack on the United States was foolhardy to an extreme. Scant forethought was given to the psychological impact the surprise attack would have on Americans; no one really anticipated the rage and thirst for revenge that Pearl Harbor triggered. Astonishingly, almost no serious systematic attention was given to the enormous industrial resources the

Fig. 3-10. *Furoshiki* (wrapping cloth), "Mitsubishi Bomber." Japan 1930s. *Yūzen*-dyed artificial silk; 29¼" × 29¼". Collection Tanaka Yoku, Tokyo. Courtesy of Bard Graduate Center: Decorative Arts, Design History, Material Culture; New York. Photographer: Nakagawa Tadaaki/Artec Studio.

The Mitsubishi Army Heavy Bomber Type (Ki-1-II) depicted on this *furoshiki* was produced between 1933 and 1936 and was subsequently superseded by a lighter and faster model. This is one of the most striking graphics to be found among wartime textiles, setting the sleek power of the war machine against a simple but captivating expanse of blue.

United States would be able to mobilize in retaliation. Still, until it was no longer possible to deny inevitable defeat, the Japanese were able to take pride in their military machine (Figs. 3-10, 3-12, and 3-13).

At their peak of conquest in 1942, the emperor's soldiers and sailors controlled a vast area extending from deep in China on the

Fig. 3-11. Artist unknown, *Graduating Students Depart for the Front.* Japan, c. 1944–45. 50" × 74 ⅛". Collection National Museum of Modern Art, Tokyo.

After the China War escalated into the larger Asia-Pacific War, the draft was extended to university students. Beginning in October 1944, many of these young men were assigned to pilot suicide missions against the advancing American forces. The veneration and heroic send-off they received is conveyed here, where the young recruit, still wearing his university uniform, has draped the Japanese flag around his neck.

west to far into the Pacific on the east, and from the Aleutians on the north to the Philippines, Dutch East Indies, and British Burma in the south. The Japanese deployed advanced new tanks in the China war, as well as sophisticated long-range bombers and (from 1940) the best fighter plane in the world—the Mitsubishi Zero, which was also used to great advantage against the Americans and British in the early stages of the Pacific War. Honed and hardened by the combat in China, Japanese pilots were as good as any in the world until their ranks were decimated. They stood as idols to un-counted numbers of boys and young men.

In the 1930s the Japanese navy developed a formidable ar-

Fig. 3-12. Unsold *omiyamairi*, "Battleships." Japan late 1930s. *Yūzen*-dyed silk with embroidery (silk and metallic threads); 40 ½" × 37". Collection Alan Marcuson and Diane Hall, Belgium. Courtesy of Bard Graduate Center: Decorative Arts, Design History, Material Culture; New York. Photographer: Nakagawa Tadaaki/Artec Studio.

This dramatic rendering of a battleship, intended for use as a boy's shrine-visiting kimono, was never sold. The piece still carries its price tag, and the three places meant to depict a family crest are covered with protective white paper.

mada of advanced cruisers, destroyers, carriers, and submarines. In 1937 they began secret construction of the largest battleships ever seen—the ultimately ill-fated *Musashi* and *Yamato*. The attack on Pearl Harbor was an astounding tactical success, not simply because of its boldness but also because of the great armada of modern warships and airplanes assembled for the attack and the use of cutting-edge torpedoes launched from the carrier-based planes. When Japanese aircraft sank the British battleship *Prince of Wales* and the cruiser *Repulse* off the coast of Malaya in the opening days of the Pacific War, they stunned the world and rang the death knell for the vaunted British empire on which the sun, it had been presumed, would never set.[11] (The Japanese had no monopoly on hubris.)

More than old-fashioned samurai or piquant cherry blossoms, it was images of heroic fighting men and their stupendous modern machines that dominated the graphic propaganda of the war years. And it was this same sort of imagery that civilians wore when they literally wrapped themselves in war.

The sumptuous textile designs that graced patriotic kimono and a range of children's clothing over the course of Japan's fifteen-year war have no real counterpart outside Japan. No other nation's civilians, young and old alike, draped themselves so elegantly with images of holy war. No one else produced so many ingenious and individual designs—clothing that frequently blurred the line between fashion and original art.

In part, of course, this clothing reflected deep aesthetic traditions: the distinctive cut of kimono and *haori* coats and other traditional garments; the flamboyant designs that appeared on not only elite costume but also commoner clothing in the cities of the late feudal era; and a general tradition of artistic creativity that drew no clear line between so-called high art and the production of beautiful everyday artifacts. But the patriotic textiles with which the Japanese beautified war in the 1930s and early 1940s reflected more than just this deeply rooted aesthetic tradition. Like the war itself, they were, and consciously so, a reflection of Japan's modernity. There was nothing anachronistic about them.

In postwar scholarship about imperial Japan's road to war, it is possible to speak (oversimply) of two antithetical lines of analysis. The more traditional approach stresses Japan's relative backwardness vis-à-vis the United States and great European powers—the persistence of "feudal remnants"; the failure to establish strong democratic institutions; the pathologies of power in a non-Western nation hell-bent on catching up to the West. More recent approaches tend to lay greater stress not only on the international milieu in which Japan went to war (imperialism, colonialism, global depression, spiraling arms races, rising nationalisms, virulent new ideologies, etc.), but also on the many manifestations of "modernism" and "modernity" that were beginning to flourish in Japan from the 1910s on.

This latter perspective has drawn renewed attention to the phenomenon known as Taishō Democracy. The term derives from the reign name (*nengō*) during which Emperor Hirohito's father, the Taishō emperor, reigned (1912–26), but its thrust is both broader than that short interlude and indifferent to the phenomenon of imperial rule per se. Taishō Democracy is a rhetorical umbrella that covers an enormous range of dynamic and non-militaristic developments. Politically it refers to the strengthening of parliamentary politics, the appearance of cabinets headed by political parties and strongly backed by big-business interests, and the emergence of opposition movements involving labor activists, feminists, socialists, Communists, and a new intelligentsia strongly influenced by Marxist as well as liberal ideas. The reason that government watchdogs labored so zealously to purge Japanese heads of Anglo-American thought in the 1930s was that such influences were becoming widespread.

Socially and culturally, Taishō Democracy was more amorphous but equally dynamic—a seemingly inexhaustible treasure house today for the historian drawn to developments such as urbanization, consumerism, entertainment, publishing for mass audiences, the fashions and frills and exuberant humor of an emergent bourgeois culture in general. The 1920s, for example, witnessed an ebullient vogue centering on the modern girl (*moga*) and modern boy (*mobo*)—sometimes alternatively referred to,

筆二堅岡吉   襲強灣珠眞イワハ

Fig. 3-13. Yoshioka Kenji, *Official Commemoration Card: Attack on Pearl Harbor.* Government-issued postcard, 1943. Photograph © 2012 Museum of Fine Arts, Boston, from the Leonard A. Lauder Collection of Japanese Post Cards (2002.4256).

through Hollywood's mirror, as the "Clara Bow girl" and "Valentino boy."[12] In the more rarefied ether of this new modernity, the Iwanami publishing house became associated with a cosmopolitan "Iwanami culture" featuring translation of European classics that included the liberal and left-wing canon. At the same time, the giant publisher Kōdansha promoted a less highbrow "Kōdansha culture" of lively publications aimed at a mass audience, including magazines that targeted housewives, young boys, and young girls. Almost overnight, a vibrant new children's culture of periodicals, books, comic strips, toys, games, and clothing began to be marketed.[13]

Much of this popular culture found expression through music. Radios and phonographs appeared on the scene, and spirited, sentimental, lachrymose tunes filled the air like birdsong. Certain composers, lyricists, and singers were accorded celebrity status. The most immediate and overwhelming impression of a new era, however, was visual. Illustrators of children's books became household names, right through the war years. Youngsters, and not a few adults as well, became devoted fans of serialized comics such as "Norakuro," which debuted in 1931 featuring a feisty black stray dog who mobilized all the white dogs in the neighborhood. A talented cadre of serious cartoonists emerged to puncture the foibles of political and social trends (led by Kitagawa Rakuten from the turn of the century, and by Kondō Hidezō from the 1920s). The dreamy painter Takehisa Yumeji attracted an adoring audience with his renderings of fragile and melancholy young women who seemed suspended between the curtained world of traditional shops and restaurants and the splashy café society of the modern girl.

As consumerism and popular entertainment flourished, a spectacular world of advertising art developed with it that would, eventually, give much graphic wartime propaganda its distinctive look. Being up-to-date did not require choosing between Western fashions and more traditional clothing such as the kimono. On the contrary, commercial artists devoted themselves to capturing a chic aesthetic that embraced both styles and both traditions. Whereas the cosmetics firm Shiseidō promoted an elegant image of feminine sophistication that highlighted the cosmopolitan, for example, department-store chains such as Mitsukoshi reached a huge audience of largely female consumers more comfortable with kimono and traditional hairstyles. The consumer could pick and choose, and the range of choices seemed to grow exponentially. Commercial artists touting almost everything under this new bourgeois sun—movies, plays, musicals, books, magazines, beverages, cafes, clubs, restaurants, department stores, travel agencies—saw their handiwork reproduced not only in magazines and posters, but even on ubiquitous little boxes of matches. One could literally carry the new culture in one's pocket or pocketbook.[14]

All this was complemented by creative innovation in photography and film-making, where the 1920s and 1930s witnessed path-breaking contributions that wedded foreign models and inspiration to indigenous visions and themes.[15] Avant-garde influences such as Surrealism permeated the arts (Fig. 3-14), and even where less radical modes of expression prevailed, fields such as painting still saw dramatic departures. Superlative work continued to be produced in the traditional Japanese style of representation

(*Nihonga*)—with women in Western dress now joining the traditional kimono-clad beauty as a standard subject—but this was now
complemented by a generation of artists trained in Western-style
oil painting (*Yōga*).[16]

Although little known to foreigners, even today, an enormous
range of Japanese artists was thus immersed in visualizing and creating a new modernity as the militarists stepped in with their own
version of what it meant to be modern. And in short order, however
reluctantly, the artists fell in line. With few exceptions, they lent
their talents to the war machine. They became part of the mobilization for total war. Even the charming comic-strip stray dog
Norakuro became a military leader (Fig. 3-15).

Victors write the histories, the old cliché tells us; and where
imperial Japan's war is concerned, that is more or less true. Postwar
histories tend to focus on Japanese aggression and atrocity, as well
they should. They dismiss the propaganda out of hand—and this is
more problematic. The propaganda was brilliant, and without confronting it squarely we are doomed never to grasp the full nature of
Japan's war—and, by extension, never to have the broad comparative perspective necessary to see how all peoples and cultures make
their wars beautiful, noble, and just.

In present-day Japan, it still remains largely taboo to exhibit
the trappings of the great propaganda machinery of the war years.
The reason why is obvious. Foreigners would denounce such displays as unrepentant neo-nationalism. Japanese critics on the political left would agree. And these critics would, indeed, be half
correct. In Asia, now over a half century removed from the end
of World War II, the wounds from imperial Japan's fifteen-year
war remain open and painful on all sides, and their presence still
defines contemporary struggles for national identity. The Chinese
in particular beat the subject of Japan's war responsibility like a
drum in pumping up their own present-day nationalism. And, on
the opposite side, many conservative Japanese do still argue that
the rhetoric of the war years was sincere and the war dead deserve
to be mourned as *eirei*, departed heroes.[17]

Fig. 3-14. Koga Harue, *Sea*. Japan, 1929. Oil on canvas; 51 ¼"× 63 ⅞". Collection National Museum of Modern Art, Tokyo.
  Koga's famous painting from the late 1920s captures the dramatic play of Western influences and indigenous engagement with the "modernity" that flourished in interwar Japan before the militarists gained control and tightened the screws of censorship and repression.

The need to mourn one's own dead is surely universal. In the case of Japan, however, it has not helped at all that since the mid-1960s many conservative prime ministers have chosen to do this by visiting Yasukuni Shrine, where the souls of those who once despoiled Asia were said to be reborn as cherry blossoms. They have usually scheduled these expressions of homage on or near the anniversary of the end of the war, without ever explaining to the outside world how such acts can be separated from homage to the holy war itself. In such an obtuse political milieu, it is only natural that suspicion will fall on any serious attempt to reconstruct the atmosphere in which an entire nation was mobilized to fight and die.

Yet how else but by revisiting the past are we to understand how such tragedy comes about? The pernicious effect of sanitizing what can be publicly reexamined from Japan's fifteen-year conflict has been to withhold from the world one of the most adroit expressions of visual propaganda ever mobilized in the cause of a modern war. In the context of the times, it was certainly more elaborate than anything the beleaguered Chinese resistance that operated out of Chungking and Yenan for eight long years was able to mount—divorced, as this resistance was, from the personnel, infrastructure, and plain physical security that made the Japanese propaganda effort so large and cohesive.[18] Beyond this, however, at almost every visual level of expression—cartoons, posters, serious paintings, feature films—the Japanese efforts also surpassed the overt propaganda of the Americans and British.

When the Hollywood director Frank Capra was recruited shortly after Pearl Harbor to prepare "documentary" propaganda films for the Army, he had the opportunity to screen many captured feature films that the Japanese had released in the course of the war in China. His response is often quoted in contemporary film circles. "We can't beat this kind of thing," Capra exclaimed. "We make a film like that maybe once in a decade. We haven't got the actors."[19]

This was high praise indeed from a director renowned for his genius evoking the dignity of ordinary folk; and, in retrospect, Capra's observation remains not only persuasive but also applicable to other areas of wartime propaganda. Most Hollywood war films from the World War II period, for example, are of primary interest today for their formulas and stereotypes (the "multiethnic platoon," the Japanese "beast in the jungle," the hero who proves himself in battle). By contrast, many Japanese feature films are distinguished by levels of realism, and even restrained tones of humanism, that run counter to what most foreigners would expect

Fig. 3-15. Child's kimono, "Norakuro." Japan, 1930s. Printed silk; 37½"
× 37¾". Collection Tanaka Yoku, Tokyo. Courtesy of Bard Graduate
Center: Decorative Arts, Design History, Material Culture; New York.
Photographer: Nakagawa Tadaaki/Artec Studio.

  Norakuro, the enormously popular stray dog hero of a cartoon strip by
Tagawa Suihō, made his debut in the monthly magazine *Shōnen Kurabu*
(Boy's Club) in 1931 but quickly captured the fancy of girls and adults as
well. As Japan became increasingly embroiled in war, Norakuro was drafted
and given one military star; by the time this textile appeared, he had been
promoted to three-star level.

from the people who perpetrated the Rape of Nanking or eventually became famous for throwing away their lives in suicidal *"ban-
zai"* charges. The films tend to focus on the sincerity, comradeship,
and stolid self-sacrifice of their Japanese protagonists, rather than
on battlefield mayhem and the killing game. They rarely zero

Fig. 3-16. Poster for the movie *The Story of Tank Commander Nishizumi* (Nishizumi seshachō-den). Commissioned by Japan's Ministry of War, directed by Yoshimura Kenzaburō, and released in 1940, this version of the film's well-known poster is directed to a Malay-speaking audience.

Japanese films were often translated for distribution in occupied areas. This advertisement for the feature film based on the life of a war hero killed in China in 1938 combines many characteristic features of wartime propaganda—the sincere and resolute hero, the awesome machinery of war, and the slick style associated with commercial advertising and popular graphics, particularly after World War I.

in at all on the enemy—whether Chinese or Caucasian. More often than not, they keep speechifying to a minimum; long moments may pass without a word being spoken. Musical scores tend toward the melodic and romantic rather than the corny or stridently martial.[20]

In *Chocolate and Soldiers*, for example—produced by the Tōhō studio in 1938 as one of the first feature-length commercial war films ever made in Japan—the protagonist is an utterly ordinary older draftee whom we never see in close combat. The film cuts back and forth between the China front and the Home Front, where the protagonist's wife and small son and daughter maintain a precarious existence in an extremely modest community. When news of his death is received (he was preparing for the advance on Nanking when last seen on screen) and the boy is told at the funeral service that his father was a hero, he responds "But who will take me fishing now?" The propaganda is subtle to a fault—a local storyteller glimpsed telling various war stories to youngsters, the orphaned son playing with a toy plane at the end, the blood debt one obviously owes to a simple, decent man who died for his country.

In *The Story of Tank Commander Nishizumi*, a 1940 Shōchiku feature based on the actual story of a young officer who was enshrined as a military god (*gunshin*), viewers were introduced to the double theme of Japan's impressive war machinery (the tanks) and the suffering and heroic sacrifice of the nation's fighting men. Nishizumi does indeed face battle again and again, but we never see him kill anyone. His fatal wound comes when he is picked off by a dying Chinese soldier while testing the depth of a body of water his tanks must cross. Although he lingers before dying, there is no death scene and he is given no rousing final words. Nishizumi's godliness lies almost entirely in a purity that reveals itself in concern for his men (that is why he personally tests the water, rather than order his subordinates to do so), and in unquestioning acceptance of his duty to the nation (which is why he feels no need to pontificate about "why we fight," a staple in most Hollywood scripts). Nishizumi and his tank would have made a splendid woodblock print of the sort that flourished during the Sino-Japanese and Russo-Japanese wars. Just as easily, they would have made a perfect subject for a boy's kimono (Fig. 3-16).

Much the same soft realism characterizes the most interesting Japanese film about the Home Front produced during the Asia-Pacific War: Kurosawa Akira's *Ichiban Utsukushiku* (The Most Beautiful). Released by Tōhō in 1944, this film focuses on very young female factory workers recruited from the countryside to produce sophisticated optical lenses for the air force. (Grinding and testing the lenses constitutes the modern machinery here.) Unlike the pretty and peppy wives, girlfriends, nurses, and the like in Hollywood war films, these young women are beautiful by virtue of their innocence and purity. The key word in the film—said, at the end, about the female protagonist—is *yasashii*, gentle. It is a quality the heroine only obtained after transcending mere dedication and discipline. It is, indeed, the same quality that made Nishizumi a figure to be venerated. As much or even more than fervid nationalism or emperor worship, it was this ethos of gentleness wedded to selfless sacrifice that pervaded the visual propaganda of the war years and made it so persuasive to so many Japanese.[21]

In the wake of Japan's defeat, American occupation authorities ordered the destruction of 236 feature films deemed "feudal and militaristic" (they were usually torched in bonfires). A less draconian fate befell the scores of war-related paintings done by artists working in both Japanese and Western styles. Most major Japanese painters, including the esteemed Paris-trained Fujita Tsuguharu, were commissioned to produce such works, and their collective contribution provides an extraordinary window on how worldly Japanese visualized the war in the Chinese, Southeast Asian, and Pacific theaters. Like many of the feature films, the paintings stand the test of time as something more than undiluted propaganda. One finds "pure" heroes here (the *Nihonga*, or Japanese-style paintings, lend themselves particularly readily to this)—but one also encounters sorrow, mourning, even intimations of the humanism and antimilitary sentiments that animated so much of the spirit of Taishō Democracy. Much of this serious artwork was confiscated by the victors and held in Washington until the 1960s, when it was returned to Japan. Some of it is exhibited there piecemeal now. Unlike the feature films, these paintings were not destroyed—but most of them, again, remain inaccessible and little known (Fig. 3-17).[22]

This is the milieu in which the remarkable textiles that appear in this catalog were produced and worn—and subsequently withdrawn from view and all but forgotten. They have no real counterpart on the Home Fronts of other combatants in World War II. The fifteen-year span of Japan's war witnessed an evolutionary refinement of martial designs and themes not seen in other countries, where those war-related textiles that were produced tended toward "sound-bite" jingoism (often, indeed, relying on words) or allusion to specific events. No one else beautified war with such panache or wore the war so literally.

Obviously, we must turn—in part—to old-fashioned notions of "culture" and "tradition" to help account for this. Traditional Japanese apparel lent itself particularly well to intricate and flam-

Fig. 3-17. Ezaki Kōhei, *Capture of Guam*. Japan, 1941. Color on paper, 76 ¼" × 105 ⅝". Collection National Museum of Modern Art, Tokyo.
The tradition of Japanese-style painting (*Nihonga*), with its delicate washes and flat, stylized renderings, proved particularly adaptable to propaganda suggesting the purity and discipline of Japan's mission as "the Light of Asia."

boyant design, and artists of genuine distinction did not hesitate to devote themselves to producing such artwork—even to hand-painting it on the fabric. Ever since late feudal times, people in all walks of life had wrapped themselves in statements and signs, always with an artist's touch. The wartime textiles, it can be said, just carried this one step further.

In a subtle and unarticulated and surely unplanned way, these garments also served to replicate a peculiarly Japanese practice of symbolically linking the Home Front to the battlefield in the most intimate, tactile manner imaginable. Most Japanese men went to war with a "thousand-stitch belly warmer" (*senninbari*) given them upon departure by their local community. This practical gift took its name from the fact that, at least in theory, every stitch—done with red thread, and each individually tied off—had been sewn by a different girl or woman. However far away Japan might be, the fighting man was figuratively and almost literally in touch with his home folk. (In a wry scene in *The Story of Tank Commander Nishizumi*, a soldier whiling away time in a barracks on the China front counts the stitches in his *senninbari* and mutters that he has been shortchanged.) Turned about, people wrapping themselves in war patterns on the Home Front could imagine a comparable sort of intimacy.

When all was said and done, however, such propagandistic artistry was far from traditional in any old-fashioned sense. The patterns were bold and chic in the way recent fashions and commercial design had become bold and chic. The airplanes and battleships and tanks depicted were state of the art. The cause—the holy mission—was the creation of a prosperous new era in Asia. It was all a beautiful expression of Japan's complex—and, at this particular moment, truly terrible—modernity.

4

"AN APTITUDE FOR BEING UNLOVED": WAR AND MEMORY IN JAPAN

It is fashionable among foreigners to say that "the Japanese" have sanitized the past and failed to acknowledge their wartime aggression and atrocities. And at the government level as well as in conservative and right-wing circles, it is not difficult to compile a damning record supporting this. A parade of officials associated with the Liberal Democratic Party that dominated politics from the 1950s into the twenty-first century routinely took turns—almost by appointment, it sometimes seemed—denying atrocities such as the Rape of Nanking. Beginning with Prime Minister Nakasone Yasuhiro in the mid-1980s, conservative leaders began visiting Yasukuni Shrine, where the souls of Japan's war dead, including World War II leaders, are enshrined. A long-running legal case extending from 1965 to 1997 (the Ienaga Saburō textbook case) that challenged the guidelines by which the Ministry of Education approved history textbooks helped sustain critical attention to such official whitewashing as reluctance to characterize Japan's invasion of China in 1937 as a "war of aggression." When the issue of Korean and other non-Japanese women being forced to serve as sexual "comfort women" (ianfu) for the imperial forces in Asia was uncovered (by Japanese researchers) in the 1990s, the government resisted acknowledging official responsibility for this, either then or now, in the form of redress. The list easily can be extended.

At a more general, nongovernmental level, a pervasive sense of victim consciousness (higaisha ishiki) *has characterized much popular recollection of the Asia-Pacific War that extended from 1937 to 1945. Some 3 million Japanese fighting men and civilians died in that conflict, and sixty-six cities were devastated in the U.S. air raids of 1945 that culminated in Hiroshima and Nagasaki. Over the decades that followed, the scores of millions of Japanese who survived naturally carried this suffering and destruction as an intimate memory. Japan's most famous museum associated with World War II is the Peace Memorial Museum in Hiroshima, where the overwhelming impression is the horrendous effects of the atomic bomb. The multistory National Shōwa Memorial Museum* (Shōwakan) *in Tokyo, which opened in 1999, features largely benign exhibits of everyday artifacts and lifestyles during the hard times of the war and early postwar years.*

Victim consciousness is hardly peculiar to Japan and the Japanese, however; and the number of private Japanese "peace" museums, exhibitions, and—most notably—publications devoted to imperial Japan's atrocities and war responsibility is in fact very large. Most major bookstores in Japan carry a shelf or so of publications, including illustrated books and magazines, dealing with Japanese atrocities such as Nanking, the ianfu, *the murderous scientific experiments conducted on prisoners by the Imperial Army's Unit 731 in Manchuria, and Japanese depredations throughout East and Southeast Asia. A major scholarly quarterly titled Sensō Sekinin Kenkyū, which carries the English subtitle "A Report on Japan's War Responsibility," dates from 1993 and features annotated research articles by meticulous scholars. To an American who came of age during the Vietnam War and has witnessed the official and popular whitewashing of this carnage in the United States in the decades since, the finger-pointing penchant for calling attention to historical sanitization in Japan is not only misleading but also hypocritical.*

The following essay, addressing the kaleidoscope of war memory in Japan, appeared in a 2002 book devoted to war crimes and denial in the twentieth century.

* * *

In mid-June 1945, as World War II was reaching its denouement in Asia, a Japanese scholar of French literature named Watanabe Kazuo mused about Germany and Japan in his diary. While bombs fell on Tokyo, Watanabe, in his early forties at the time, was reading Romain Rolland's 1915 account of writings taken from the corpses of German soldiers in World War I. He was particularly struck by the observation of a Prussian officer that the Germans had an aptitude for being unloved. Was this not true, Watanabe wrote, of his own country and compatriots as well?

Watanabe, later esteemed as one of postwar Japan's most engaging "progressive intellectuals," deplored the war. His "diary of defeat," which begins in March 1945 and ends the following November (but was not published until fifty years later), is one of the more intimate and evocative lamentations about the insanity of their "holy war" that has come down to us from the Japanese side. Obviously, the murderous behavior of the odd couple of the Axis Alliance helped prompt Watanabe's observation of shared unlovable national personalities. In his view, however, there was more behind this than just militarism and atrocity. The Japanese, he feared, alienated others because they had difficulty thinking in terms of equality, and lacked any true sense of "responsibility." In January 1946, five months after the war ended, Watanabe devoted a short essay to this aptitude for being unloved, specifically relating it to the issue of "repentance" and his fear that Japanese comprehension of such matters remained superficial.[1]

Would Watanabe draw such an analogy about Germany and Japan today? Would we ourselves do so? Over half a century has passed since World War II ended, and it is surely fair to say that the former Axis partners have developed in ways that most of their non-Communist adversaries in 1945 only hoped and dreamed might be possible.[2] They have become fundamentally democratic societies. They have brought prosperity to a majority of their peoples. Although both have reemerged as great economic workshops, neither has menaced the peace of its neighbors.

And yet, where war and memory are concerned, it also seems

fair to say that, in the eyes of most outsiders, Germany and Japan have gone separate ways. Deservedly or not, "the Germans" have been generally praised for confronting their Nazi past. "The Japanese," by contrast, are more usually castigated—not only by Americans and Europeans, but by Asian commentators as well—for sanitizing the war they waged in the emperor's name so many decades ago. Indeed, it is a commonplace of contemporary polemics to compare the Japanese unfavorably to the Germans when it comes to confronting war responsibility. On this particular issue, the Japanese aptitude for being mistrusted and unloved is truly singular.

There are easy explanations for this. For all practical purposes, the Japanese cabinet and Diet (parliament) have been dominated by the same conservative political lineage since 1949 (it took the name Liberal Democratic Party in 1955). The electoral base of the conservatives lies in a constituency that still feels an intimate sense of bereavement for the 2 million Japanese soldiers and sailors who died in World War II. Such a constituency is, unsurprisingly, hostile to any blanket condemnation of Japanese war crimes that denies honor and respect to those who died for their country.

This electorate, rather than outsiders, is the audience the conservatives most care about. This helps explain, at least in part, why official statements of war responsibility, repentance, and apology so often seem lukewarm to non-Japanese.[3] At the same time, the ranks of the conservatives do indeed include many die-hard nationalists who still subscribe to some of the propaganda under which imperial Japan was mobilized for war. In one form or another, they would argue that their country was engaged in a legitimate war of self-defense against the "Red Peril" of Communism and the "White Peril" of European and American imperialism and colonialism in Asia. Japan's war may have been ill advised, in this view, but neither in motive nor in conduct can it be fairly deemed to have been peculiarly criminal.

Until recently, it seemed possible to suggest (or at least hope) that much of the more intemperate nationalistic rhetoric that older conservative politicians continued to spout at regular intervals was simply the carryover of wartime indoctrination by a cohort of largely unrepentant patriots. Then Japan entered the twenty-first century with a new conservative leader who made it embarrassingly clear that this was not the case. In a widely publicized speech to an association of Shinto priests, Prime Minister Mori Yoshirō, born in 1937, saw fit to evoke the most extreme and exclusionist nationalistic rhetoric of the militaristic past by referring to Japan as an "emperor-centered land of the gods" (*tennō chūshin to suru kami no kuni*). On another occasion, addressing another purely domestic audience, he spoke of Japan's present-day mission in terms of defending the *kokutai*, or "national polity"—thereby resurrecting the central code word in prewar emperor-worship. In a trice, Japan's new leader had established himself as the international community's most notorious practitioner of rhetorical necrophilia. He became, overnight, the latest personification of the Japanese aptitude for being unloved.

The rub in all this, however, is that Mori's reactionary language (which he attempted to explain away, but did not retract) led him to be unloved by most of his compatriots as well. The media flayed him, and his personal approval rating plummeted to between 10 and 20 percent in opinion polls. More tellingly, his Liberal Democratic Party dropped from 271 to 229 seats in the House of Representatives in the general election of June 2000, maintaining but a narrow minority over a polyglot opposition. While factors such as Japan's continuing economic doldrums also contributed to this precipitous decline, the prime minister had clearly crossed the line where acceptable patriotic rhetoric is concerned. He misread the depth to which even a conservative electorate recalls the war years with horror.[4]

Non-Japanese, fixated as they usually are on the pronouncements of Japan's most bombastic nationalists, also tend to misread the tenor and complexity of popular Japanese recollections of World War II. Whereas Europeans commonly date the war from the German invasion of Poland in 1939, and Americans from the

Japanese attack on Pearl Harbor in 1941, in Japan the war is usually dated from the Japanese invasion of Manchuria in 1931. In a name promoted by leftist scholars shortly after Japan's defeat, World War II in Asia is widely referred to as "the Fifteen-Year War."

Most Japanese now also acknowledge that this fifteen-year conflict was a war of aggression. To non-Japanese, this may seem surprising, for the litany of right-wing Japanese pronouncements that the foreign press highlights leaves little room for anticipating serious critical popular consciousness about the war. If Japanese were asked "Was Japan an 'Aggressor' in World War II?" most foreigners would probably predict that the response would be negative. In fact, this very question was posed to a random sample of people by the conservative *Yomiuri* newspaper in 1993. Fifty-three-point-one percent answered "Yes" and 24.8 percent "No," while the remainder had no response. Among the wartime generation itself (people over seventy), whom one might expect to be most firmly indoctrinated in the propaganda of the holy war, only 39.5 percent responded that Japan was not an aggressor (41.1 percent said it was, and the rest had no response). Among respondents in their twenties, 61.7 percent agreed Japan had been an aggressor, and only 17.1 percent disagreed with this label.[5]

This fracture of memory and perception accounts for much of the fervor of present-day nationalistic pronouncements in Japan. Whereas foreigners tend to isolate the most inflammatory right-wing utterances and interpret them as being representative of deep trends, the spokesmen for a new Japanese nationalism actually speak in almost apocalyptic terms of the *death* of patriotism in their country. Here, for example, is a representative passage from a pamphlet issued in 1998 by the Japanese Society for History Textbook Reform, one of the most influential associations of "revisionist" conservative academics:

> When the young people of Japan were asked if they would
> defend their country if invaded by another nation, 10% of
> them answered "yes." Ninety percent replied that they would

not. Over 70% of the world's young people say that they would defend their countries. When Americans and Koreans were asked if they would sacrifice their interests to serve their countries, 56.9% and 54.4% answered "yes," respectively. Only 5.5% of Japanese respondents answered that question in the affirmative. That figure is suggestive of what is at the depth of our national psychology. The foolish obsession with economic matters on the part of the Japanese, and their failure to contemplate the proper way for humans to live, have characterized the 50 years since World War II ended. The result is that the very future of our nation is in jeopardy. I am reminded of the last days of Carthage.

This is, indeed, alarmingly reactionary language. It suggests that serious engagement with "the proper way for humans to live" was lost in Japan only after the defeat in World War II, when the war was belittled and overt patriotism came to be viewed with deep and widespread skepticism. Such rhetoric is of a piece with Prime Minister Mori's suggestion that Japan's true identity is to be found elsewhere than in postwar professions of a commitment to peace and democracy. To escape this perceived crisis of national identity, those associated with the movement to create a "correct" national history have declared that the very purpose of historical writing and education is to instill pride in the nation. Professor Fujioka Nobukatsu, one of the best-known spokesmen for the movement, puts it this way: "It is precisely its way of teaching its modern history that is the crucial determinant of the constitution of a people as a nation. The people that does not have a history to be proud of cannot constitute itself as a nation."[6]

Such assertions are heard with increasing frequency as Japan enters a new century as perplexed and tormented as ever concerning its identity as a modern nation. At the same time, however, we should not lose sight of the panic that runs through these pronouncements: the near-hysterical perception, that is, that since their defeat the Japanese, and especially the younger generations, have become the *least* patriotic of contemporary peoples. How can one account for this? To individuals like those associated with the conservative "textbook reform" movement, the answer is clear. It is precisely because negative impressions of Japan as an aggressor in the wars of the mid-twentieth century run so deep that postwar Japanese have been unable to look upon their modern history and accomplishments with pride.

The interplay of war and memory in contemporary Japan is, in fact, even more complicated and convoluted than this dichotomy suggests. It is "kaleidoscopic" in the fullest sense, in that we can identify a great range of attitudes and opinions—and, with slight interpretive twists, make any number of patterns out of them. Five such patterns are singled out in the discussion that follows—five kinds of memory, as it were, that seem especially prominent in shaping the popular consciousness and public histories of Japan's war. They are [1] denial, [2] evocations of moral (or immoral) equivalence, [3] victim consciousness, [4] binational (U.S.-Japan) sanitizing of Japanese war crimes, and [5] popular discourses acknowledging guilt and responsibility.[7]

1. DENIAL

It is reasonable to speak of a collection of Japanese ranging from right-wing thugs through conservative politicians, bureaucrats, and businessmen to nationalistic journalists, academics, and even cartoonists that is devoted to "denying" Japan's war crimes. But what, specifically, is being denied?

The answer varies. The most extreme position, as might be expected, simply counters the notion of Japan's grievous responsibility for engaging in militaristic aggression by resurrecting the propaganda of the war years. It argues, that is, that the emperor's loyal soldiers and sailors, fired by both love of country and pan-Asian idealism, were engaged in the mission of simultaneously defending their homeland and establishing a "Greater East Asia Co-Prosperity Sphere."

Japan, from this perspective, was driven to war by strategic, ideological, and economic threats that came from all directions: the Soviet Union in the north; Soviet-led "international" Communism spilling into China, Korea, and Japan itself; chaos and violation of Japan's treaty rights in China (including Manchuria); global economic depression, and the rise of anti-Japanese trade policies that followed in the wake of this; American and European opposition to the establishment of a Japanese-style "Monroe sphere" in Asia; unfair and destabilizing treatment by the United States and Great Britain in international naval armaments treaties in the 1930s; "economic strangulation" by the so-called ABCD powers (America, Britain, China, and the Dutch) as the crisis in Asia intensified; etc. In responding to these multiple threats, the argument continues, imperial Japan's leaders did not just act in legitimate self-defense. They turned the crisis into a genuinely moral campaign to liberate all Asia from the oppressive Europeans and Americans, and to simultaneously create an impregnable bulwark against the rising tide of Communism. The "holy war" was thus both inescapable and altruistic.

Even among those who maintain that Japan was not an aggressor, however, relatively few subscribe to such undiluted jingoism. Here one encounters one of the more entertaining anomalies of the patriotic agenda. For whereas the heart and soul of old-fashioned Japanese-style nationalism lies in extolling the country's "peculiarly unique uniqueness" (as exemplified in Prime Minister Mori's archaic emperor-centered and Shinto-centered rhetoric), when it comes to the question of aggression and atrocity in World War II, uniqueness is more usually explicitly denied. In a world order that was collapsing into chaos everywhere, and in a global conflict that witnessed unspeakable brutality in all theaters and on all sides, this more modulated mode of denial goes, it is absurd to single out the Japanese as sole bearers of responsibility for the outbreak of conflict in Asia, or as sole perpetuators of acts of barbarism there. To do so amounts to simply perpetuating the victors' version of the war.

Those who deem it imperative to restore love of country by promoting a positive appreciation of Japan's twentieth-century experience are not concerned with merely downplaying or denying specific wartime horrors (such as the Rape of Nanking, abuse of POWs, or large-scale exploitation of "comfort women" to service the imperial forces sexually). They are very precise in identifying what constitutes the "old" historiography that must be repudiated. It takes two forms. One is the Marxist analysis of modern Japanese history that had an enormous impact in scholarly, journalistic, and educational circles for several decades after the war (emphasizing the authoritarian emperor system, *zaibatsu*-led capitalist "dual structure," and other pernicious "feudal remnants" that all lay behind the domestic repression and overseas aggression of imperial Japan). The second target of revisionist ire is the outlook and values allegedly imposed on Japan during the postsurrender occupation by the American-led victors that lasted from 1945 to 1952. A target of particularly impassioned derision here is "the Tokyo War Crimes Trial view of history."[8]

This critical notion of "victor's history"—or victor's justice, or victor's double standards—entails a subtle turn in the kaleidoscope of war consciousness, amounting to an argument of moral relativism.

2. EVOCATIONS OF MORAL (OR IMMORAL) EQUIVALENCE

The Tokyo trial (formally, the International Military Tribunal for the Far East) is the great sitting duck of conservative Japanese revisionism, and for understandable reasons. These proceedings against accused "Class A" war criminals lasted almost three times as long as the counterpart Nuremberg trial of Nazi leaders; and when they limped to a close at the end of 1948, it already was apparent that the judgment imposed would not withstand the test of time very well. All twenty-five defendants were found guilty of war crimes, and seven were executed within a month after the courtroom proceedings came to an end. Even the Allied judges themselves, however, were unable to come to unanimous agreement. Thus, the decisive "majority judgment" of the tribunal (supported by eight of eleven justices) was accompanied by five separate opinions criticizing the proceedings and sentences from one perspective or another. The most detailed and dramatic of these separate opinions came from the Indian justice, Radhabinod Pal, who found the very premises of the trial unsound and acquitted all twenty-five defendants.

Pal's detailed dissent, which ran to many hundreds of pages, was published in Japanese in 1952 (as soon as the post-defeat Allied occupation ended), and has remained the bible for Japanese critics of "victor's justice" ever since. His critique is substantive. Pal challenged the juridical premises of the tribunal on the grounds that the defendants were being tried for ex post facto "crimes" (that is, offenses such as "crimes against peace" that did not exist in international law before the Nuremberg and Tokyo tribunals were convened). He rejected as absurd the basic argument on which the prosecution rested its case in Tokyo: namely, the charge that Japan's leaders had been engaged in a "conspiracy to commit aggression" that dated back to 1928 (which meant that the defendants could not argue that they were acting in accordance with their perception of legitimate self-defense, and that all military actions by the Japanese from 1928 on thereby constituted "murder"). And, good Indian nationalist that he was, Pal took seriously the defendants' arguments that they were intent on liberating Asia from Western colonialism (or, at least, the argument that Asia needed such liberation). Unsurprisingly, he managed to smuggle more than a few sharp comments about European and American hypocrisy into his dissenting opinion.

Justice Pal has proven a godsend to those who have devoted themselves to repudiating "the Tokyo War Crimes Trial view of history," for he gives their argument not merely a non-Japanese face (and, just as important, a non-Caucasian one), but also a dense theoretical scaffolding. They have used him sedulously, but not, in fact, fairly. The Tokyo trial was undeniably a poorly conceived affair; but what the deniers of grievous Japanese war responsibility have done is use this vulnerable exercise in victor's justice—and Pal's stinging technical dissent from its premises and conclusions—as a smokescreen for covering up the real war crimes and acts of aggression the Japanese did commit in the course of their fifteen-year war.[9] Repudiating the trial has become a synecdoche for implying that imperial Japan was, after all, an "innocent" participant in the cataclysmic breakdown of world order—or, at least, no more guilty than other nations, and no more brutal on the battlefield and in occupied areas than other combatants.

It is within this larger context of repudiating "victor's justice" that the denial of more specific accusations of Japan's egregious acts of aggression and atrocity takes place. At a still grand level, and still within the framework of the war crimes trials, the revisionists vehemently reject the argument that imperial Japan was in any fundamental way comparable to its German ally. There was no Japanese counterpart to Hitler, they argue, or to the Nazi Party (which made charges of conspiracy more tenable at the Nuremberg trials). There was nothing comparable to the planned genocide we now speak of as the Holocaust. Thus, references to the 1937 Japanese massacre of civilians in Nanking as "the forgotten Holocaust of World War II" provoke especially emotional denials—which, again, become a smokescreen that obscures the terrible rape of the city that did occur, not to mention the systematic abuse of prisoners and civilians by the imperial forces in all theaters.[10]

In calling attention to the double standards of the victors who sat in judgment at Tokyo—and who still sit in judgment of Japan today—the revisionists, as might be anticipated, are able to move with near abandon from the nineteenth century through the war itself right up to the present day. Justice Pal set the pattern for some of this argumentation, and in ways beyond simply calling attention to the deep (and, as of the time of the trial, ongoing) history of Western imperialism and colonial oppression. He ridiculed the prosecution's repudiation of the "anti-Communism" defense offered by former war minister and prime minister Tōjō Hideki and his cohorts, pointing out that most of the governments represented on the bench at the Tokyo trial were at that very moment themselves obsessed by the need to contain Communism (Pal was himself strongly anti-Communist). He was less than impressed when white prosecutors accused the Japanese of racial prejudice. And, in one of his most controversial and frequently cited passages, Pal suggested that the closest counterpart to Nazi atrocities in the war in Asia may well have been the American use of the atomic bombs. Pal did acknowledge heinous behavior by the Japanese. His point was that they were not alone in this.

Japan's neo-nationalists deploy such arguments as another form of diversion, even as a kind of historiographic *cancellation* of immorality—as if the transgressions of others exonerate one's own crimes. In American, British, and Australian circles, for example, the strongest and most ineradicable "memory" of Japanese atrocity is surely the abuse of prisoners of war (coupled, in the American case, with the "treachery" and "infamy" of the attack on Pearl Harbor). It was estimated at the Tokyo trial that over one-quarter of the Anglo-American servicemen who fell into Japanese hands died in captivity—a vastly greater percentage than died under Japan's Axis allies on the Western Front. Japanese conservatives, in their turn, "cancel" this by emphasizing not merely the wanton killing of Japanese civilians in American air raids, but—a more exact counterthrust—the much greater number of Japanese prisoners who surrendered to the Soviets in the final week of the war and suffered prolonged incarceration and a massive death toll in the Siberian gulags. Unlike many Americans and Europeans, Japanese conservatives never forget that the Allied victors who stood in self-righteous judgment of Japan included the Soviet Union.[11]

This sense of victor's hypocrisy has grown stronger with the years. Most of the nations that sat in judgment in Nuremberg and Tokyo were, even at the time of these trials, embroiled in their own acts of violence, aggression, and political and racial repression.

Most engaged in subsequent mayhem and atrocity. None ever dreamed of allowing themselves to be held accountable to the new standards of international law that had ostensibly been established in the showcase trials in Germany and Japan. And—as our contemporary scrutiny of World War II "as history" reveals—*all* countries have engaged in the manipulation and obfuscation of public memory of their wartime conduct. Look at wartime anti-Semitism in the United States, for instance, and the vapid "Enola Gay" exhibition commemorating the atomic bomb that was installed in the Air and Space Museum of the Smithsonian Institution in 1995. Look at the exaggerated "myth of the Resistance" in collaborationist France, exposed so belatedly in the trials of Paul Touvier and Maurice Papon; the Nazi bank accounts in "neutral" Switzerland; the popularity of the xenophobic Jorg Haider in Austria; and the Vatican's sustained refusal to acknowledge Pope Pius XII's appeasement of Hitler. And in Germany itself, to give but one recent example, look at the public honoring of the historian Ernst Nolte as the new millennium opened, for his recognition of the "rational core" of Hitler's anti-Semitism and anti-Communism.

Why, in such a world, the neo-nationalist "revisionists" ask, are the Japanese still singled out for particular censure? Does this not reflect plain anti-Japanese racism more than any innate propensity for being unloved?

3. VICTIM CONSCIOUSNESS

The Japanese are hardly alone in their acute sense of victimization. Nor, where World War II is concerned, are they unique in conveying such victim consciousness through highly evocative, proper-name catchphrases. "Remember Hiroshima" has its obvious American analogue in "Remember Pearl Harbor" (or "Remember the Bataan Death March"). In British memory, "Singapore" and the "Burma-Thailand Railway" are comparable signatures of suffering from the war in Asia. For the Chinese, the encryption is "Nanking." For Filipinos, "Manila."

In Japan, however, postwar victim consciousness is inevitably coupled with the traumatic recollection of shattering defeat—with memory of futile death, that is, and the destruction in air raids of some sixty-six cities, culminating in Hiroshima and Nagasaki. All told, around 3 million Japanese, some 4 percent of the population, died in the war or as a result of it—leaving those who survived bereft of even the psychological consolation of ultimate victory. There could be no heroes for the losing side. It became commonplace to speak of the war dead themselves—and, indeed, of virtually all ordinary Japanese—as being "victims" and "sacrifices."[12]

The decisive period when the Japanese might have been expected to learn about and acknowledge the true nature of their "holy war" was, of course, during the American-led occupation that followed the defeat and lasted until April 1952. As in the Nuremberg trial of Nazis, one explicit purpose of the "Class A" Tokyo trial was heuristic: to establish a body of evidence and testimony that would persuasively demonstrate the extent to which Japan had waged an atrocious war of aggression. As long as the Tokyo trial lasted, the Americans used their control of the Japanese mass media to ensure that the details of such "war crimes" were well publicized.

Many Japanese at the time were in fact deeply shocked by the revelation of barbaric behavior on the part of their fighting men. (Atrocities against Chinese civilians, the Japanese rape of Manila in 1945, and reported incidents of cannibalism by members of the imperial forces appear to have made a particularly strong impression.) Indeed, in scenes that almost seem to foreshadow the plight a few decades later of U.S. servicemen who had served in Vietnam, demobilized Japanese soldiers and sailors often complained bitterly about returning to their homeland only to be reviled as criminals by their own compatriots. The impact of this early publicity about Japanese war crimes, however, was severely blunted by the hardship of everyday life that most Japanese continued to confront for many years after the surrender. The repatriation from overseas of millions of demoralized military men and civilians took years to complete, leaving many families at home in a state of enervating uncertainty. Those who made it back encountered, until around 1949, a country racked by industrial stagnation, massive unemployment, hyperinflation, severe food shortages, and a ravenous black market.

In this milieu, the plight of Japan's Asian victims, even when acknowledged, seemed remote and abstract. And it was difficult even to imagine yesterday's Caucasian enemies as having been victims at all. On the contrary, the well-fed, splendidly equipped, victorious Americans who now occupied Japan (together with a small U.K. contingent) were obviously people to be *envied*.

The second circumstance that blunted development of a deeper Japanese sense of war responsibility was the Cold War. By the time the Korean War erupted in 1950 (and sparked Japanese economic recovery with a vigorous war boom), the Cold War had long since intervened to destroy not merely the old wartime Allied alliance but the old wartime enmities as well. Japan, like West Germany, became central to U.S. anti-Communist strategy militarily as well as economically; and, in this context, both forgetting the recent atrocities of the former Axis partners and *playing up* the danger of them becoming victimized by Soviet-led Communism served U.S. purposes. It is a bad joke, but Tōjō might well have been recruited as a ghostwriter for the new "Pacific partners."

Until the Cold War ended, the U.S.-Japan relationship provided Japan's conservative leaders with a clear, fixed, almost myopic sense of security and national identity. Tokyo's relationship with Washington was the great axis around which all of Japan's international activities revolved—to a much greater degree than was to be seen in the relationship between Germany and the United States. Whereas Germany was part of the larger NATO alliance, Japan took particular pride in being America's critical *bilateral* partner in Asia. And whereas Germany, over the decades, found it imperative to carefully build constructive relationships with its continental neighbors and former enemies, Japan's conservative governments followed a less independently creative course. Locked in the American embrace, their archipelago studded with U.S. military bases like a monstrous stationary battleship off the coast of Asia (the "battleship" metaphor is beloved of strategic planners), and their economy geared more to the United States and Europe than to Asia, they seem to have built more fragile bridges to their neighbors. Certainly, the end of the bipolar certainties of the Cold War, coupled with the dramatic rise of China as a formidable rival to Japan in the struggle for leadership in Asia, has created a mounting sense of insecurity in the last decade. The recent emergence of more strident nationalistic voices can be interpreted, at least in considerable part, as one manifestation of this new sense of vulnerability.

Even before the end of the Cold War, however, the peculiarly ingrown nature of the U.S.-Japan relationship had the paradoxical effect of enhancing Japanese victim consciousness even as it provided the security of strategic protection under the U.S. nuclear umbrella. The relationship has never been a genuinely equal one. (From the beginning, one mission of the U.S. military forces in Japan—almost never stated publicly—has been to ensure strategic control of Japan.) One can, of course, qualify this in various ways. Obviously, for instance, Japan has exercised considerable autonomy—considerable "economic nationalism," some would say—within the Pax Americana. Be that as it may, it is still difficult to deny the unusual degree to which the nation's status vis-à-vis the United States has been one of dependent, or subordinate, independence ever since the occupation ended in 1952. Even the zealous spokesmen for the "Pacific partnership" who deny this must acknowledge that many observers, both in and outside Japan, take it for granted that this is the case.

This is a wearying psychological situation under which to operate for so long. Nor is it the end of this complicated story. For even at the height of the Cold War, the peculiar imbalances in the bilateral relationship operated in ways that tended to turn the very phenomenon of "victim consciousness" itself into yet one more example of the double standards by which Japan tends to be judged. The American war in Indochina provides the most vivid example of this. It is not unreasonable to see this war, in its ferocity and futility, as a rough American counterpart to Japan's own atrocious lost war of several decades earlier. (U.S. planners in the 1960s even went so far as to study Japan's scorched-earth anti-Communist tactics in rural China in the 1930s and early 1940s for lessons pertinent to their own "pacification" campaign in Vietnam.) At the same time, it is obviously not politically acceptable to suggest such a comparison in the United States. The deep sense of suffering and victimization that defines mainstream American recollections and commemorations of this conflict is carved in stone in the Vietnam War Memorial in Washington. By the same token, visitors who come to pay their respects here are almost literally walled off from imagining the millions of Vietnamese and Cambodians and Laotians who also died in that tragedy. During the Gulf War, President George H.W. Bush went so far as to speak of there being a "statute of limitations" on self-recrimination where America's terrible war of a mere few decades earlier was concerned.

And so, Americans have their commemorative memorial, even for an atrocious and lost war, and the Japanese do not. Again, the point is not whether drawing such a parallel between Japan in World War II and the United States in the Indochina War is accurate in every respect. Rather, this is but one more example of how Americans (and others) are seen as holding the Japanese to standards they themselves do not in practice observe. The veneration of Confederate soldiers and battlefield sites in the United States—despite (or even because of) their pro-slavery cause—is another such example. All people honor their war dead, but it seems particularly difficult to do so publicly in Japan.

In one form or another, this issue has percolated through all the debates on war and memory that have taken place since 1945. It came to a boil in the 1990s, when individuals and interest groups across the ideological spectrum vigorously debated the construction of a national museum that appropriately addressed the World War II years as "public history." Powerful conservative lobbyists led by the Association of War Bereaved Families (*Nihon Izokukai*) had long promoted such a museum as a vehicle for honoring the spirits of the Japanese war dead (*eirei*) and reminding younger generations of the hardship and sacrifices of these years. In opposition, Japanese associated with peace movements, the liberal media, and the academic left argued that any such facility must devote major attention to imperial Japan's aggression and atrocity. Names such as "Peace Prayer Hall" and "War Dead Peace Memorial Hall" were proposed as a way of turning such commemorative space into an overtly pacifist statement.

In the end, caution and conservatism prevailed. A multistory National Shōwa Memorial Museum (Shōwakan) opened its doors in Tokyo in 1999, with exhibits and programs designed to minimize controversial explicit interpretation of Japan's war and focus instead on the suffering of the Japanese people between 1935 and 1955.[13]

4. BINATIONAL (U.S.-JAPAN) SANITIZING OF JAPANESE WAR CRIMES

Even before the Cold War intruded to distort public memories of World War II, the United States had taken care to suppress certain aspects of Japan's war responsibility. This took place in the context of the Tokyo war crimes trial, and amounted to an exercise in "victor's justice" just the opposite of the anti-Japanese bias that Japanese nationalists decry. For purely expedient political reasons, the Americans concealed the true nature and full enormity of Japanese war crimes.

This unfinished business has come back to haunt Japan, and properly so. At the same time, however, non-Japanese usually approach this as but one more example of "Japanese" perfidy: the thoroughly binational nature of the cover-up does not play well outside Japan. The major issues and crimes the American-led prosecution chose to ignore and/or suppress were [1] the emperor's knowledge of and responsibility for his country's aggression and acts of atrocity; [2] lethal "medical" experiments conducted on at least 3,000 prisoners in Manchuria by the notorious "Unit 731"; [3] recruitment and virtual enslavement of many tens of thousands of so-called comfort women (*ianfu*) to service the emperor's soldiers and sailors sexually, the majority of them young Korean women; and [4] the full extent of Japan's use of chemical warfare in China. In the light of recent inquiries into the use of Caucasian and other POWs as slave labor in Japanese coal mines and other operations, it should be noted that the victors also formally decided to exclude any representatives of *zaibatsu* oligopolies from actual indictment for war crimes in the "Class A" trial in Tokyo. So substantial are these omissions that it does not seem too harsh to speak of criminal neglect, or even collusion, on the part of the prosecution itself.[14]

The most appalling of these cover-ups was the case of Unit 731, involving high-level officers and scientific researchers whose practice of official, institutionalized murder is comparable to the crimes of the "Nazi doctors." Unlike the German case, Japanese participants in these grotesque experiments on human subjects were granted secret immunity from prosecution in exchange for divulging their procedures and findings to the Americans. It naturally followed that the very existence of such practices within the formal structure of the Imperial Army had to be carefully suppressed by the Americans themselves thereafter.

Less sensational but more consequential where the question of popular Japanese consciousness of "war responsibility" is concerned was the exoneration of Emperor Hirohito from any responsibility whatsoever for the policies and actions undertaken in his name. Unlike Germany, where the Nazi regime was eliminated, there was no decisive break with the past in defeated Japan. Maintaining the same monarch on the throne under whom a decade and a half of Japanese aggression had been carried out was but the crowning symbol of this institutional and even personal continuity.

This was a pragmatic decision on the part of the American victors, who deemed it expedient to use Emperor Hirohito to ensure popular acquiescence to the occupation. However reasonable this may have seemed at the time, the negative consequences of such a policy have been far-reaching. No serious investigation of the emperor's actual wartime role and responsibility was ever undertaken. Carefully choreographed pronouncements by both Japanese royalists and the American occupation command made clear that Hirohito did not even bear *moral* responsibility for whatever had been done in his name. In a remarkable act of collusive intrigue that brought together high occupation officers, court circles, members of both the prosecution and defense staffs in the Tokyo trial, the "Class A" defendants, and the emperor himself, the Tokyo trial was "fixed" from the very outset to exclude any possible testimony that might seem to incriminate the sovereign. As two of the separate critical opinions that emerged from the trial noted, the emperor's exemption made these judicial proceedings farcical.[15]

It is difficult to exaggerate how subtly but significantly this binational imperial cover-up impeded serious Japanese engagement with the issue of war responsibility, both at the time and in the decades that followed. Hirohito had been commander in chief of the imperial forces and the most exalted political figure in the nation. If *he* was deemed to have no responsibility whatsoever for the horrors and disasters that took place between his ascension to the throne in 1926 and the end of the war in 1945, why should ordinary Japanese even think of taking responsibility on themselves? Emperor Hirohito became postwar Japan's preeminent symbol, and facilitator, of non-responsibility and non-accountability.

This was compounded by his longevity. Hirohito outlived any of the other major national leaders of World War II by far, and remained on the throne until his death in 1989 at the age of eighty-nine. So long as he was alive, it was generally taboo to discuss his personal war responsibility in the mass media (though this did take place, often vigorously, in left-wing and certain liberal publications). When a journalist did make so bold as to ask Hirohito his thoughts about "war responsibility" in a famous press conference in 1975, following an unprecedented state visit to the United States, the emperor's response was revealing. "Concerning such a figure of speech," he said, "I have not done much study of these literary matters and so do not understand well and am unable to answer."

Here was a sobering window not only on the emperor personally, but also on his country and the new "Pacific partnership" he was commemorating with his visit.

As the years passed and the emperor became an increasingly fragile and hollowed-out figure, it became understandably difficult for younger generations to associate his long "Shōwa" era (1926–1989) with anything but a kind of innocuous banality. War, peace, prosperity blurred into one—so thoroughly, in fact, that as Japan entered the present century conservative politicians introduced an astonishingly reactionary proposal to establish "Shōwa Day" (*Shōwa no Hi*) as a national holiday in commemoration of the late sovereign. Nothing of this sort has taken place in Germany, of course; and if contemporary Japan still maintains a peculiar "aptitude for being unloved," the binational imperial taboo must be factored in as a significant part of the explanation.[16]

The Cold War impact on *American* thinking about Japanese war crimes and war responsibility was openly apparent by 1948. Although hundreds of Japanese had been arrested as potential "Class A" war criminals between 1945 and 1946, only twenty-eight were actually indicted (two died during the trial, and one was excused on grounds of mental incompetence). By the time the Tokyo trial ended in November 1948, only a handful of the others still remained in jail. When the Tokyo judgment came down, that small number too was immediately exempted from prosecution. Unlike Germany, where the showcase Nuremberg trial was followed by ongoing prosecution of Nazi war criminals, there was no ongoing prosecution, or even investigation, of possible top-level Japanese war criminals. No indigenous Japanese system was ever established to pursue these issues.

Quite the opposite took place. By around 1949, former members of the imperial forces were being recruited by the Americans to assist in anti-Communist intelligence activity vis-à-vis China in particular. The outbreak of the Korean War in June 1950 prompted initiation of Japanese rearmament under the U.S. occupation forces—and with this, of course, a concerted binational campaign to *suppress* recollection of Japanese behavior in the "old" war that had ended (as of 1950) only a scant five years earlier. In the new imagery of the Cold War, "Red China" now replaced Japan as the truly threatening and atrocious menace in Asia.

The peace settlement under which Japan regained sovereignty in 1952 included most of the nations of the world but excluded the Soviet Union and the People's Republic of China. For these reasons, it was known at the time as a "separate" (as opposed to "over-all") peace, and strongly criticized as such by left-wing elements within Japan. Where the issue of war responsibility is concerned, perhaps the most consequential aspect of the peace settlement lay in the handling of reparations.

In the immediate aftermath of Japan's defeat, the concept of reparations was essentially punitive. Existing industrial plants were to be transferred to other countries in Asia that had been ravaged by the Japanese war machine. Not only would this help compensate these countries for their losses, the argument went. It could also serve as a mechanism whereby a "leveling" of industrial productivity throughout Asia might be promoted. For technical as well as political reasons, these initial plans proved stillborn. And by 1951–1952, when the peace settlement was being finalized, U.S. planners, led by John Foster Dulles, had completely turned about the very purpose of reparations. Such compensation would now be taken out of current Japanese production, or in the form of financial arrangements, with the fundamental objective of promoting economic integration between Japan and the less developed anti-Communist nations of Asia. These state-to-state agreements were to be directed at rehabilitating Japan as the "workshop" of Asia (just as Germany was to become the workshop of Europe) and, at one and the same time, at strengthening Asian participation in the economic containment of China. The last thing anyone in Washington or Tokyo wished to see was a Japan left vulnerable to subsequent claims for compensation for its wartime abuses and atrocities.

Over the decade that followed, the Japanese government fulfilled its obligations under the 1952 peace treaty by negotiating bilateral "reparations" settlements with former enemy nations such as the Philippines, Burma, Indonesia, and South Vietnam. (The United States waived its right to reparations, as did the Kuomintang-led Republic of China on Taiwan, with which Japan had been forced to deal, rather than the Communist regime, at the time of the peace treaty.) Normalization of diplomatic relations with South Korea, delayed until 1965, was accompanied by a reparations agreement. (This rapprochement between Japan and the southern half of its former colony was promoted as part of the larger U.S. strategy of containment in Asia, coincident with the intensification of military engagement in Vietnam.) When Japan belatedly normalized relations with the People's Republic of China in 1972, on the other hand, the Chinese agreed not to pursue the issue of reparations. Through these various state-to-state transactions, all supported by the United States, Japan in theory formally addressed and resolved all outstanding war claims.[17]

The bilateral "Pacific partnership" that arose on the foundations of the 1952 peace settlement was characterized, on the Japanese side, by the consolidation of a conservative "iron triangle" of politicians, bureaucrats, and businessmen that has, for all practical purposes, maintained power to the present day. This coalition has always been racked with conflict and factionalism, and Japan scholars usually take care to repudiate the myth of a monolithic "Japan, Inc." Nonetheless, in yet another suggestive contrast to the situation in postwar Germany, it can still be said that the Japanese government has essentially been controlled by the same conservative political lineage since 1949. The creation of the misnamed Liberal Democratic Party in 1955 established a tradition of "one-party" dominance that, with the exception of two weak non-LDP prime ministers between August 1993 and January 1996, carried through the Cold War up to 2009, when the fragile Democratic Party of Japan took over the premiership.*

---

* This page has been lightly edited to take into account the electoral defeats of the Liberal Democratic Party, especially in 2009 (seven years after this essay was published).

LDP prime ministers usually, in one form or another, expressed generalized "regret" for Japanese behavior during the war years. Still, this is also the party that supported Kishi Nobusuke, an accused (but never indicted) "Class A" war criminal, as prime minister from 1957 to 1960. It is the party of former prime minister Nakasone Yasuhiro, who breached a long-standing taboo by officially visiting Yasukuni Shrine with his entire cabinet on the anniversary of the war's end in 1985, to pay homage to those who had died for the emperor in World War II. It is the LDP that secretly arranged for the seven defendants condemned to death in the Tokyo trial to be enshrined at Yasukuni; that supported watered-down textbook treatments of the war; that time and again appointed cabinet ministers given to inflammatory statements such as the denial of the Rape of Nanking.

And it is the LDP that for over half a century provided the United States with its "men in Japan"—staunch conservatives, virulent anti-Communists, loyal supporters of the U.S.-Japan security agreement, steadfast proponents of the necessity of gradually expanding Japan's military role under the Pax Americana. Their more extreme nationalistic statements occasionally embarrassed their American patrons, but the larger *function* of their attempts to downplay the atrocious nature of Japanese behavior in World War II served the perceived interests of both governments. For if the Japanese populace is to be persuaded to support greater and more diversified remilitarization under the bilateral security treaty—as both Washington and Tokyo desire—it remains necessary to dispel the critical perception of past Japanese militarism and "aggression" that remains so strong in popular consciousness.[18]

5. POPULAR DISCOURSES ACKNOWLEDGING GUILT AND RESPONSIBILITY

Why *is* "patriotism" still so suspect in Japan?

This question returns us to the phenomenon of victim consciousness and, more precisely, the manner in which this can be turned in positive and constructive directions. It also returns us to the Japan of half a century ago—not merely to defeat and occupation, but to the broader experience of war itself. To speak of having been victimized, or having been "sacrificed," was not merely a lament or rationalization or excuse. It opened up a world of interrogation.

It is difficult to exaggerate how bitter, heartfelt, and widespread such questioning was in the wake of the surrender, when it became possible to speak openly about such matters. Victimized, people asked, *by whom?* Or *by what?* Sacrifices *to what end?* And how, indeed, could one make atonement to the war dead so that their great sacrifice would not be in vain?

Being victims of the American air raids, or the atomic bombs, or the perceived double standards of the victorious powers was but one aspect of such consciousness. More potent and pervasive was a sense of having been victimized by war itself, by the stupidity of militarist leaders who had plunged the nation into the hopeless "holy war," and by the ignorance of the general populace for having allowed itself to be so brainwashed.

These attitudes were not imposed by the victors. They erupted from within, and quickly coalesced in a set of widely accepted articles of faith. The country must not become embroiled in war in the future. The way to avoid being deceived again was to create a more rational and open society. To create such a society, committed to "peace and democracy," was not only the path through which to regain national pride and international respect. It was also the only conceivable way by which the living could assure the dead that they had not perished in vain.

Such sentiments found expression at all levels. Teachers and scholars who had failed to speak out against the war experienced deep feelings of guilt for having thereby contributed to the deaths of kin and compatriots and, perhaps most poignantly, former students. Almost instinctively, many of them came together in what the influential political scientist Maruyama Masao later described as a "community of remorse" (*kaikon kyōdōtai*). More than a few academics turned to one form or another of Marxism to explain not merely the structural dynamics that had propelled Japan to war, but also the false consciousness that had led most Japanese to go along with the militarists. The Communist Party, legalized under the occupation, made strong inroads into the ranks of organized labor, including the national teachers' union. Socialists, feminists, "old liberals," religious leaders, academics, literary figures, media people in radio, journalism, and filmmaking who had chafed under the wartime censorship—all joined in a chorus of criticism and self-criticism.

Contempt for the militarists who had led the country to destruction was quite extraordinary in the half year or more that preceded the convening of the Tokyo trial in June 1946. It is striking to return to the public record of these years. Political cartoonists ridiculed yesterday's honorable leaders. Editorials and letters to the press complained that the victors were not arresting *more* top-level individuals. People expressed regret that the Japanese themselves had been excluded from participating directly in the investigation and prosecution of war criminals.

There were certainly elements of superficiality and outright deceit in this—"repainting signs," as one of the cynical sayings of the time put it. The unregenerate did not speak their minds in public, and much sincere early criticism and self-criticism faded under the sheer pressures of daily life, the new fashions of the Cold War, and the accumulating sense of victor's double standards. Still, there have also been notable countertrends to the dilution of critical consciousness. In the years and decades that followed, engagement with issues of war memory and responsibility has been kept alive through a number of domestic controversies and confrontations. Notable among these are seemingly interminable debates concerning constitutional revision, the content of nationally certified textbooks, proper language for official "apologies" for imperial Japan's depredations, and the appropriate mission of the nation's still benignly labeled "self-defense forces." To these has been added, in the last decade, the question of redress or reparations to individuals such as "comfort women," prisoners of war, and civilians in occupied areas who were personally victimized by Japan's "crimes against humanity."

These topics, all deserving of extended treatment, constitute a kind of "contested institutionalized memory" that has kept critical consciousness of World War II just as alive in Japan as the "triumphal" consciousness and mythologizing of that same conflict is kept alive in the United States. Heated clashes over revising the decidedly pacifistic provisions of the "no war" constitution, for example, have continued ever since the occupation ended in 1952. Invariably, these provoke evocation of the horrors of war in general and the irresponsibility of the prewar Japanese military machine in particular.[19] In much the same way, the textbook controversies that have drawn strong criticism from abroad since the mid-1960s do indeed reflect official attempts to downplay the "dark" aspects of Japan's modern history. At the same time, however, the cyclical nature of textbook certification—and the snail's-pace court cases deriving from legal challenges to the government's position—have served as an ongoing domestic education in the clash between orthodoxy and its critics.[20]

These contentious forms of institutionalized memory, running like a leitmotiv through postwar political discourse, have been given emphatic counterpoint by discrete incidents and occasions that likewise force war and peace issues to the forefront of popular consciousness. The end of the occupation in 1952, for instance, was accompanied by shocking "Bloody May Day" demonstrations protesting the Cold War nature of the peace settlement, with its attendant remilitarization of Japan and demonization of China. The mid-1950s witnessed the emergence of a broad-based antinuclear movement (sparked by the 1954 "Bikini incident," in which Japanese fishermen were irradiated by fallout from a U.S. hydrogen-bomb test on the Bikini atoll). In 1959–60, pending renewal of the bilateral U.S.-Japan security treaty provoked massive protests in Tokyo, in which the issue of Japan's accelerated remilitarization under the eagle's wing was again dramatically called in question. (Prime Minister Kishi Nobusuke, America's "man in

Japan" on this occasion, was one of the accused "Class A" war criminals who escaped indictment in the Tokyo trial and was released
from prison in its immediate wake.)[21]

In the latter half of the 1960s, war and peace issues were com-
pellingly reformulated in the context of nationwide protests against
Japan's complicity in U.S. aggression in Indochina. Spearheaded
by the highly articulate and media-savvy League for Peace in
Vietnam (*Beheiren*), this New Left movement entailed not only
placing U.S. behavior in the mirror of Japan's own atrocious war a
quarter century earlier, but also reexamining the very notions of
"victim" and "victimizer" (and the possibility, for Japanese then
and now, of being simultaneously both).[22] Hard on the heels of
this, Japan's opening to China in the early 1970s paved the way for
a truly wrenching confrontation with the debaucheries of imperial
forces in the now resurrected China War. From this time on, a
cadre of prolific scholars and journalists has continued to produce
detailed accounts of Japanese war crimes, including the Rape of
Nanking and the activities of Unit 731—materials that tend to
pass under the radar of most non-Japanese observers and popular
commentators.[23] In some circles, it is true, the lingering presence
of Emperor Hirohito on the throne continued to put a damper
on forthright discussion of Japanese war responsibility. Ironically
enough, the emperor's death in 1989 simultaneously rang the death
knell for this particular royalist taboo. His passing was followed
by the appearance of a number of hitherto repressed diaries and
memoirs from the war years, and, once again, gave new impetus to
public discussion of the issue of Japanese war responsibility.[24]

Can we draw some kind of "balance sheet" based on all this?
Perhaps, but it is risky business. Watanabe Kazuo's despon-
dent observation concerning Japan's peculiar "aptitude for being unloved" does seem as apposite now as it did in 1945, but why
this is so where the issue of repentance is concerned is not easily explained. Watanabe's own explanation—that Japanese have

difficulty thinking in terms of equality and lack a genuinely deep sense of responsibility—is not very persuasive. To our ears today, such a note of cultural determinism sounds very much like a self-referential, self-deprecating sort of Orientalism. Watanabe himself was not trapped in such a world. Many of his compatriots escaped it as well, as the persistence of postwar discourses of responsibility and repentance attests. Or, to take an entirely different tack can it not be said that most nations, states, peoples, collectivities fall short when it comes to thinking in terms of equality and assuming a sense of responsibility for historical transgressions? Wherever we turn, "repentance" rarely holds a candle to self-righteousness or victim consciousness or parochial loyalties or, indeed, indifference to the sins of the past. The situation in Japan, on either side of the ledger, does not really seem exceptional.

Within Japan, it is fair to speak of other kinds of balance sheets. One must certainly look to the general public rather than to the conservative tripod of ruling party, bureaucracy, and big business for genuine engagement with the issue of war responsibility—that "figure of speech" Emperor Hirohito found too literary for his tastes. Japan's deeply entrenched elites have proven steadfastly disinclined to seriously open either their minds or their archives on these matters; and where their pocketbooks are concerned, they remain wedded to the narrowest technical notions of reparations and redress. Here again, opinion polls suggest a public far readier than its leaders to acknowledge past wrongdoings, and to attend to them. A 1994 survey, for example, found that 80 percent of Japanese polled agreed that the government "has not adequately compensated the people of countries Japan invaded or colonized."[25]

It is precisely this general receptivity to such "unpatriotic" notions that has given a desperate edge to the rise of a new wave of reactive neo-nationalism in the last decade, spearheaded by conservative academics who have learned to use the mass media quite masterfully. They have also learned to play the racial card adroitly—against Americans, Chinese, and Koreans in particular, whom they unsurprisingly portray as being prejudiced against the Japanese. There is an ominous circularity in all this—and, to outsiders, a certain perverse reinforcement of Watanabe's old notion of an aptitude for being unloved.

5

THE BOMBED:
HIROSHIMAS AND NAGASAKIS
IN JAPANESE MEMORY

World War II is branded the Good War in American popular conscious-
ness, and for many reasons this will never change. Eradicating the men-
ace of Nazi Germany and militaristic imperial Japan was a great and
necessary accomplishment, and the United States played a major role in
bringing this about. It also helps that most Americans, despite their coun-
try's postwar global engagement, are parochial when it comes to think-
ing about history. From this insular perspective, World War II began
with Japan's attack on Pearl Harbor in December 1941 and ended with
the emperor's surrender broadcast in August 1945, shortly after the
atomic bombing of Hiroshima and Nagasaki. Japan's invasion of China
in 1937 and Germany's blitzkrieg in Europe in 1939 barely figure in
this account; the major role of the Soviet Union in defeating Nazi forces,
and massive Soviet losses incurred in the process, scarcely register in the
American psyche; and marginalized, virtually forgotten, too, is the role
that Chinese Nationalist and Communist resistance movements played
in sapping Japan's military strength and focus between 1937 and 1945,
again at a cost of many millions killed. Beyond this, of course, World War
II was America's last victorious war—as Korea, then Vietnam, and then
Iraq and Afghanistan made painfully clear. No patriotic American is go-
ing to jettison this *consoling counter-memory.*

The use of the atomic bombs against two densely populated Japanese cities slots neatly into the triumphal Good War narrative. In this telling, the bombs were necessary to persuade Japan's militarist leaders to surrender, and they saved countless thousands of American lives that otherwise would have been lost attempting to invade the Japanese home islands. Americans tend to think cinematically—we all do, really—and the standard scenario here is clear and simple. The United States is confronted by a fanatic enemy determined to fight to the bitter end; heroic airmen take off in their majestic Superfortress bombers without any fighter-plane escorts; they drop their bombs from miles above the two urban targets, cut away, and look back to behold awesome, multicolored, almost supernatural mushroom clouds rising to towering heights. Quick on this follows the sonorous, triumphal summing-up: the omniscient narrative voice-over telling us that eight days after Hiroshima, five days after Nagasaki, the emperor and his militarist advisers capitulated. "Thank God for the atomic bombs," as the writer Paul Fussell later put it in a famous essay, to great approbation.

Reconstructing and remembering the atomic bombs as experienced at the two ground zeros are, of course, an utterly different narrative. The insubstantial mushroom clouds disappear. Abstractions concerning material destruction and human casualties are replaced by children, women, and men with names. No one thanks God for the carnage. The emergence of popular memory about the atomic bombs took time in Japan, however. Japanese nationwide had more pressing things to think about when the war ended, like daily survival. U.S. occupation authorities censored writings, photographs, and pictorial depictions of Hiroshima and Nagasaki for many years, out of fear these would provoke anti-American hostility. The first compilation of photographs from the two ground zeros was not published in Japan until August 1952, after the occupation ended, and the first famous Japanese photographers did not visit the two cities to photograph scarred survivors until 1960. The earliest intimate drawings by hibakusha of what they had experienced at ground zero and could not erase from memory were not promoted and publicized until 1970, a quarter century after the bombings.

It is fatuous, no matter what the specific topic, to speak of "Japan"

*or "the Japanese" or Japanese culture or society as if these were homo-
genous and all of a piece; and this applies to how the atomic bombs are
remembered. There is no monolithic way of remembering Hiroshima and
Nagasaki. Thus the plurals ("Hiroshimas" and "Nagasakis") in the title
of the essay that follows, which first appeared in a special anniversary issue
on the bombs in the journal* Diplomatic History *in 1995.*

*   *   *

Hara Mieko, who was a youngster in Hiroshima when the city
was bombed, later wrote of herself that "the Mieko of today
is completely different from the Mieko of the past."[1] Most *hibakusha* experienced this fracturing of identity, and for Japan as a whole
the very meaning of time was altered by the atomic bombings of
August 6 and 9, 1945.

Such a profound sense of disjuncture was, of course, not peculiar to Japan. For much of the world, the Holocaust in Europe
and the nuclear genocide of Hiroshima/Nagasaki signified the
closure of "modernity" as it had been known and dreamed about
until then and the advent of a new world of terrible and awesome
potentialities. In Japan, however, the situation was unique in two
ways. Only the Japanese actually had experienced nuclear destruction. And in the years immediately following, only they were not
allowed to publicly engage the nature and meaning of this new
world. Beginning in mid-September 1945, U.S. authorities in occupied Japan censored virtually all discussion of the bombs.

Such censorship reflected both the general U.S. policy of se-
crecy concerning nuclear matters and, on a different plane, the
broad agenda of media control pursued as part of U.S. occupation
policy in defeated Japan itself. Where Hiroshima and Nagasaki
specifically were concerned, the rationale for censorship within
Japan was essentially twofold. American occupation authorities
feared that unrestrained discussion of the effects of the bombs
might incite "public unrest" against them (the most elastic and all-
encompassing rationale of censors everywhere). More specifically,

statements by Japanese politicians and the print media early in September conveyed the impression that the Allied policy of publicizing Japanese war atrocities and conducting war-crimes trials might confront a Japanese countercampaign that called attention to the allies' own atrocious policies, most graphically exemplified by the nuclear destruction of the two essentially civilian targets.[2]

Such a hypothetical countercampaign was plausible. Shigemitsu Mamoru, a once and future foreign minister (and future convicted war criminal in the interim), authored an early internal memorandum explicitly proposing that the Japanese use the atomic bombs as counterpropaganda to Allied accusations of Japanese war crimes. Hatoyama Ichirō, an ambitious conservative politician who aspired to the premiership (the occupation-period purge disrupted his timetable, but he did serve as prime minister from the end of 1954 to 1956), rashly voiced similar opinions in public.[3] In the opening weeks of occupation, the Dōmei news agency and leading newspapers, such as the *Asahi*, also naively attempted to balance the record of war behavior in this manner. With the advantage of hindsight, however, it can be said that the censorship of Japanese discussion of the bombs and their human consequences was misguided, perhaps counterproductive, certainly disdainful of the needs of the survivors themselves.

Between August 6 and 9, when the bombs were dropped, and mid-September, when censorship was imposed by the U.S. occupation force, Japanese responses to the new weapon actually were varied and provocative. Until the American victors established their presence in defeated Japan, of course, the media was censored by Japan's own imperial government. Thus, the historian faces a biased public record both before and after the occupation commenced. Still, it is possible to re-create a kaleidoscope of responses beyond the overwhelming sense of horror and shock experienced by those who suffered the bombings directly, and apart from the political notion of playing Allied atrocities against Japanese ones.

Initially, rage was one such response. In Hiroshima immediately after the bombing, for example, survivors came upon

uninjured American POWs (they had been confined in underground cells) and beat them to death.[4] In a makeshift Hiroshima
medical facility, the rumor spread that Japan had retaliated by
bombing the United States with its own secret weapon, causing
comparable atrocious death and suffering—and the Japanese survivors, it was reported, were pleased. The government and media
naturally condemned the new weapon as evidence of the enemy's
barbaric and demonic nature. Early in September, before occupation censorship was imposed, the *Asahi* ran a vivid article about the
hatred of Americans visible in the eyes of Hiroshima survivors.
Later, in one of the countless unnoticed individual tragedies of
the occupation period, a Nisei soldier affiliated with the U.S. force
visited relatives in Hiroshima, where his parents came from, and
was so shattered by their hostility to him as an American "mur-
derer" that he committed suicide soon afterward in his quarters
in Tokyo.[5]

Perhaps surprisingly, however, at least at first glance, hatred
against the Americans did not become a dominant sentiment in
the weeks, months, and years that followed. The destructiveness of the bombs was so awesome that many Japanese initially
regarded them—much like the calamitous losing war itself—
almost as if they were a natural disaster. Then, as the man-
made nature of the disaster sank in, what riveted attention was
the realization that science and technology suddenly had leapt
to hitherto unimagined levels. Such attitudes soon became conspicuous even in the two bombed cities themselves (although
the Americans still took care to assign British and Australian
forces to oversee local occupation administration in Hiroshima).
Certainly they were prevalent throughout defeated Japan as
a whole, where rage dissipated quickly in the face of the urgent challenges of recovery—and, indeed, simple daily survival.

The Japanese identified the new weapon as a nuclear bomb
within a matter of days. Their own scientists had investigated the
possibility of developing such weapons after Pearl Harbor and had
concluded that doing so was technically feasible but practically im-

possible for many decades to come.[6] Nishina Yoshio, an eminent physicist who had studied with Niels Bohr and supervised some of the wartime research on the military application of nuclear fission, was sent to Hiroshima right after the attack and immediately recognized that these long-term projections had been naive. (Nishina died of cancer in 1951, and it is popularly believed that his illness resulted from his exposure to residual radiation in Hiroshima.)

By August 15, when Japan capitulated, it was widely known throughout the country that a weapon of entirely new dimensions had devastated the two cities. The emperor himself, in his careful, self-serving address of this date announcing acceptance of the Potsdam Declaration, took care to emphasize this. "The enemy has for the first time used cruel bombs to kill and maim extremely large numbers of the innocent," Hirohito informed his subjects, "and the heavy casualties are beyond measure; if the war were continued, it would lead not only to the downfall of our nation but also to the destruction of all human civilization."[7] Japan's capitulation, in the official imperial rendering, thus became a magnanimous act that saved humanity itself from possible annihilation.

By the time the first contingent of U.S. occupation forces actually arrived in Japan at the very end of August, popular responses to the defeat and unconditional surrender had begun to assume complex configurations politically. The bombs quickly became a symbol of America's material might and scientific prowess—and this symbol was all the more stunning because it contrasted so sharply with Japan's relative material backwardness. While the Americans had been perfecting nuclear weapons, Japan's militaristic government had been exhorting the emperor's loyal subjects to take up bamboo spears and fight to the bitter end to defend the homeland. A year after the surrender, Katō Etsurō, a famous cartoonist, perfectly captured this dichotomy in the opening pages of a little book of illustrations chronicling the first year of occupation. An exhausted Japanese man and woman lay on the ground on August 15, fire buckets discarded beside them, contemplating the absurdity of pitting bamboo spears and little pails against atomic bombs.[8]

Katō's juxtaposition of atomic bombs against bamboo spears captured a widespread and politically explosive sentiment. In sum, it amounted to this: Japan's ideologues and military spokesmen had deceived the people and led the country into a hopeless war against a vastly superior United States. Personally, they obviously were fools (thus there was not much popular Japanese hand-wringing about the showcase Tokyo war-crimes trials). More generally, one clearly could not trust military appeals or military solutions in the future (thus the "no-war clause" of the new 1947 Japanese constitution, originally drafted by the Americans, found strong support among ordinary Japanese).[9]

The popular antimilitary sentiment that has influenced so much of postwar Japanese politics has its genesis in such visceral feelings. The "fifteen-year war" in general was devastating for Japan. Close to 3 million Japanese soldiers, sailors, and civilians were killed between the Manchurian Incident of 1931 and Japan's surrender in 1945, and a total of sixty-six cities, including Hiroshima and Nagasaki, were bombed. In the end, misery and humiliation were the only conspicuous legacies of the so-called holy war.[10] The atomic bombs quickly came to exemplify this tragic absurdity.

In these various ways, a complex symbolic field already had begun to resonate around the bomb by the time the victorious Americans arrived. The horror of a war brought home with unimagined destructiveness was one aspect of this, Japan's own backwardness another, the immense potentiality of science yet another. The Japanese did not place a negative construction on "science" in this context, but on the contrary singled out deficiency in science and technology as an obvious explanation for their defeat and an immediately accessible means by which the country could be rebuilt.

Scarcely a day passed between Japan's capitulation and the imposition of censorship by the Americans in mid-September that did not see a statement by the government or press about the urgent necessity of promoting science. On August 16, in his first broadcast after being named prime minister, Prince Higashikuni Naruhiko declared that "science and technology" had been Japan's biggest shortcoming in the war. A day later, the outgoing minister of education thanked schoolchildren for their wartime efforts and urged them to dedicate themselves to elevating Japan's "science power and spiritual power" to the highest possible levels. On August 19, the press reported that under the new minister of education, Maeda Tamon, the postwar school system would place "emphasis on basic science." "We lost to the enemy's science," the *Asahi* declared bluntly in a August 20 article, going on to observe that "this was made clear by a single bomb dropped on Hiroshima." The article was headlined "Toward a Country Built on Science."[11] In the years that followed, improving science education remained one of the country's foremost priorities.

In Japan, as elsewhere, the bomb thus became Janus: simultaneously a symbol of the terror of nuclear war and the promise of science. More than in other countries, however, the peculiar circumstances of the nuclear bombings, unconditional surrender, and, later, the new pacifist constitution created a postwar milieu in which "building a nation of science" almost invariably was coupled with an emotional emphasis on "peace" maintained through nonmilitary pursuits. Economically, the long-term consequences of this development were spectacular. Japan's emergence as an economic superpower by the 1980s resulted in considerable part from the fact that, after the surrender, the vast majority of talented Japanese scientists, businessmen, and bureaucrats devoted themselves to promoting *civilian* applications of science. Unlike the United States, where many scientists and engineers found the sweetest problems and most lucrative funding in weapons-related research, in Japan such work carried a social stigma.[12]

The immediate sanguine linkage between the tragedy of Hiroshima/Nagasaki and the promise of a "country built on science" had ramifications beyond just the material promotion of science and technology. Science itself became equated with the development of more "rational" modes of thinking in general. The disastrous folly of the lost war, that is, was attributed to a weakness in critical thought and "conceptual ability" throughout Japanese society. From this perspective, it was only a short but momentous step into linking promotion of science to promotion of democracy in postwar Japan, on the grounds that scientific progress was possible only in a "rational" environment that encouraged genuinely free inquiry and expression. In this manner, a seemingly technological response to defeat contained within itself a political logic that contributed greatly to support for casting off the shackles of the imperial state and instituting progressive reforms.[13]

At the same time, the trauma of nuclear devastation and unconditional surrender also reinforced an abiding sense of Japan's peculiar vulnerability and victimization. As the bombs came to symbolize the tragic absurdity of war, the recent war itself became perceived as fundamentally a *Japanese* tragedy. Hiroshima and Nagasaki became icons of Japanese suffering—perverse national treasures, of a sort, capable of fixating Japanese memory of the war on what had happened to Japan and simultaneously blotting out recollection of the Japanese victimization of others. Remembering Hiroshima and Nagasaki, that is, easily became a way of forgetting Nanking, Bataan, the Burma-Siam railway, Manila, and the countless Japanese atrocities these and other place names signified to non-Japanese.

"Victim consciousness" (*higaisha ishiki*) is a popular euphemism in postwar and contemporary Japan, and the bombs occupy a central place in this consciousness. From this perspective, it can be observed that nuclear victimization spawned new forms of nationalism in postwar Japan—a neo-nationalism that coexists in complex ways with antimilitarism and even the "one-country pacifism" long espoused by many individuals and groups associated with the political left.

Such considerations leave out the fate of the nuclear victims themselves; and, in fact, most Americans and Japanese at the time were happy to ignore these victims. Official U.S. reports about the two stricken cities tended to emphasize physical damage and minimize human loss and suffering. Prescient early journalistic accounts about the horrible consequences of radiation sickness were repudiated or repressed by occupation authorities. Japanese film footage was confiscated. Accounts of fatalities were conservative.

The U.S. policy of prohibiting open reporting from Hiroshima and Nagasaki was made clear at an early date, in a celebrated incident involving the Australian journalist Wilfred Burchett. Burchett made his way to Hiroshima early in September and succeeded in dispatching a graphic description of victims of an "atomic plague" to the London *Daily Express*. This was the first Western account of the fatal effects of radiation, and occupation officials immediately mounted an attack on what Burchett had reported. He was temporarily stripped of his press accreditation, and his camera, containing film with yet undeveloped Hiroshima exposures, mysteriously "disappeared." A comparable early account by an American journalist in Nagasaki never cleared General Douglas MacArthur's press headquarters, and reports to the outside world thereafter were carefully controlled through complacent, officially approved mouthpieces such as William Laurence, the science editor of the *New York Times*.[14] Some eleven thousand feet of movie film shot in the two cities between August and December by a thirty-man Japanese camera crew was confiscated by U.S. authorities in February 1946 and not returned to Japan until two decades later, in 1966.[15]

Accurate estimates of atomic-bomb fatalities also have been difficult to come by over the years. In June 1946, the prestigious U.S. Strategic Bombing Survey placed the number of deaths at approximately seventy to eighty thousand individuals in Hiroshima and thirty-five to forty thousand in Nagasaki. An honest estimate at the time, these figures have been perpetuated in most subsequent commentary about the bombs, although they are conservative in themselves and obviously fail to take into account bomb-related deaths subsequent to mid-1946. For the usual political reasons,

after 1946 neither the U.S. nor Japanese governments chose to revise the initial estimates or call attention to the ongoing toll of
hibakusha deaths. It now appears that the total of immediate and
longer-term deaths caused by the bombing of the two cities is well
over 200,000—probably around 140,000 in Hiroshima and 75,000
in Nagasaki—with the great majority of these deaths occurring
during or shortly after the bombings. Some estimates are considerably higher.[16]*

Disregard for the victims extended beyond sanitized reporting, suppressed film footage of the human aftermath, and disregard of the real death toll. Unsurprisingly, the United States
extended no aid to survivors of the atomic bombs. Among other
considerations, to do so could have been construed as acknowledging that use of the bombs had been improper. Aid to victims
also might have opened the door to claims for compensation or
special treatment by victims of conventional U.S. incendiary
bombing. The well-known Atomic Bomb Casualty Commission
(ABCC) established by the U.S. government in Japan at the beginning of 1947 was set up exclusively to collect scientific data on
the long-term biological effects of the bombs. Whether fairly or
not, to many Japanese the ABCC thereby earned the onus of simply treating the *hibakusha* residents of Hiroshima and Nagasaki as
experimental subjects or guinea pigs a second time.[17]

More surprisingly, perhaps, the Japanese government only
began extending special assistance to the bomb victims after the
occupation ended in 1952. In the aftermath of the devastation of
Hiroshima and Nagasaki, local treatment was largely dependent

---

* I have revised this sentence about atomic bomb fatalities to indicate
the most plausible estimates at the time this present collection of essays
is being compiled. As indicated in the endnote, in 1994, when this article was written, Japanese government deliberations concerning death-
benefits compensation to the families of *hibakusha* put the total number
of deaths prior to 1969 at upwards of 300,000.

on local resources—and this from municipalities that had come close to annihilation. One of the several legacies of this callous early history of neglect has been to make identification of victims and precise quantification of the effects of the bombs even more problematic than might otherwise have been the case.[18]

In the localities themselves, suffering was compounded not merely by the unprecedented nature of the catastrophe, as well as by the absence of large-scale governmental assistance, but also by the fact that public struggle with this traumatic experience was *not permitted*. It is at the local level that U.S. censorship was most inhumane. With but rare exceptions, survivors of the bombs could not grieve publicly, could not share their experiences through the written word, could not be offered public counsel and support. Psychological traumas we now associate with the bomb experience—psychic numbing and the guilt of survivors, for example, along with simply coping with massive bereavement and mutilation and grotesque protracted death—could not be addressed in open media forums. Nor could Japanese medical researchers working with survivors publish their findings so that other doctors and scientists might make use of them in treating the *hibakusha*. U.S. occupation authorities began easing restrictions on the publication of personal accounts by survivors only after more than three years had passed since the bombings. And it was not until February 1952—two months before the occupation ended, and six and one-half years after the residents of Hiroshima and Nagasaki were bombed and irradiated—that Japanese academic associations were able to engage freely, openly, and independently in investigating atomic-bomb injuries.[19]

American isolation of the *hibakusha* was compounded by ostracism within Japanese society itself, for the bomb, of course, stigmatized its victims. Some were disfigured. Some were consigned to slow death. Some, in utero on those fateful midsummer days, were mentally retarded. Many could not cope well with the so-called real world to which most other Japanese (including survivors of combat as well as conventional incendiary bombing) returned after the war. And all initially were presumed to carry the curse of the bombs in their blood. *Hibakusha* were not welcome compatriots in the new Japan. Psychologically if not physically, they were deformed reminders of a miserable past. Given the unknown generic consequences of irradiation, they were shunned as marriage prospects. The great majority of Japanese, overwhelmed by their own struggles for daily survival, were happy to put them out of mind. So was the Japanese government, which did not even establish its own research council to conduct surveys of bomb survivors until November 1953.[20]

In this milieu, where time was so peculiarly warped, the Japanese as a whole did not begin to really *visualize* the human consequences of the bombs in concrete, vivid ways until three or four years after Hiroshima and Nagasaki had been destroyed. The first graphic depictions of victims seen in occupied Japan were not photographs but drawings and paintings by the wife-and-husband artists Maruki Toshi and Maruki Iri, who had rushed to Hiroshima, where they had relatives, as soon as news of the bomb arrived. The Marukis published a booklet of black-and-white Hiroshima drawings in 1950 under the title *Pika-don* ("Flash-bang," a euphemism peculiar to the blinding flash and ensuing blast of the atomic bombs). In 1950 and 1951, they were permitted to exhibit five large murals of *hibakusha* entitled "Ghosts," "Fire," "Water," "Rainbow," and "Boys and Girls." This was the beginning, as it turned out, of a lifelong series of collaborative paintings addressing the human dimensions of World War II in Asia.[21]

As the Marukis later recalled, they began attempting to paint Hiroshima in 1948 not merely because they remained haunted by what they had witnessed but also because they believed that if they did not put brush to paper there might never be a visual eyewitness record of these events for Japanese to see. Actual photographs of the effects of the bombs in Hiroshima and Nagasaki were not published nationwide until after the occupation ended in the spring of 1952—and in theory never should have been available from Japanese sources to publish at all, since occupation policy forbade even possessing such negatives or prints.

In the print media, the easing of censorship in late 1948 finally paved the way for publication of reminiscences, poems, essays, and fictional re-creations by *hibakusha*. A minor publishing boom developed in this area, led by a remarkable outpouring of writings by Nagai Takashi, a widowed young father dying of radiation sickness in Nagasaki. Nagai, ironically enough, had been a medical researcher specializing in radiology and was a devout Catholic. His wife had been killed outright in the Nagasaki blast. He lived in a tiny hut in the ruins of Nagasaki with his young son and daughter—reflecting on the meaning of his city's fate, writing furiously before death caught him (which it did on April 30, 1951, killing him with heart failure caused by leukemia). Nagai was extraordinarily charismatic in his prolonged death agony and captured popular imagination to a degree unsurpassed by any other Japanese writer about the bombs until the mid-1960s, when the distinguished elderly novelist Ibuse Masuji, a native son of Hiroshima prefecture, published *Kuroi Ame* (Black Rain).

Nagai's interpretation of the nuclear holocaust was apocalyptically Christian. The bombs were part of God's providence, a divine act of suffering and death out of which world redemption would arise. And in his view, it was not mere happenstance that the second and last nuclear weapon fell on Nagasaki, a city with a long Christian tradition—exploded, indeed, above the great cathedral at Urakami. "Was not Nagasaki the chosen victim," Nagai wrote in a typically passionate passage, "the lamb without blemish, slain as a whole-burnt offering on an altar of sacrifice, atoning for the sins of all the nations during World War II?"

There is no evidence that the Japanese who flocked to buy Nagai's writings, or wrote him in great numbers, or made pilgrimages to his bedside, were fundamentally moved by his Christianity. More obviously, they were moved by his courage, his struggle to make sense of his fate, and the pathos of the two youngsters he soon would leave orphaned. And regardless of what one made of messianic Christian theology, Nagai's sermon that Japan had been divinely chosen to endure unique and world-redemptive suffering clearly struck a resonant chord in the Japanese psyche. Even

Emperor Hirohito, who had been formally recostumed as "the symbol of the State and the unity of the people" under the new constitution, undertook a pilgrimage to Nagai's bedside in 1949.[22]

In his own telling, Nagai conceived the idea for his most famous book, *Nagasaki no Kane* (The Bells of Nagasaki), on Christmas eve of 1945 and completed the manuscript around August 9, 1946—the first anniversary of the Nagasaki bomb that had killed his beloved wife, also a Christian, and scores of medical coworkers. The book was not approved for publication until the beginning of 1949, however, and its handling as that time captured the lingering nervousness of U.S. occupation authorities on these matters. Between the same covers, the publisher was required to pair Nagai's abstract and emotional reflections with an extended graphic account of Japanese atrocities in the Philippines. This coupling was extremely ironic, for it unwittingly subverted the official U.S. position that use of the bombs had been necessary and just. Japanese readers, that is, could just as easily see the juxtaposition of the Hiroshima/Nagasaki bombs and the rape of Manila as suggesting an equivalence between American and Japanese atrocities. Despite this crude and revealing intervention, in any case, *Nagasaki no Kane* not only became a best-seller but also soon was turned into a popular movie with an equally well-known theme song.[23]

Nagai's breakthrough essentially opened the door to the publication of books, articles, poems, and personal recollections by *hibakusha* beginning in 1949.[24] By the time the occupation ended, a distinctive genre of atomic-bomb literature had begun to impress itself on popular consciousness—often, as in Nagai's case, associated with a vivid sense of martyrdom. In 1951, two years after completing "Summer Flowers," one of the classic first-hand accounts about Hiroshima, Hara Tamiki committed suicide by lying down on a railway crossing near his Tokyo home. Tōge Sankichi, by far the most esteemed poet of the atomic-bomb experience, wrote most of his verses in an extraordinary burst of creativity while hospitalized in 1951 for a chronic bronchial condition complicated by exposure to radiation in Hiroshima. Tōge died on the operating table in March 1953, with friends from the Japan Communist Party clustered nearby while a compatriot read the "Prelude" of his *Genbaku Shishū* (Poems of the Atomic Bomb). Later engraved on a memorial in the peace park in Hiroshima, "Prelude" became the single best-known Japanese cry of protest against the bombs:

> *Bring back the fathers! Bring back the mothers!*
> *Bring back the old people!*
> *Bring back the children!*
> *Bring me back!*
> *Bring back the human beings I had contact with!*
>
> *For as long as there are human beings, a world of human beings,*
> *bring back peace,*
> *unbroken peace.*[25]

Among the many things that the paintings of the Marukis and the writings and reminiscences by *hibakusha* provided was a vocabulary and iconography of nuclear annihilation that soon became familiar to most Japanese. Textually and visually, the closest existing approximation to the experience of August 6 and 9, 1945 was to be found in medieval writings and pictorial scrolls depicting the horrors of the Buddhist hell. Phrases such as "it was like hell," or "hell could not be more terrible than this," were the most commonly heard refrain in recollections by survivors. The first detailed Japanese survey of the effects of the atomic bomb—made public on August 23, 1945, a week before the American victors arrived—described Hiroshima and Nagasaki as a "living hell."[26] In the Marukis' paintings, the fire that consumed men, women and children in Hiroshima was painted in the same manner that medieval artists had used in rendering the flames of the underworld—and, indeed, the only real Japanese precedents for the naked, mutilated figures in the Marukis' depictions of atomic-bomb victims were the tormented sinners in these old Buddhist hell scrolls. Years later, in selecting a title for a collection of drawings by *hibakusha*, Japan's public television network turned naturally to the phrase "unforgettable fire."[27]

The "procession of ghosts" that was the subject of the Marukis' first, stark, India-ink mural—depicting naked, stunned, maimed *hibakusha* with hands outstretched, skin peeling from them—captured another enduring image of the bomb experience. In this instance, the nuclear reality resonated with traditional depictions of ghosts and ghouls, who also moved with eerie slowness, hands stretched before them (many bomb survivors had their hands severely burned when they covered their eyes against the blinding flash of the bombs, and almost invariably walked holding their hands palms down in front of them because this eased the pain).

Benign images grotesquely transformed also emerged as unforgettable metaphors of the nuclear disaster. Water, for example, became a central fixation in several forms—the parching thirst that victims felt (the most often heard last words spoken by victims were "*mizu kudasai*," or "water please"); the enduring guilt that survivors experienced because they did not heed these pleas (the Japanese had been told, as a matter of general principle, not to give water to injured people); the seven great rivers of Hiroshima, running out to the beautiful Inland Sea when the bomb fell, all clogged with corpses (people threw themselves into the rivers to escape the fires, and drowned or died there of their injuries).

Black rain fell after the bombs had transformed the clear-day atmosphere. The ominous rainfall stained skin and clothing and became in time an indelible metaphor of the unprecedented aftereffects of the new weapons. Although subsequent research by the ABCC found no lethal connection between the black rain and radioactive fallout in Hiroshima and Nagasaki, in popular consciousness the rain became associated with the terrible radiation sickness that soon killed thousands of individuals who appeared to have survived the bombings. After a few hours or days, they experienced fever, nausea, vomiting, diarrhea, abnormal thirst, and sometimes convulsions and delirium. Beginning in the second week after the bombs were dropped, apparent survivors found blood in their spit, urine, and stools; bruise-like discolorations (*purpura*) appeared on their bodies; their hair fell out in clumps. At the time no one knew what such grotesqueries portended. The Japanese government report made public on August 23 captured the local horror by describing what we now know to be radiation sickness as an "evil spirit."[28]

Other traditionally benign symbols also were transmogrified. Mother and infant, universal icon of love and life, were transposed into a symbol of the broken life bond—mothers attempting to nurse dead babies, infants attempting to suck at the breasts of dead mothers. (Classic medieval texts such as the early thirteenth-century *Hōjōki* had offered such fractured images as evidence of *mappō*, the Buddhist apocalypse or "latter days of the Buddhist law.") Bizarre iconographies became commonplace in August 1945: monstrously mutilated people, of course, unrecognized by neighbors and loved ones—but also a man holding his eyeball in his hand; hopping birds with their wings burned off; live horses on fire; permanent white shadows on scorched walls where what had made the shadow (grass, ladders, people) no longer existed; people standing like black statues, burned to a crisp but still seemingly engaged in a last energetic act; legs standing upright, without bodies; survivors as well as corpses with their hair literally standing on end; maggots swarming in the wounds of the living.

All this, and much more, became familiar to most Japanese when those who witnessed Hiroshima and Nagasaki belatedly began to express what they had experienced.

The delayed timing of these first intense Japanese encounters with the human tragedy of Hiroshima and Nagasaki had unanticipated consequences. For example, censorship began to be lifted at approximately the same time that the Tokyo war-crimes trials ended (December 1948). The culminating moments of the protracted

Allied juridical campaign to impress Japanese with the enormity of their wartime transgressions thus coincided with the moment that many Japanese had their first encounters with detailed personal descriptions of the nuclear devastation that the Americans had visited upon them. While former Japanese leaders were being convicted of war crimes, sentenced to death, and hanged, the Japanese public simultaneously was beginning to learn the details of Hiroshima and Nagasaki for the first time. For many Japanese, there seemed an immoral equivalence here.

Of even greater political consequence, the Japanese really confronted the horrors of nuclear war three years or more after Americans and other unoccupied peoples did—at a time when China was being won by the Communists, the Soviet Union was detonating its first bomb, hysteria in the United States had given rise to rhetoric about preventive war and preemptive strikes, runways all over occupied Japan and Okinawa were being lengthened to accommodate America's biggest bombers, and, in short time, war came to Korea. In effect, the Japanese confronted the bombs and the most intense and threatening moments of the Cold War simultaneously. They did so, moreover, at a level of intimate concern with the human consequences of nuclear weapons that ran deeper than the generally superficial American impressions of a large mushroom cloud, ruined cityscapes, and vague numbers of abstract "casualties."

The impact of John Hersey's classic text *Hiroshima* in the United States and Japan can be taken as a small example of the ramifications of this aberrant collapse of time. Hersey's terse portraits of six victims of the Hiroshima bomb stunned American readers when first published in 1946. His account originally was written for the urbane *New Yorker* magazine, however, and reached a rather narrow upper-level stratum of the American public. By 1949, moreover, when anti-Communist hysteria had take possession of the American media, the initial impact of the book had eroded. By this time, Hersey's masterwork had no conspicuous hold on the American mind. A Japanese translation of *Hiroshima*, on the other hand, was not permitted until occupation censorship was terminated in 1949. The translation became a best-seller in 1950—four years after Hersey's account first appeared in the United States—and reinforced popular Japanese sentiment against active commitment to U.S. military policy in the Cold War.

It was in this context that the Japanese "peace movement" (*heiwa undō*) took shape between 1949 and the mid-1950s. Vivid recollections and re-creations of the old war coincided with confrontation with new Cold War realities—including, beginning in July 1950, Japanese rearmament and, beginning in April 1952, the indefinite maintenance of U.S. military bases in sovereign Japan. In attempting to mobilize public support behind a more neutral position for their country, liberal and leftist intellectuals starting with the prestigious "Peace Problems Symposium" (Heiwa Mondai Danwakai) adopted a policy of promoting pacifism by appealing to the personal experiences of Japanese in the war just past—essentially appealing, that is, to the Japanese sense of victimization.

An internationalist peace consciousness, this liberal and left-wing argument went, was like the outermost ring in a series of concentric circles. To promote such a consciousness, one had to begin at the center with the intimate experience of suffering in the recent war, and strive to extend this aversion to war to the outer rings of a national and ultimately international outlook. The atomic-bomb literature contributed to this. So did a complementary vogue of publications evoking the experiences of other Japanese who had suffered in the war. Conspicuous here were collections of the wartime letters of student conscripts killed in battle.[29] Even on the left, in short, victim consciousness was seen as the essential core of a pacifist and ultimately internationalist consciousness.

By the early 1950s, fear of a nuclear World War III had become almost palpable in Japan. President Truman's threat to use nuclear weapons in the Korean conflict in November 1950 inflamed these fears; and even after a truce had been arranged on the battlegrounds next door, a great number of Japanese remained alarmed by the continued testing of nuclear weapons by the American and

Soviet superpowers, extending now to hydrogen bombs. When fallout from a U.S. thermonuclear test on the Bikini atoll irradiated the crew of a Japanese fishing boat misnamed *Lucky Dragon* 5 on March 1, 1954, the public was primed to respond with intense emotion to this concrete presentiment of a second cycle of nuclear victimization (one fisherman eventually died from exposure to these "ashes of death").

A campaign to ban all nuclear weapons, initiated by Japanese housewives in May 1954, for example, soon collected an astonishing 30 million signatures.[30] This same turbulent period also saw the birth, in November 1954, of Godzilla, Japan's enduring contribution to the cinematic world of mutant science-fiction monsters spawned by a nuclear explosion. In serious cinema, the director Kurosawa Akira followed his triumphant *Seven Samurai*, a 1954 production, with an almost incoherent 1955 film entitled *Record of a Living Being*, in which fear of atomic extinction drives an elderly man insane.

This was the milieu in which, in 1955, a memorial peace museum and peace park were opened in Hiroshima and the first national coalition against atomic and hydrogen bombs was established. The latter development gave temporary coherence to the antinuclear movement—and simultaneously delivered the movement into the hand of fractious political professionals and ideologues.[31] As a consequence, in the decades that followed, popular remembrance of Hiroshima and Nagasaki can be characterized as having gone through cycles of renewal—or, put differently, through cycles of rehumanization, in which individuals or grass-roots movements reacted against the ritualization and gross politicization of remembrance. While the professional peace advocates warred over whether socialist nuclear weapons were as objectionable as capitalist ones, and while the organizers of formal antinuclear observances negotiated the seating on the speakers' platforms, certain writers, artists, and projects succeeded in casting new perspectives on the human costs of the bombs.

Beginning in 1963, for example, the gifted young writer Ōe Kenzaburō began to use reports about the annual peace observances in Hiroshima as a vehicle for criticizing "the strong odor of politics" that hovered over the peace park, and rediscovering "the true Hiroshima" in the ordinary citizens who still lived with and died from the legacies of the bomb.[32] Ibuse Masuji's *Black Rain*, a masterful fictional reconstruction of death from radiation sickness based on the diary of a Hiroshima survivor plus interviews with some fifty *hibakusha*, was serialized in 1965–66 and enjoyed perennial strong sales in book form thereafter. Ibuse himself had been born in Hiroshima prefecture in 1898, and his evocation of the rhythms and rituals of ordinary life restored the human dimension of the horror of nuclear destruction with immense dignity.[33]

In the early 1970s, Nakazawa Keiji, a cartoonist for children's publications who had been a seven-year-old in Hiroshima when the bomb was dropped, achieved improbable success with a graphic serial built on his family's own experiences as victims and survivors. Nakazawa's *Hadashi no Gen* (Barefoot Gen) was serialized in a boy's magazine with a circulation of over 2 million and ran to some one thousand pages before the series was terminated—surviving thereafter as both an animated film and a multivolume collection.[34] In a very different form of popular graphics, Japanese public television solicited visual representations by *hibakusha* in the 1970s and received several thousand drawings and paintings of scenes that had remained burned in the memories of the survivors. These intensely personal images became the basis of television broadcasts, traveling exhibitions, and publications.[35]

As time passed, popular perceptions of Hiroshima and Nagasaki were transformed in ways both predictable and unpredictable. Through painstaking demographic reconstructions—an immense task, since entire families and neighborhoods and all their records had been obliterated—higher estimates of nuclear fatalities became generally accepted. And with the passing of years, the "late effect" medical consequences of the bombs became apparent in higher incidences among survivors of leukemia, thyroid cancer, breast cancer, lung cancer, stomach cancer, malignant lymphoma, salivary gland tumors, hematological disorders, and cataracts.

Belated sensitivity to the enduring social and psychological legacies of the bombs introduced new euphemisms into the lexicon of nuclear victimization. One spoke not merely of "A-bomb orphans," such as the children Nagai Takashi left behind, but also of the "elderly orphaned," in reference to old people bereft of the children who ordinarily would have supported them in old age. The painful disfiguring scars known as keloids were said to have a spiritual counterpart in "keloids of the heart," just as the radiation-caused leukemia had its psychological counterpart in a "leukemia of the spirit" among survivors. In the cruel vernacular of everyday discourse, youngsters who were born mentally retarded due to exposure to radiation while in the womb became known as *"pika* babies," in reference to the blinding flash of the bombs.[36]

Such new information and perceptions gave greater concreteness to the victim consciousness that always had accompanied popular recollections of Hiroshima and Nagasaki. At the same time, however, fixation on Japan's nuclear victimization proved unexpectedly subversive—for the closer the Japanese looked at Hiroshima and Nagasaki, the clearer it became that more nationalities than just the Japanese had been killed there. Hiroshima prefecture was one of the major areas from which Japanese emigrated to the United States. After Pearl Harbor, many second-generation Japanese Americans who had temporarily gone to Japan were stranded there—and it is estimated that around thirty-two hundred may have been in Hiroshima when the bomb was dropped. If that is true, then extrapolating from overall casualty rates it is probable that at least one thousand American citizens were killed by the Hiroshima bomb.[37]

While these American deaths in Hiroshima are of slight interest in Japan (and, involving ethnic Japanese, of negligible interest to most Americans), by the early 1970s the Japanese found themselves confronting a more troublesome question of victimization. For it had become apparent by then that thousands of Koreans also were killed in Hiroshima and Nagasaki. As a Japanese colony, Korea was a source of extensively conscripted and heavily abused labor in wartime Japan, and it was belatedly estimated that between five and eight thousand Koreans may have been killed in Hiroshima, and fifteen hundred to two thousand in Nagasaki.[38] Such laborers were, in effect, double victims—exploited by the Japanese and incinerated by the Americans. By the same token, the Japanese were revealed as being simultaneously victims and victimizers. Indeed, as the story unraveled, it was learned that even in the immediate aftermath of the nuclear holocaust, Korean survivors were discriminated against when it came to medical treatment and even cremation and burial.

A small number of Japanese read a large lesson in this, concerning the complexities of both victimization and responsibility. In 1972, for example—over two decades after they first started portraying the Japanese victims of the bombs in their collaborative paintings—the Marukis exhibited a stark mural entitled "Ravens," depicting the black scavengers descending on a mound of Korean dead, plucking out eyes. In the Hiroshima peace park itself, however, the guardians of memory thus far have succeeded in keeping a memorial to the Korean victims from violating the central, sacred ground. Even in the peace park, the Japanese unwittingly reveal themselves to be both victims and victimizers.

These tensions—racial and ethnic bias and dual identity as victim and victimizer—never will be entirely resolved in Japan. Since the 1970s, however, they have become more transparent and openly debated. Acknowledgment of the Korean victims of the atomic bombs in the early 1970s, for example, coincided with restoration of Japanese relations with the People's Republic of China—and, with this, renewed attention by liberal and left-wing writers to Japanese atrocities in China, beginning with the Rape of Nanking. Until then, and despite the zealous didacticism associated with the war-crimes trials conducted by the Allied victors during the occupation period, it seems fair to say that most Japanese regarded Hiroshima and Nagasaki as the preeminent moments of atrocity in World War II in Asia, towering above all other acts of war just as the mushroom clouds had towered over Hiroshima and Nagasaki in August 1945.

Belatedly reencountering China changed this. Here, again, memory was reconstructed after an abnormal interlude of silence, during which defeat followed by Cold War politics isolated Japan from China and essentially smothered recollections of Japan's aggression and atrocious war behavior there.[39] The struggle to reshape memory of the war has become more intense since then—increasingly so as other Japanese atrocities have been exposed, such as the murderous medical experiments carried out by Unit 731 in Manchuria and the forced recruitment of Asian women to serve as prostitutes (*ianfu*, or "comfort women") for the emperor's loyal troops. To the extent that popular consciousness of victimization and atrocity has changed in contemporary Japan, this has entailed greater general acknowledgment of Japan's own war crimes vis-à-vis fellow Asians.[40]

Even this remains contested, of course, as the May 1994 resignation of the newly appointed minister of Justice, Nagano Shigeto, attests. Nagano was forced to step down after calling the Nanking massacre a "fabrication," characterizing the *ianfu* as "public prostitutes," and referring to the war in Asia by the patriotic old name "Great East Asia War" (*Dai Tōa Sensō*)[41] In all this, he was repudiated by his government, which formally acknowledged that the war against Asia had been a war of aggression. That same month, however, in the face of considerable domestic pressure, the same conservative coalition government also canceled plans for the emperor, Hirohito's son, to visit Pearl Harbor while on a state visit to Hawaii. This, it was argued, was too great a concession—for, after all, no American head of state ever had visited Hiroshima or Nagasaki, or even expressed regrets for those terrible deaths.[42]

For most Japanese, the war against other Asians was different and more regrettable in a moral sense than that against the Americans, and Hiroshima and Nagasaki account for much of this difference.[43]

6

A DOCTOR'S DIARY OF HIROSHIMA, FIFTY YEARS LATER

For several decades after World War II, doing "proper" history in the American academic milieu generally was understood to involve working with official documents and pronouncements; with formal decisions and developments; with "hard," quantitative data; with the writings, including memoirs, letters, and diaries, of prominent individuals. Attentiveness to "lesser names"—the aspect of E.H. Norman's pioneer scholarship that Japanese scholars admired—was seldom regarded as worthwhile. The vast numbers who left no names at all to history remained ignored and invisible. "People's history" had yet to become a respectable professional preoccupation.

There were, of course, ways to rectify and counterbalance this academic elitism; and where the intimate human experience of the atomic bombs was concerned, the most accessible gateway to lesser names and hitherto invisible people was through journalism and trade publications. By far the most influential English-language portal of this nature was John Hersey's Hiroshima, *based on interviews with six survivors and originally published in an August 1946 issue of the* New Yorker. *(U.S. occupation authorities blocked publication of a Japanese translation of this for several years.) In 1955, an engrossing survivor's account was published in English and a score or more European languages under the title* Hiroshima Diary. *The author, Hachiya Michihiko, was a medical doctor whose hospital was shattered by the bomb and who was himself seriously injured. His diary, focusing on the surviving staff and patients in the ruined hospital, covered the weeks between August 8 and the end of September and had been serialized in a Japanese medical journal between 1950 and 1952.*

The essay that follows was written as an introduction to the reissue of Hiroshima Diary *in 1995, on the fiftieth anniversary of the bombing.*

* * *

A half century has passed since Dr. Michihiko Hachiya wrote his diary in the ruins of Hiroshima. Forty years have gone by since his observations became available to English-language readers through the devoted translating and editing of an American doctor, Warner Wells. The translation was hailed as an extraordinary literary event when it first appeared in the United States in 1955, and it retains its capacity to move us today.

This is a remarkable accomplishment, for what we encounter here is an account of the end of a ferocious war that is intimately Japanese and simultaneously transcends national, cultural, and racial boundaries. The diary speaks to the human heart and human condition, and does so without artifice, for it was not intended to be published. Dr. Hachiya himself was severely injured by the blast effects of the atomic bombing. At one point he notes in passing that his face and body still showed around 150 scars. By August 8, 1945, however—two days after Hiroshima was devastated—he was well enough to begin keeping a record of his convalescence in the hospital he himself administered. That record is what we have here, and there is nothing comparable to it.

As a rule, Westerners, and Americans in particular, have been reluctant to look closely at the world in which Dr. Hachiya lived between August 6 and the last day of September, when his diary ends. In the heroic American narrative of the war, the destruction of Hiroshima commonly ends with the mushroom cloud, followed by a quick fast-forward to Japan's surrender nine days later. The

Soviet declaration of war against Japan on August 8 receives little mention in this narrative. The dropping of a second atomic bomb on Nagasaki on August 9 is similarly neglected. The power of the Hiroshima bomb receives lavish, even loving, attention. By contrast, commentary about the human consequences of the bombs on the largely civilian populations of Hiroshima and Nagasaki generally is shunned, for this undermines the heroic narrative and raises troubling questions about "the good war."

Episodically, almost in a cyclical manner, it is true that the American public has shown interest and sensitivity concerning what took place beneath the mushroom cloud. John Hersey's *Hiroshima*, a terse collection of portraits of atomic bomb victims, deeply affected many readers in 1946. Dr. Hachiya's *Hiroshima Diary* was seriously received in the mid-1950s, and over a decade later the translation of the greatest Japanese account of death from radiation sickness, Masuji Ibuse's *Black Rain*, was hailed as a classic in the United States and Britain. In the early 1980s, the apocalyptic spectacle of nuclear death and devastation witnessed in Hiroshima and Nagasaki was transposed to the global level in an extraordinarily successful futuristic best-seller by Jonathan Schell entitled *The Fate of the Earth*.

The averted gaze has been the easier, more persistent response to Hiroshima and Nagasaki, however, and in mainstream U.S. circles commemoration of the fiftieth anniversary of the end of World War II in Asia has strengthened this tendency. For understandable reasons, Americans wish to celebrate victory over an aggressive, fanatic, atrocious enemy. Most choose to see the atomic bombs as weapons that *saved* countless lives. In this heroic rendering, Hiroshima and Nagasaki simply hastened the end of a terrible global conflagration.

These sentiments emerged strongly in the closing months of 1994 and opening months of 1995, when the Smithsonian Institution in Washington, D.C., was forced to drop plans for a major exhibition on the atomic bombs that would have included photographs and artifacts from ground zero. These were, critics declared, "emotionally loaded." Intimate depiction of civilian Japanese victims (in the parlance of the heroic American narrative they are "casualties"), it was argued, distorted the reality of a war in which the Japanese over and over again had victimized others atrociously. The chief historian of the U.S. Air Force publicly asked how the Smithsonian could have blundered so badly on such a "morally unambiguous" subject. The U.S. Senate unanimously approved a resolution condemning the institution for failing to celebrate the manner in which the atomic bombs had brought the war to a "merciful" end.

In this highly charged emotional and ideological climate, the reissue of Dr. Hachiya's diary is a salutary event. His simple account tells us, as no one but the Japanese who experienced the bombs can, about the human consequences of nuclear weapons. It reminds us of the larger tragic narrative of World War II, in which heroism coexisted with moral ambiguity, and the same act could seem simultaneously merciful and merciless.

From the Japanese perspective, Hiroshima and Nagasaki were not only an end but also a beginning: the beginning of grotesque lingering deaths, lifelong bereavement, unprecedented physical harm from radiation, and ceaseless psychological trauma, of course—but also the beginning of a new sense of the preciousness of life. Shuffling through the filth and debris of his ruined, overcrowded hospital; watching patients and acquaintances die, often mysteriously; assailed by the stench of bodies being cremated wafting through the hospital's shattered windows—through all this Dr. Hachiya moved with composure, compassion, and keen appreciation of the smallest pleasures of so-called normal life.

To turn a chronicle of nuclear horror into an affirmation of life in this manner is no small accomplishment, and the triumph of Dr. Hachiya's *Hiroshima Diary* lies in his ability to do this so naturally—without preaching, usually without philosophizing, just by being himself and setting down his daily thoughts and activities. That his thoughts and feelings are entirely accessible to non-Japanese, despite numerous small references to things peculiar to everyday Japanese culture, is the ultimate measure of his triumph. Somehow, in August 1945, when the rhetoric of war hate and race hate was at fever pitch and the most devastating weapon in history had just shattered his life, this modest and conspicuously patriotic physician managed to express himself almost entirely in the language of a common humanity.

These matters bear spelling out a bit, for as the cyclical nature of American memory suggests, they are easily forgotten. Of course, the images of nuclear hell that Dr. Hachiya depicts may in the end remain most indelibly etched in many readers' minds. In this regard his chronicle is typical of other *hibakusha*, or survivor, accounts, where the same haunting images of nuclear destruction appear. The stunning flash (*pika*) of the bomb, followed by a colossal blast (*don*) that shattered buildings kilometers away. Nakedness or seminakedness, from the blast stripping clothing away. Eerie silence. People walking in lines with their hands outstretched and skin peeling off—like automatons, dream-walkers, scarecrows, a line of ants. Corpses "frozen by death while in the full action of flight." A dead man on a bicycle. A burned and blinded horse. Youngsters huddled together awaiting death. Mothers with dead children. Infants with dying mothers. Corpses without faces. Water everywhere—in firefighting cisterns, swimming pools, the rivers that fed the city—clogged with dead bodies. Fires like the infernos of hell. A man holding his eyeball in his hand. Survivors in crowded ruined buildings, lying in vomit, urine, and feces. Everywhere flies and maggots.

This is the familiar iconography of the immediate aftermath of the atomic bombing, although at this early date Dr. Hachiya, largely cut off from the outside world, was simply recording what he saw or others told him. Some of his descriptions are unusually vivid. A visitor comments about how roasted corpses become smaller. Burned people smell like drying squid or look like boiled octopuses. The odor of bodies being cremated is likened to that of burning sardines. In perhaps the most haunting of all the diary's images, as Dr. Hachiya makes his daily rounds we frequently encounter a nameless beautiful girl—she is always identified simply as "the beautiful girl"—who has been severely burned everywhere except her face. In early entries, she lies in a puddle of old blood and pus, soiled with urine and excrement. As time passes, she is able to smile when the doctor visits. By the end of the diary she can stand and go to the toilet by herself. What became of her? We will never know.

Because he is a physician, Dr. Hachiya quickly moves, and the reader with him, to the next level of the nuclear trauma: the emergence of inexplicable symptoms and unanticipated deaths. Patients who seemed to be improving suddenly worsen and die. People who appeared to have escaped harm entirely are stricken: they become speckled with subcutaneous bleeding, their hair falls out, and they have bloody diarrhea, vomit blood, pass blood from their genitals and rectum. Autopsies reveal massive internal hemorrhages that are erratic but seem to affect every organ. Belated acquisition of a microscope shows alarmingly low white blood cell counts, as well as the destruction of platelets in the blood. Could this have something to do with the bomb changing atmospheric pressure? Could it be a poison gas? In the course of these weeks Dr. Hachiya himself helps identify the mysterious scourge as radiation sickness and determines that all of the patients dying in this manner were within one kilometer of the bomb's hypocenter.

The intellectual satisfaction of understanding these deaths is part of Dr. Hachiya's own coming alive again, and he does not disguise the pleasure he takes in helping clarify this dreadful riddle. As early as August 9 he records the delight he feels in finding that his scientific curiosity is returning. Scientific understanding does not eliminate the horror, he indicates throughout, but it can mitigate the terror of the unknown and help dampen irrational fears—help dispel, for example, the rumor that Hiroshima would be uninhabitable for seventy-five years. Those dying of radiation sickness, he takes pains to explain publicly, were exposed to the *pika*. (What the diary does not reveal, for it stops too soon, is the appalling fact that from late 1945 until 1952 Japanese medical researchers were prohibited by U.S. occupation authorities from publishing scientific articles on the effects of the atomic bombs.)

Even in these earliest grim days after the bomb was dropped, Dr. Hachiya emerges as remarkably frank. Within two days, he regretfully observes how quickly he and his colleagues had come to accept massive death and cease to respect its awfulness. In time, the smell of cremations outside the window does not even disturb people's appetites. In one of his most stunning entries, he dryly records (on August 11) how the rumor spread within his miserably crowded hospital that Japan possessed the same weapon that had devastated Hiroshima and Nagasaki and had retaliated against the west coast of the United States. The whole atmosphere in the ward changed, and those patients who were most severely hurt were happiest. People sang songs of victory. They were convinced the tide of the war had changed. In all the literature about the bombs there are few scenes more Dickensian than this.

To historians of these days and weeks, Dr. Hachiya's response to the emperor's surrender broadcast on August 15 also is of considerable interest. Like many of his countryfolk, he had expected to be urged to fight to the end and was stunned to hear that Japan had capitulated. The shock of surrender, he writes, was even greater than the shock of the atomic bombing. He was overwhelmed with despair. Here and frequently afterward, in language redolent of the emperor worship under which the Japanese were marshaled for war, he reiterates his veneration of the throne and deep concern about the emperor's personal well-being. If there is a second Dickensian vignette in the diary, it is surely the scene in which Dr. Hachiya admiringly records how acquaintances of his stumbled through the dead and dying to bring the emperor's sacred photograph from the hospital to a safer place.

Such a response to the surrender was commonplace but not ubiquitous in Japan at this time. Many other Japanese greeted the capitulation with tears of relief; some even celebrated. But the obverse side of Dr. Hachiya's emperor worship was indeed widespread: namely, contempt for Japan's military leaders. With characteristic frankness, Dr. Hachiya acknowledges that hitherto he had been sympathetic toward the military. Now he despises them, for they had betrayed the emperor and deceived the people.

This was a widespread sentiment in Japan in the months and years following the defeat. While Emperor Hirohito by and large was exonerated from responsibility for war and defeat, his generals and admirals were widely condemned as having been ruthless, duplicitous, and stupid. With but one exception, Dr. Hachiya never openly expresses hatred in the diary. The exception is not, as might be expected, toward the Americans who dropped the atomic bombs, but rather toward General Hideki Tōjō and the Imperial Army, whose arrogant and unbounded stupidity brought disgrace and disaster upon their country.

Obliquely, too, the diary conveys these same sentiments. When Dr. Hachiya writes about digging in the rubble left by the atomic bomb and finding wooden bullets and broken bamboo spears, he knows full well what an absurd juxtaposition he is recording. And when, early in September, he prepares a report on the bomb effects for a newspaper and declares that the Japanese "were defeated in a scientific war," once again he is offering an observation that was widespread at the time and implicitly critical of Japan's irrational wartime leaders.

The ramifications of such attitudes were far-reaching. Although Dr. Hachiya and his little community were cut off from newspapers and radio for many weeks, their observations resonated strongly with what Japanese throughout the defeated country were saying. The angry exclamation that Tōjō deserved to die for his transgressions, for example, was reified in the form of widespread popular indifference to the fate of Japanese leaders in the Tokyo war crimes trials in subsequent years. More generally, this immediate contempt for the folly of the military leadership that led Japan to disastrous defeat survived in the postwar political culture in the form of deep antimilitary and even pacifist sentiments.

On the other hand, unbeknownst to Dr. Hachiya, the profound respect for science that emerges in his diary also was being widely trumpeted throughout Japan in these very same days as a force to be developed in reconstructing a peaceful Japan.

The contempt for the military that emerges so strongly in *Hiroshima Diary* did not extend to the victorious Americans. This seems astonishing given the direct suffering all the figures who appear in the diary had experienced from the Hiroshima bombing. In fact, this too was a fairly common response to the defeat throughout Japan. Initially, there was widespread apprehension about how the conquerors would behave when they occupied the country. Soon, however, this gave way to awkward but remarkably amicable relations. In the cataclysmic moment of staggering defeat, the "evil" enemy for most Japanese became Japan's own military. Throughout Japan, even ordinary demobilized servicemen often were treated with contempt or plain derision.

When word of the impending arrival of occupation forces in Hiroshima reached Dr. Hachiya's hospital, the initial response was typical. Many local women, including even some patients, fled out of fear that they might be raped. Dr. Hachiya's personal response, however, was remarkably composed. "I felt we had nothing to worry about," he recorded on September 13, "because westerners were a cultured people, not given to pilfering and marauding." His initial encounter with an American officer soon after he made this comment was strained but was quickly followed by a conspicuously positive evaluation of the young Americans who came to his hospital. They were, in his estimation, warm, friendly, kind, and amusing. They were gentlemen. They impressed him "as citizens of a great country."

This ability of antagonists on both sides of the atrocious Japanese-American war to move so abruptly from bitter hostility to cordial relationships has often been commented on and puzzled over. Dr. Hachiya's journal offers a subtle perspective on this turn from enmity to amity in which, once again, Japanese behavior is contrasted unfavorably to that of the victorious Anglo-Americans.

When one of his medical colleagues rushes to the hospital to urge him to evacuate the women because Americans were coming, for example, Dr. Hachiya jots down a telling aside. His colleague was so agitated, he observes, because of his awareness of how Japan's own soldiers had conducted themselves in China. Such initial fears about American rapacity by many Japanese, especially males, that is, in considerable part was a projection based on painful knowledge of how badly the Japanese themselves had behaved in alien and occupied lands. It is rare in Japanese writings from this time to see this submerged line of thinking exposed so incisively. And when the arriving Allied conquerors did in fact generally behave with restraint and even generosity toward the local population, the favorable impression of the visitors was strengthened.

Where the contemporary scene in defeated Japan is concerned, the diary offers vivid testimony to two particularly debilitating aspects of the postsurrender scene that similarly were not peculiar to Hiroshima or Nagasaki but rather persisted throughout the country. One was the condition widely known as *kyodatsu*, an overall state of demoralization and psychological prostration. The despair and confusion that Dr. Hachiya witnessed on his brief forays outside the hospital certainly reflected the staggering trauma of the nuclear devastation. They were, however, scenes repeated to greater or lesser degrees everywhere. Thus the "panorama" around Hiroshima station that Dr. Hachiya describes on September 15, exactly a month after the emperor's surrender broadcast, is a scene that could have been duplicated in countless other Japanese towns and cities: "tired war victims, demobilized soldiers, old people leaning against the burnt pillars, people walking aimlessly, heedless of all around them, and beggars." These, Dr. Hachiya comments, "were the *real* conquerors!" His stunning image on the same day of a poor woman walking through the rubble wearing her wedding kimono and carrying a sack of sweet potatoes could stand as an emblematic symbol of the *kyodatsu* condition that shrouded the entire country in these days.

In this milieu of exhaustion and despair, venality and corruption flourished like rank weeds. On this matter too, the diary is a valuable intimate source, for time and again as the days pass Dr. Hachiya records his mounting dismay at Japanese behavior in the wake of catastrophic defeat. Drunken ex-soldiers ride the trolley. Looting and burglary are widespread. Local officials are mostly inept and corrupt, and massive pillaging of military supplies is taking place. Inflation has made money almost meaningless. "People with evil faces and foul tongues" suddenly appear on the scene, profiting from others' misery. Disreputable men fondle uncouth girls. Greed rules the day. "Evil influences" are everywhere. The country appears to have fallen into "the clutches of the mean and unintelligent." Hiroshima, the doctor notes when supplies are even stolen from his hospital, was "becoming a wicked town."

This too was a widespread phenomenon in immediate post-surrender Japan, particularly in the weeks that elapsed between the surrender and the actual arrival of Allied occupation authorities and their belated consolidation of authority. Indeed, in the country at large during the eight weeks covered by *Hiroshima Diary*, military authorities as well as politicians and businessmen at both the national and local levels spent a major portion of their time destroying records and looting the massive storehouses of military matériel that had been stockpiled in anticipation of prolonged war and a last-ditch defense of the home islands. Like his striking vignettes of the *kyodatsu* condition of exhaustion and despair, Dr. Hachiya's terse observations of corruption and venality open a window not simply on the local scene in Hiroshima after the bomb, but—really unknown to him at the time—on Japan as a whole.

It is in this broader milieu of *internal* degradation coupled with staggering defeat that the conquering Americans emerge as unexpectedly positive figures. Even old Mrs. Saeki, a quiet figure of strength and comfort throughout the diary, whose daughter-in-law and three sons all had been killed, concludes after friendly young American officers visit the hospital that "Amerika-san is kind. I think they are very nice." This is an astonishing comment, and yet in the extraordinary environment that Dr. Hachiya portrays, it does not really surprise us.

*   *   *

In various ways, Dr. Hachiya's deceptively simple account of the Hiroshima bombing and its aftermath thus reveals a world of many layers of complexity. His diary is not merely an unusually intimate record of nuclear death and destruction. It is now clearer in retrospect that it also provides an unusually broad window on the psychology and social pathology of defeat. Beyond all this, however—and this is what ultimately gives *Hiroshima Diary* its enduring quality—it is a chronicle about coming alive, about cherishing life after tasting the bitterest kinds of death.

On several occasions Dr. Hachiya makes clear that he was as passionate a patriot as anyone, ready to throw down his life and die for the country if and when the emperor called on him to do so. At one point he quotes with understanding and even approval a fanatic fight-to-the-bitter-end entry from the diary of a close friend whose young son has just been killed in the bombing. But the destruction of Hiroshima, the loss of all his possessions, the near loss of his own life, the daily spectacle of war-wrought misery and death in the hospital all lead Dr. Hachiya, and many around him, to repudiate ultranationalism and war and linger instead on the preciousness of personal relationships and private blessings.

Tucked away in the diary, sometimes almost as passing thoughts, are lines that speak more or less directly to this. "How hard for a man to die," Dr. Hachiya muses while lying in bed eight days after the bomb, "whose life has once before been miraculously spared. On the day of the *pika* I gave no thought to my life, but today I wanted to live and death became a spectacle of terror." Three weeks later, he reflects again on "how precious" small things are—thoughts sparked, in this instance, by the destruction of an old plaque with calligraphy quoting words of wisdom from the Chinese classics. "When I was filled with faith in the certainty of victory and when I was working with thoughts only for the emperor," he confides on this occasion, "nothing was precious." It seemed entirely appropriate to sacrifice everything for the country. Now, however, "things had changed. Since the *pika* we had all become desperate and our fight was the fight of defeat even if we had to fight on stones. Our homes and our precious family possessions were no longer meaningless, but now they were gone. . . . I felt lonesome and alone because I no longer had even a home."

Old Mrs. Saeki, widowed and bereft of all her children, expresses similar sentiments when recounting where she was when the bomb fell. All was darkness, she recalls, and she thought she had died. What a joy to find she was still alive! This is the sentiment that keeps Dr. Hachiya's small group in the hospital going; and it is, indeed, the sentiment that ennobles the greatest Japanese writings on the atomic bomb experience, such as Ibuse's *Black Rain*. The overwhelming horror of man-made death is countered, placed in perspective, and ultimately transcended by evocation of the simplest activities of human intercourse and normal daily life (or, as in Ibuse's chronologically longer account, by the nurturing, cyclical rhythms of nature).

This healing process, this transcendence through the seemingly plainest of activities, occurs over and over again in the diary. Dr. Hachiya never moves away from the dead and dying, but he simultaneously creates an alternative, life-affirming world by recognizing the wonder of what in other circumstances would be taken for granted. Fruit and vegetables become treasures—someone brings peaches, and on another day there are tomatoes, or grapes. One day the ragged contingent in the ruined hospital room dines on the river fish *ayu*. Obtaining sugar is a cause for celebration. Cigarettes bring near ecstasy. Baths are recorded, and so is the happy discovery of a clean and intact toilet. Restoration of electricity is a signal event, as is the first arrival of mail and the first newspaper. A good bowel movement is deeply satisfying. This was no small matter when others were passing blood, an ominous sign of the radiation sickness. Still, the small group in the hospital managed to buoy their spirits with seemingly endless repartee involving toilet jokes.

In Japan as a whole, the broader social and cultural literature of these weeks and months reveals similar preoccupations. There they are linked to what in the Japanese idiom would be called "transcending *kyodatsu*"—that is, moving beyond the immediate trauma of the defeat. Taking heart, regaining hope, recovering a taste for life—this was all a familiar part of becoming psychologically whole again. And what this ultimately involved was a restoration of personal connections and pursuits that the war had all but obliterated. From this perspective—and *Hiroshima Diary* is a representative example of this way of thinking—the atomic bombs were the ultimate symbol of the horror of war itself. In the Japanese context, this meant that they were simultaneously a symbol of the folly of superpatriotism as well as the fatuousness of those who sought to mobilize people for military crusades in the name of the state.

In this sense, Dr. Hachiya's chronicle can also be read as an account of returning to an essentially private world—a world of intensely human and personal connections. Friendship is cherished. So are family relations. Every individual life is precious. Work—in this instance, scientific and medical work—is redemptive. One works to heal, to construct, and not to harm. One thinks of the former enemy not in terms of past horrors but rather terms of personal acquaintance and, later, professional collaboration.

There is both modesty and dignity here. And, of course, pathos—because now, a half century later, we know things Dr. Hachiya could not anticipate. The richness of his deceptively simple chronicle is such that each reader surely will come away with different lasting impressions, different moments or images that stay in the mind.

I find myself thinking of one such moment: when, on the last day of August, old Mrs. Saeki chides Dr. Hachiya for working so long at his microscope, trying to understand the strange and terrible symptoms that radiation sickness had caused in his patients. He has forgotten to eat lunch, she reminds him, and smoked too much, and is harming his body. This is the passage.

"*Baba-san,*" I answered softly, "we now understand some of the things which puzzled us before."

"Is that so," she retorted. "Will you be able to cure the disease now?"

We know, of course, that the answer was no. What the atomic bomb did could never be undone. Our only hope is to face it squarely and learn from Hiroshima.

7

HOW A GENUINE DEMOCRACY
SHOULD CELEBRATE ITS PAST

Commemorating the past is in good part triggered by numerology in our modern mass cultures, as certain magic anniversary numbers induce intense spasms of attention. There are, of course, annual spasms. December 7 is the key such date in the United States where World War II is concerned; in Japan, the end of the war on August 15 (Japan time) annually prompts a more reflective and critical media attentiveness to the war and its legacies. The big anniversary numbers, in any case, are five, ten, twenty-five, fifty, and one hundred. At fifty, one can still locate some survivors to interview. At one hundred, no one is left.

In 1994 and 1995, the impending fiftieth anniversary of the end of the Pacific War gave rise to an unusually harsh dispute over how to treat this milestone in the public arena in the United States. Controversy centered on plans for a major exhibition at the Smithsonian Institution's National Air and Space Museum featuring the Enola Gay, *the B-29 bomber that dropped the Hiroshima bomb. Initial support for such an exhibit came from air force enthusiasts and aerospace lobbyists; early working scripts by the museum's curators and advisers were widely distributed for outside comment; and an uproar ensued when critics accused the authors of these early drafts of attempting to besmirch recollection of the heroic mission that brought a horrendous war to an end.*

In retrospect, it was naive to imagine that serious treatment of the dropping of the first atomic bomb would be possible in a public space in the United States. As the exhibition's initial enthusiasts saw it, the anniversary would be an occasion for celebration—for retelling the story of a stupendous mobilization of scientific and technological expertise (building the great bombers as well as the atomic bomb) and a heroic strategic mission (using the bomb to end the war). The museum's early draft plans, in their eyes, subverted such patriotic remembrance in numerous ways—by introducing controversies over whether it was necessary to use the bombs, for example, and by carrying the projected treatment beyond the Enola Gay *and mushroom cloud to look, first, at Japanese casualties at ground zero; and, second, at the nuclear arms race that followed as one legacy of this watershed moment. The heroic narrative, as the critics saw it, was being sabotaged by a complicated, ambiguous, tragic narrative that would lead the visiting public to question the decision to use the atomic bombs or, at the very least, restrain their applause.*

As this controversy unfolded, I was particularly taken by the difficulty of doing "public history" in the United States in the balanced and self-critical way we usually argue that other countries (like Japan) should do public history. I was struck, that is, by the political and institutional constraints under which museums like the Smithsonian operate. This was conveyed in brusque language in a resolution introduced in the Senate in September 1994 (Resolution 257) that condemned the Air and Space Museum's script for being "revisionist and offensive to many World War II veterans," and went on to observe that federal law stipulates that "the valor and sacrificial service of the men and women of the Armed Forces shall be portrayed as an inspiration to the present and future generations of America." The resolution began by describing "the role of the Enola Gay" *as "momentous in helping to bring World War II to a merciful end, which resulted in saving the lives of Americans and Japanese."*

The exhibition that eventually materialized did conclude with a small number of displays about the destruction at ground zero. Compared to what might have been, however, this gelded presentation was an insult to the thoughtful individuals who visit museums to learn and are perfectly capable of handling complexity. There was an obverse side to all this, of course, in the vigorous and often fact-filled exchanges that the *patriotic attack on the original plans provoked; this was a serendipitous contribution to public education. Still, one sobering lesson of the* Enola Gay *controversy was the realization that one cannot expect great publicly funded institutions like the Smithsonian to turn future attention to America's other controversial wars, such as Korea, Vietnam, Iraq, and Afghanistan. What sort of inspiration could one expect to find here?* *

The short piece that follows appeared as an op-ed essay in the Chronicle of Higher Education *in June 1995.*

* * *

I had an unusual experience shortly after the Smithsonian Institution surrendered unconditionally to critics in late January and abandoned its plans for a major exhibition at the National Air and Space Museum on the use of the atomic bomb to end World War II. I was, to coin a phrase, "disinvited" from giving two public, off-campus talks, both of which had been roughly framed in terms of "thinking about the bomb."

The disinvitations were conveyed in a genteel manner, of course. I remained welcome, my erstwhile sponsors explained. I should just come prepared to focus on a different aspect of American-Japanese relations. The bombs that the United States dropped on Japan simply had become "too controversial" a topic.

Thus, in ways that have gone virtually unreported by the mass media, the dispute over the Smithsonian's exhibit has emerged as a case study of the many levels at which censorship can operate

---

* In 2003, the stripped-down *Enola Gay* exhibition was transferred for permanent display to an annex of the National Air and Space Museum near Dulles International Airport. For a diversified collection of critical essays about the *Enola Gay* controversy, see Edward T. Linenthal and Tom Englehardt, eds., *History Wars: The* Enola Gay *and Other Battles for the American Past* (New York: Metropolitan Books, 1996). I contributed an essay titled "Three Narratives of Our Humanity" to this volume.

in an ostensibly democratic society—ranging from overt political repression (epitomized by Congressional pressure to change the Smithsonian exhibit and threats to cut the institution's appropriations) to subtle forms of self-censorship.

Confounded by a vitriolic campaign against "revisionist" interpretations of a "good war" by conservative forces both inside and outside government, the nation's premier institution of public history did more than just jettison its plans for a serious retrospective look at the use and consequences of the atomic bomb. The Smithsonian also indefinitely postponed plans for an exhibition on an even more controversial moment in recent American history: the Vietnam War. In addition, it announced that the current exhibition on "Science in American Life" (at its National Museum of American History) would be revised, in yet unspecified ways, to modify critical mention of negative by-products and consequences of twentieth-century science. In the latter instance, the Smithsonian is responding to criticism by professional scientific societies.

Not content with these victories, the Smithsonian's critics have demanded that heads roll. Curators have been placed under intense political scrutiny. Congress has held hostile hearings on the planning for the original *Enola Gay* exhibit. The director of the National Air and Space Museum recently resigned under pressure, and it is an open secret that morale among members of the Smithsonian's professional staff has been shattered. In this new McCarthyism, the catchall indictment is no longer "Communism" but rather "political correctness" or even just plain "revisionism." Few people in the media or among the general public seem to find the enforcement of a purely celebratory national history alarming.

We praise other countries, especially those in the former Communist camp, for engaging in critical reappraisal of the past. We castigate the Japanese when they sanitize the war years and succumb to "historical amnesia." Yet, at the same time, we skewer our own public historians for deviating from Fourth of July historiography. We are so besieged by polemics and sound bites that almost no one has time to dwell on the irony of demanding a pristine, heroic official version of a war that presumably was fought to protect principled contention and the free play of ideas.

It is in this milieu that the chill of self-censorship has appeared. My "disinvitations" do not appear to be isolated events. After the Smithsonian was brought to its knees, a fellow historian similarly was disinvited by the newsletter of a major archive from contributing a critical essay on President Harry S. Truman's decision to use the bomb. A television program to mark the anniversary of the devastating Tokyo air raids of March 9 and 10, 1945—in which the United States inaugurated the policy of targeting Japanese civilians—was canceled by the network.

A scholarly symposium on the use of the atomic bomb, scheduled to be held at one of the service academies, was abruptly moved, at the last moment, to the campus of a private college (and the military officers who participated appeared in civilian dress). Officials at an archive devoted to World War II reportedly considered addressing the topic of the postwar Allied war-crimes trials of our German and Japanese adversaries at the archive's annual conference in 1996, but quickly rejected the idea as "too controversial." Such inquiry presumably would have led to a discussion of the miscarriages of justice that sometimes occurred in the Allied trials of Japanese military men.

In this climate of political pressure and self-censorship, academics should attempt, at the very least, to do four things. First, we must convey to the public how we go about historical scholarship. Second, we must make more broadly known what we have learned or concluded from our specialized studies. Third, we must try to define what "celebrating" the American experience ideally should mean. Finally, in light of the Smithsonian's sad capitulation to the purveyors of an official historical orthodoxy, academics—social scientists and humanists in particular—must give serious attention to the appropriate mission of "public history."

* * *

What, in brief, do these tasks entail?

As the Smithsonian controversy and the larger "culture wars" have revealed, "revisionism" has become a mark of political incorrectness, according to conservatives. There have been miserable excesses on all sides of this debate, and, in our present age of invective and unreason, it is a daunting task to try to convey to the public the idea that critical inquiry and responsible revision remain the lifeblood of every serious intellectual enterprise.

Serious historians, like serious intellectuals generally, draw on new perspectives and data to reconsider and rethink received wisdom. The challenge of this task is difficult to convey to people who believe in fixed, inviolable historical truths. It is doubly difficult where patriotic gore and a "good war" are concerned.

The same people who speak of inviolable truths, however, also generally are receptive to language that evokes "the perspective of time" or the "judgment of history." Popular wisdom thus holds open a door through which historians can enter to try to explain—judiciously and painstakingly—how the passage of time, the discovery of new information, the posing of new questions all may lead to revised understanding and reconstruction of past events. (The Smithsonian's own spokesmen, caught in the whirlwind, never vigorously tried publicly to explain and defend the serious historical considerations on which their original plans rested.)

In the case of the fiftieth anniversary of the end of World War II, what we scholars *know* in our specialized areas of expertise is certainly conspicuously different from what viewers will encounter at the stripped-down display at the Air and Space Museum, which consists of little more than a section of the fuselage of the *Enola Gay*, the B-29 Superfortress that dropped the atomic bomb on Hiroshima, and the taped reminiscences of the bomber's crew. We now know, for example, that many imperatives, in addition to saving American lives, propelled the decision to drop the bombs on Hiroshima and Nagasaki in August 1945. We also know that the American military had not planned to invade Japan until several months after the bombs were dropped; that Japan was on the verge of collapse before the atomic bomb was used; and that alternatives to the bomb were considered and rejected.

We know, too, that the dead in Hiroshima and Nagasaki included not only Japanese but also many thousands of Koreans, who had been conscripted for hard labor by their Japanese overlords; more than 1,000 Nisei, who were trapped in Japan after Pearl Harbor; a small number of white American prisoners of war, most of them beaten to death by Japanese survivors of the bombing of Hiroshima; and smaller numbers of Chinese, Southeast Asians, and Europeans. We now also know that the total number of people killed in Hiroshima and Nagasaki, most of them civilians, was considerably greater than initial estimates—more than 300,000 by current official Japanese calculations (and thus more than triple the total number of U.S. fighting men killed in the entire course of the Pacific War).*

Through film, photographs, and personal accounts, we gradually have become better able to visualize the peculiar grotesqueries of death from nuclear radiation. Much of the documentary record of the human consequences of the bombing was initially censored by U.S. authorities. (Atomic-bomb survivors in occupied Japan were not allowed to publish accounts of their experience until late 1948, for example, and film footage from Hiroshima and Nagasaki remained classified for two decades.)

Moreover, years passed before many survivors found it psychologically possible to articulate their traumatic experiences in words or drawings—some of which have become accessible to Americans only in recent decades. The horror of the early deaths from radiation poisoning was initially concealed from the world. It is still little known outside Japan. Similarly, the long-term medical con-

---

* See the footnote on page 146 in chapter 5 for the official source for this figure. The most plausible atomic-bombs fatality estimate now appears to be more than 200,000—that is, double the number of U.S. fatalities in the Pacific War.

sequences of exposure to radiation from the bombs remain known mainly to specialists. These legacies range from mental retardation among infants in utero at the time to a higher-than-normal incidence of various cancers, especially leukemia, among survivors.

"Lack of context" is an argument hitherto monopolized by the Smithsonian's critics, who charged that the institution's original plans for its exhibition failed to convey adequately the nature of the war before 1945 and the aggressive, atrocious, fanatical behavior of the Japanese military machine. Such criticism was reasonable. Instead of leading to a fuller exhibition, however, it has resulted in a "commemorative" display, in which basic knowledge about the use and consequences of the bomb itself has been completely excised. Thus it has become the responsibility of academics and ordinary citizens to publicly convey the knowledge, perspectives, and controversies deemed unpatriotic and improper in official circles.

And indeed, in recent months, many academics and universities have taken up the challenge, through lectures and symposia on the war and the bombs. In the most politically visible and courageous example of such assumption of responsibility, American University in Washington, D.C., is sponsoring an exhibition on the human consequences of a nuclear strike, based in major part on materials from Hiroshima that were to be included in the Smithsonian's exhibition.

Such activities are crucial to countering the chill of self-censorship. At the same time, they also should be understood as an attempt to promote a true celebration of what America ideally stands for—namely, tolerance of dissenting voices and the capacity to confront and transcend past evils. This may be a dream, but it is a dream worth struggling for. The alternative is to accept the current public definition of celebration: the parroting of nationalistic myths and honking of patriotic horns.

If this more radical notion of celebration is to be honored, however, we must turn serious attention to what we mean by "public history." The argument that has temporarily won the day is clear and explicit: tax-supported institutions such as the Smithsonian (or the National Endowment for the Humanities or the National Endowment for the Arts) have no business endorsing criticism of our national experience. Their mission is to praise, exalt, beautify, and glorify all that America has been and has done.

This is precisely what we criticize and ridicule when espoused by other nations and other cultures, and we would be better off practicing what we preach. America has much to be proud of and a great deal to think critically about. Sometimes, as in the case of the last "good war" and the almost nonchalant incineration of hundreds of thousands of enemy civilians that accompanied it, it seems excruciatingly difficult to separate our truly heroic from our horrendous deeds. Yet we must face these terrible ambiguities squarely—and do so at our public, as well as our private, institutions—or else stop pretending to be an honest and open society.

That is the kind of "public history" worth struggling for in a genuine democracy.

8

PEACE AND DEMOCRACY IN TWO SYSTEMS: EXTERNAL POLICY AND INTERNAL CONFLICT

One of my more folksy memories of navigating the transition from student to teacher involves attending the annual conference of the American Historical Association as a dissertation-writing graduate student in 1970, for the sole purpose of interviewing for an entry-level college or university position. Early the first morning I went to breakfast at the restaurant in the conference hotel, sat at the counter, and had a genial gentleman sit next to me and inquire where my research interests lay. When I told him they extended to the postwar occupation of Japan, he declared "that's too recent to be history," stood up, and reseated himself several stools away. This was a less than upbeat way to begin job-hunting, but an instructive lesson in collegiality and open-mindedness within my chosen profession.

I have no idea who this middle-aged professor was; in all likelihood, he himself is now history. In any case, he was wrong in arguing that it was too soon to take on the postwar period as an historian. Rich material for venturing an early draft of recent events was everywhere. Memoirs, interviews, and archived oral histories were piling up in great abundance, in both English and Japanese; government documents were being declassified; and even in these pre-Internet years, all manner of illuminating popular-culture resources like newspapers, magazines, yearbooks, and official company and bureaucracy histories were accessible to anyone willing to put in a little legwork in libraries and used bookstores. (In postwar Japan, getting "current" and recent history into print became an almost compulsive practice at every level, public and private—often simultaneously with solemn published disquisitions about how Japanese culture was fundamentally taciturn and nondiscursive.)

When E.H. Norman published his pioneer study of politics and economics in the Meiji period in 1940, he was writing at a remove of only twenty-eight years from the end of the Meiji era in 1912. By 1989, when Emperor Hirohito died and thus brought to an end the long Shōwa era that began with his ascension to the throne in 1926, forty-four years separated us from Japan's surrender in 1945; and by then, no one moved several stools away when the phrase "postwar Japan as history" came up. That is the title of the edited book in which the long essay that follows appears. The book was published in 1993, and my "two systems" contribution was an attempt to delineate concretely a dynamism we often talk about abstractly: the dialectical relationship between domestic and international structures, policies, and conflicts. Some of the contributors to this volume felt my paradigm was overly simplistic. They were right: nothing in Japan, or anywhere else, is so tidy.

Still, the catchphrases on which I rest my analysis here—"peace and democracy" on the one hand, and on the other hand the domestic "1955 system" and international "San Francisco system"—were central to Japanese scholarly and popular discourse at that date. Historians, political scientists, and journalists in Japan still routinely use this language, for despite many changes these ideals and configurations of power are still with us. However oversimple, this concise way of highlighting the integration of domestic and international structures gives us a handle by which to open the way to more nuanced inquiry.

There are, of course, things obviously missing from this early-1990s treatment of Japan's postwar political history. We now know a little more about the U.S. role in abetting the consolidation of conservative hegemony in Japanese politics, for example, including C.I.A. subsidies to Prime Minister Kishi Nobusuke in the late 1950s. Over the years, more-

*over, there have been various leaks of documents involving secret agree-
ments or understandings between Tokyo and Washington—mitsuyaku,
in Japanese parlance—mostly revealing the extent to which the Liberal
Democratic Party's conservative governments gave assurance that, whatever they might be saying for public consumption, they supported U.S.
policy on controversial key issues such as Okinawa and the development
and deployment of nuclear weapons.*

*Most conspicuously absent from this analysis is any anticipation that
Japan would spend the 1990s and opening decade and more of the twenty-
first century in the financial doldrums, while China took its place as the
mesmerizing great emerging power in Asia. That is another story; and if
there is any virtue in it not being addressed here, it lies in focusing attention on the often-forgotten turbulence and tensions that characterized the
transition from a shattered land in 1945 to erstwhile superpower under
the American aegis in little more than a generation.*

* * *

Ever since Japan's seclusion was ruptured by the Western nations
in 1853, domestic and international politics have been inter-
woven for the Japanese. Slogans used to mobilize succeeding generations convey this interconnection. Thus, the forces that eventually
overthrew the feudal regime in 1868 rallied around the cry "Revere
the Emperor and Expel the Barbarians." The Meiji government
(1868–1912) socialized citizens for Westernization, industrialization, and empire building under the slogan "Rich Country, Strong
Military." Militant expansionists of the 1930s and early 1940s,
equally concerned with renovation at home and autarky abroad,
paired creation of a domestic "New Structure" with establishment
of a "New Order" overseas. They saw the solution to domestic ills
in the creation of a broader imperium in Asia, which they glossed
with the rhetoric of "Coexistence and Coprosperity."

Although Japan ostensibly pursued a low posture diplomati-
cally after World War II, the intimate relationship between international and domestic politics remained central. Again, catchphrases

capture this. Immediately after the war, exhausted Japanese were rallied—and frequently inspired—by an idealistic agenda of "Demilitarization and Democratization." From the outset these ideals were recognized to be inseparable: destruction of the militarized state was essential to democratize Japan, and only the creation of a genuinely democratic nation could prevent the danger of future Japanese militarism. Once formal demilitarization had been accomplished, the enduring goal became to create and maintain "Peace and Democracy." Even exhortations such as the popular postsurrender slogan "Construction of a Nation of Culture" (*Bunka Kokka no Kensetsu*) were understood to be synonymous with the paired ideals of peace and democracy. For example, when Prime Minister Katayama Tetsu addressed the first Diet session held under the new postwar constitution in 1947, he concluded with an appeal to advance toward "the construction of a democratic nation of peace, a nation of culture" (*minshuteki na heiwa kokka, bunka kokka no kensetsu*).[1]

These key terms—*democracy*, *peace*, and *culture*—were subject to reinterpretation in the years that followed, and *culture*, by and large, was uncoupled from the other two. Throughout the postwar period, however, a large portion of political policy and contention continued to be contained, like a crackling electric current, within the polemical poles of *peace* and *democracy*. These are not rhetorical ideals peculiar to Japan, but they assumed a particular vitality there. *Peace* became the magnetic pole for both legitimization and criticism of external policy; *democracy* served the same function for highly contested domestic issues. And postwar controversies over military and international policy almost invariably became entangled with internal struggles concerning power, participation, national priorities, and competing visions of fairness, well-being, and social justice.

Where the actual structures of postwar power are concerned, two additional and uniquely Japanese phrases command attention. One is the "San Francisco System," which refers to the international posture Japan assumed formally when it signed a peace treaty with forty-eight nations in San Francisco in September 1951 and simultaneously aligned itself with the Cold War policy of the United States through the bilateral Treaty of Mutual Cooperation and Security. To the end of the Shōwa period, which effectively symbolized the end of the "postwar" era for Japan, the country continued to operate within the strategic parameters of the San Francisco System, although its global role and influence changed conspicuously after it emerged as an economic power in the 1970s. The second phrase, coined to designate the nature of domestic power relations, is the "1955 System." Here the reference is to a concatenation of political and socioeconomic developments in 1955, including the establishment of the Liberal Democratic Party (LDP) which governed Japan uninterruptedly over the ensuing decades. More generally, "1955 System" signifies a domestic political structure characterized by an internally competitive but nonetheless hegemonic conservative establishment and a marginalized but sometimes influential liberal and Marxist opposition.

Like all fashionable political phrases, "San Francisco System" and "1955 System" obscure as much as they reveal. Both Japan's incorporation into U.S. cold-war policy and the triumph of the conservative elites were evident from the late 1940s, when U.S. policy toward occupied Japan underwent a so-called reverse course, in which emphasis was shifted from demilitarization and democratization to economic reconstruction, rearmament, and integration into the U.S. anti-Communist containment policy. The real genesis of both systems is thus much earlier than a literal reading of the popular labels would suggest. Moreover, the domestic as well as international milieu in which the Japanese operated changed constantly during the postwar period, and dramatically so after the early 1970s. From this perspective, it is argued, both "San Francisco System" and "1955 System" have an anachronistic ring when applied to the years after the mid-1970s or so. And, indeed, they do.[2]

Still, the two phrases remain highly suggestive for anyone who wishes to re-create postwar Japan as history. They reflect a worldview, looking both outward and inward, that was defined and described (and criticized) by the Japanese themselves. And, like all popular phrases that survive for more than a passing moment, they capture—certainly for Japanese analysts—a wealth of complicated and even contradictory associations. They are code words for the peculiar capitalist context, overseas and at home, in which postwar Japan developed. They are closely associated with the impressive international and domestic prosperity Japan attained between the 1950s and 1980s. At the same time, they evoke the internal schism and tension and even violence that accompanied Japan's attainment of wealth and power. For Japanese, "San Francisco System" and "1955 System" vividly symbolize the intense political conflicts over issues of peace and democracy that characterized Japan's emergence as a rich consumer society and powerful capitalist state.

Essentially, these conflicts pitted liberal and left-wing critics against the dominant conservative elites. At the peak of their influence in the 1950s and 1960s these critics constituted an effective minority, capable of capturing popular imagination and influencing the national agenda. By the mid-1970s, though, the left appeared spent as an intellectually compelling political force. Partly, the opposition simply had lost some of its most fundamental arguments: prosperity at home undermined the critique of capitalism, and economic superpower status abroad discredited the argument of subordination to the U.S. economy. Partly again, however, the antiestablishment critics had won some of their arguments or, more commonly, had seen their positions on social and geopolitical issues effectively co-opted by the conservatives. Despite polemics of the most vitriolic sort, postwar Japan never was split into completely unbridgeable ideological camps. The pro-American conservatives nursed many resentments against the United States, for example, while the liberal and leftist "internationalists" were susceptible to nationalist appeals. Schism in both camps, as well as accommodation between the camps, were thus persistent subtexts in the debates over peace and democracy. This ideological softness, as it were, helps explain the transition to the less polemical decades of the 1970s and 1980s. As the debates over peace and democracy receded, their place was taken by a rising tide of neo-nationalist thinking that stressed Japanese uniqueness and superiority. Although this late-Shōwa cult of exceptionalism had Japanese critics, it tapped a line of thought with strong left-wing as well as conservative roots.

Contention over global and domestic policies did not disappear in the last decades of Shōwa. Rather, it took different forms. Although Japan's emergence as an economic superpower resulted in undreamed-of influence, it also created unanticipated tensions—not only with the United States and the European community but also within Japan. At the elite level Japan's new capitalism spawned new contenders for power and influence within the conservative establishment. And at the popular level the almost catatonic fixation of the ruling groups on industrial productivity and economic nationalism stimulated citizens' protest movements that eschewed doctrinaire ideologies and focused on specific issues such as quality of life, environmental protection, community services, and the like. Less sweeping in vision than the earlier "peace and democracy" struggles, such extraparliamentary activities represented a new kind of grassroots democracy.

In these various ways, it can be said that Japan entered a new stage in the early 1970s. Yet the old military and economic imbrication with the United States symbolized by the San Francisco System remained at the heart of Japan's external policy. The conservative hegemony—the bedrock of the 1955 System—continued to rule Japan, juggling more balls than in the past, bickering and backbiting within its own ranks, but in no real danger of being removed from center stage. And the great issues of peace and democracy, however muted by prosperity and national pride, remained just beneath the surface. Was the new superstate really democratic, really a constructive force for peace? In the 1970s and 1980s, as the old debates faded from the scene, these questions were asked from new perspectives by the world at large.

These broad areas of concern—the San Francisco System,

the 1955 System, the conflicts within them and linkages between them, and the uncertain world that Japan stumbled into as an economic, financial, and technological superpower beginning in the 1970s—are addressed in the pages that follow.

THE SAN FRANCISCO SYSTEM

The intersection of "peace" and "democracy" in postwar Japan begins with the Allied occupation of 1945–52 and its evolution into the San Francisco System. Under the U.S.-dominated occupation, defeated Japan was initially demilitarized. The Imperial Army and Navy ministries were abolished. Former military officers were purged from public life, ostensibly "for all time." Under the famous Article 9 of the 1947 constitution, Japan pledged to "forever renounce war as a sovereign right of the nation and the threat or use of force as a means of settling international disputes." What this meant, it was explained at the time, was exactly what it seemed to mean. As Prime Minister Yoshida Shigeru put it, taking a colorful metaphor from the days of the samurai, under the new peace constitution the Japanese were prohibited from picking up even two swords in the name of self-defense.[3]

At this early stage Yoshida and his colleagues anticipated that for the foreseeable future Japan would fare best as an unarmed nation dedicated to restoring peaceful relations with the rest of the world, including China and the Soviet Union. Its security, the earliest scenarios went, might be guaranteed by the United Nations, or by a Great Power agreement, or if necessary by a bilateral agreement with the United States under which the main islands of Japan were protected by U.S. forces stationed elsewhere (possibly including Okinawa.)[4] This was not to be. The peace treaty signed in San Francisco in 1951 was in fact generous and nonpunitive, including no provisions for future international oversight of Japan. Under the Security Treaty with the United States, however, Japan agreed to the retention of U.S. military bases throughout the country after restoration of sovereignty and was understood to have committed itself to rearmament. The United States retained de facto control of the Ryukyu Islands, including Okinawa, which by then had become its major nuclear base in Asia, while "residual sovereignty" was acknowledged to lie with Japan.

As anticipated, because of the military alignment with the United States, which Japan agreed to in order to regain its sovereignty, the Soviet Union refused to sign the peace treaty. Neither the People's Republic of China nor the Kuomintang regime on Taiwan were invited to the San Francisco conference, but subsequently, contrary to its hopes and expectations, the Yoshida government was placed under severe U.S. pressure to establish relations with the Kuomintang and join in the containment of China. In the terms of those times the peace settlement at San Francisco was thus a "separate peace." In the years that followed the formal restoration of sovereignty to Japan in April 1952, these Cold War arrangements remained a central focus of opposition by domestic critics of the government and a source of friction within the U.S.-Japan partnership itself.[5]

At the time the Security Treaty was negotiated and came into effect, U.S. projections for a future Japanese military focused on ground forces and were exceedingly ambitious. The Japanese were told they should create an army of 325,000 to 350,000 men by 1954—a figure larger than the Imperial Army on the eve of the Manchurian Incident in 1931, and larger than ever actually was reached in the postwar period. It was assumed from the outset in U.S. circles that Japanese remilitarization should and would entail constitutional revision. This assumption emerged in secret U.S. projections in the late 1940s, before the Americans actually began rearming Japan, and was first publicly emphasized by Vice President Richard Nixon in November 1953. For many reasons—including not only fear of economic dislocation and social unrest in Japan but also fear that the zealots in Washington would go on to demand that Japan send this projected army to fight in the Korean War—Yoshida resisted these U.S. pressures and established a more modest pattern of incremental Japanese rearmament. Privately, he and his aides agreed with the Americans that constitutional revision would have to accompany any rapid and large-scale military buildup, and they argued that such revision was politically impossible at the time. After all, only five years or so earlier the Japanese had seen a war—and nuclear weapons—brought home to them. This, indeed, was and remained the critical card: because of popular support for the liberal 1947 "peace constitution," constitutional revision remained politically impossible in postwar Japan.[6]

As counterpoint to the permissive agreements on remilitarization reached between the U.S. and Japanese governments in the early 1950s, Article 9 thus survived as an ambiguous but critical element within the San Francisco System. It was reinterpreted cavalierly by the government to permit piecemeal Japanese rearmament, but at the same time it was effectively utilized to restrain the speed and scope of remilitarization. Successive Shōwa-era cabinets repeatedly evoked the constitution to resist U.S. pressure not merely for large troop increases but also for participation in collective security arrangements and overseas missions. As Prime Minister Satō Eisaku stated in 1970, "The provisions of the Constitution make overseas service impossible."[7] Because revision of Article 9 would open the door to conservative revision of other parts of the national charter as well, especially concerning guarantees of individual rights and possibly also the purely "symbolic" status of the emperor, debates over constitutional revision became the most dramatic single example of the intersection of postwar concerns about peace and democracy.

The text of the peace treaty was not made public until it was signed in September 1951, and details of the U.S.-Japan military relationship were worked out between the two governments only in the months that intervened between then and the end of the occupation in April 1952. Nonetheless, the general policy of incorporating Japan into U.S. Cold War policy was clear well before the outbreak of the Korean War in June 1950, and opposition within Japan mobilized accordingly. The political left was factionalized in its analysis of these developments, but many of the basic principles that would underlie criticism of the San Francisco System in the years to follow were introduced by the left-wing parties and liberal and "progressive" (*kakushin*) intellectuals between 1949 and 1951. In December 1949 the Socialist Party adopted "Three Principles of Peace" for Japan: an overall peace settlement with all former enemies, opposition to bilateral military pacts or foreign military bases in Japan, and neutrality in the Cold War. In 1951, after hard wrangling between the right and left wings of the party, the Socialists added, as a fourth peace principle, opposition to Japanese rearmament.

By far the most influential intellectual endorsement of these principles came from the Peace Problems Symposium (Heiwa Mondai Danwakai), a loose grouping of highly respected academics who first collaborated in November 1948 to issue a general statement on war, peace, and social justice signed by fifty-five scholars in the natural and social sciences. In a "Statement on the Peace Problem" released in January 1950 and signed by thirty-five intellectuals, the group elaborated on the three peace principles, warned that a separate peace could contribute to war, and emphasized the importance of avoiding dependency on the United States. The third Peace Problems Symposium statement, drafted largely by Maruyama Masao and Ukai Nobushige and published as usual in the monthly magazine *Sekai*, was issued in December 1950, after the outbreak of the Korean War and open commencement of Japanese rearmament. So great was the response that *Sekai* was said to have doubled its circulation.

The long third statement, signed by thirty-one intellectuals in the Tokyo chapter of the Peace Problems Symposium and twenty-one in the Kyoto chapter, dwelled on the flawed vision of those self-styled "realists" who adhered to a rigidly bipolar worldview and anticipated inevitable conflict between "liberal democracy" and "Communism." The United States and Soviet Union both came under criticism, while the Cold War premise of the emerging U.S.-Japan military relationship—the argument that the Soviet Union was committed to fostering world Communism through military means—was rejected. Japan, it was argued, could best contribute to peaceful coexistence by adopting a strict course of unarmed non-alignment under the United Nations. The final section of the statement was devoted explicitly to "the relationship between peace and the domestic structure" and argued that Japan's contribution to a world without war, as well as its best opportunity to attain economic independence, could be most effectively furthered by promoting social-democratic domestic reforms that were guided by neither Soviet ideology nor American-style cold-war objectives. The language was guarded here, referring in general and quite idealistic terms to fairness in the sharing of wealth and income, creation of a mature level of democracy, and supplementing the principles of a free economy (*jiyū keizai no genri*) with principles of planning (*keikaku genri*).[8]

These statements survived over the years as probably the best-known manifestoes of the Japanese peace movement. Neither then nor later was much attention given to undercurrents within them that seemed to run counter to a truly internationalistic and universalistic outlook. The famous third statement, for example, adopted terms faintly reminiscent of Japan's pan-Asian rhetoric in World War II by praising the neutrality espoused by India's Prime Minister Nehru as representing "the very essence of the Asian people's historic position and mission." At the same time, the statement introduced a subtle appeal to nationalism in arguing that neutrality represented "the only true position of self-reliance and independence for Japan." Most striking of all, however, was the attempt of the Peace Problems Symposium intellectuals to nurture antiwar sentiments in Japan by appealing directly to the suffering experienced by the Japanese in the recent war. "In view of the pitiful experience that our fatherland underwent during the war," the third statement declared, "it is only too clear to us what it can mean to sacrifice peace."[9] From the perspective of Japan's Asian victims, of course, such an appeal would seem shockingly parochial rather than internationalist. In the Japanese milieu, however, it tapped an almost instinctual strain of "victim consciousness" (*higaisha ishiki*) that cut across the political spectrum.

As the precise nature of the San Francisco System unfolded between 1951 and 1954, it became apparent to conservatives as well as the opposition that Japan had paid a considerable price for sovereignty. It now possessed a military of questionable legality and a bilateral security treaty that was unquestionably inequitable. "Preposterously unequal" was the phrase used by Foreign Minister Fujiyama Aiichi in 1958, and when treaty revision came on the agenda in 1960, U.S. officials agreed that the 1951 Security Treaty with Japan was the most inequitable bilateral agreement the United States had entered into after the war. It also became painfully clear to the Japanese that the price of peace was a divided country—indeed, a doubly divided country in the sense of both territorial and spiritual division. The detachment of Okinawa from the rest of Japan turned Okinawan society and economy into a grotesque appendage to the U.S. nuclear strategy in Asia. Edwin Reischauer, ambassador to Japan in the early 1960s, later characterized Okinawa as "the only 'semi-colonial' territory created in Asia since the war," and the resentments generated by this territorial division persisted until the reversion of Okinawa to Japan in 1972, and even after. The spiritual division of the country was manifested in the political and ideological polarization caused in considerable part by the San Francisco System itself. As Yoshida put it, with another graphic military metaphor, this time from the Allied division of Korea at the end of World War II, the occupation and its Cold War settlement drew a "thirty-eighth parallel" through the very heart of the Japanese people.[10] This was hardly a trauma or tragedy comparable to the postwar divisions of Korea, China, Germany, or Vietnam. It suggests, nonetheless, the emotional and politically charged climate of the years that followed Japan's accommodation to American Cold War policy.

Most fundamentally, the San Francisco System subordinated Japan to the United States in psychological as well as structural ways and ate at Japanese pride, year after year, like a slow-working acid. In official U.S. circles it was acknowledged frankly, if confidentially, that the military relationship with Japan was double-edged: it integrated Japan into the anti-Communist camp and simultaneously created a permanent structure of U.S. control over Japan. Even passionately anti-Soviet politicians like Yoshida did not regard the USSR as a direct threat to Japan and reluctantly accepted the continued presence of U.S. troops and bases as an unavoidable price for obtaining sovereignty along with assurances of U.S. protection. The primary mission of U.S. forces and bases in Japan including Okinawa was never to defend Japan directly but rather to project U.S. power in Asia and to "support our commitments elsewhere," as one high U.S. official later testified.[11] To many observers the argument that this U.S. presence also acted as a deterrent to external threats to Japan was less persuasive than its counterargument: that the external threat was negligible without the bases, but considerable with them. If war occurred between the United States and the Soviet Union, Japan inevitably would be drawn into it. At the same time, the U.S. military presence throughout the Japanese islands established an on-site deterrent against hostile remilitarization by Japan itself. Subordination of Japanese military planning to U.S. grand strategy was another and more subtle way of ensuring long-term U.S. control over Japan. So also was the technological integration of the U.S. and Japanese military forces—a process of institutionalized dependency that actually deepened after the mid-1950s, when priorities shifted from ground forces to the creation of a technologically sophisticated Japanese navy and air force.

Early critics of the San Francisco System characterized Japan's place within it as one of "subordinate independence" (*jūzokuteki dokuritsu*), including economic as well as diplomatic and military dependency. Although the phrase arose on the political left, it was echoed throughout Japanese society—and at top levels in Washington and Tokyo as well. When U.S. planners in the Army, Navy, and State departments first turned serious attention to incorporating Japan into Cold War strategy in 1947, for example, they rejected not merely the premise that Japan could be neutral but also that it could ever regain an "independent identity." In this fiercely bipolar worldview, Japan realistically could be expected to "function only as an American or Soviet satellite." In November 1951, two months after the peace conference, Joseph Dodge, the key American adviser on economic policy toward Japan, bluntly told representatives of the Ministry of International Trade and Industry (MITI) that "Japan can be independent politically but dependent economically." When Japan was forced to participate in the economic containment of China and seek alternative markets elsewhere, especially in Southeast Asia, fear that Japan was doomed to an exceedingly precarious economic future was palpable throughout the country. At this stage almost no one anticipated that Japan had a serious future in the advanced markets of the West. Thus, as we learn from "Top Secret" records of the U.S. National Security Council, in September 1954 Secretary of State John Foster Dulles "told Yoshida frankly that Japan should not expect to find a big U.S. market because the Japanese don't make the things we want. Japan must find markets elsewhere for the goods they export."[12]

Such comments may be amusing in retrospect, but they remind us that Japan's emergence as a global economic power came late and abruptly and astonished almost everyone concerned. It involved a great deal of skill and hard work, to be sure, but also a large measure of good fortune. In the long run U.S. Cold War policies abetted Japanese economic growth at home and abroad in unanticipated ways. In return for acquiescing in the containment policy, for example, Japan received favored access to U.S. patents and licenses and technical expertise, as well as U.S. patronage in international economic organizations. At the same time, despite American rhetoric about free trade and an open international economic order, these remained ultimate ideals rather than immediate practices. In the early postwar decades U.S. policy actually sanctioned import restrictions by the Western European allies as well as Japan to facilitate their recovery from the war, and these trade barriers were tolerated longer in Japan's case than they were in Europe. Also tolerated, until the early 1970s, was an undervalued yen exchange rate—that is, an overvalued dollar, which benefited Japanese export industries. Japan, more than Europe, also was permitted to retain tight restrictions on foreign exchange and capital investment that had been approved as "temporary" measures during the occupation. The closed Japanese domestic economy, which grew so rapidly in the late 1950s and 1960s and became a source of great friction between Japan and the United States and Europe by the end of the 1960s, reflected these protectionist policies sanctioned by the United States in the naive days when Japan was believed to have no serious future in Western markets—and when, by U.S. demand, Japan also was prohibited from establishing close economic ties with China. Although it is doubtful that the U.S. "nuclear umbrella" ever really protected Japan from a serious external threat, it is incontrovertible that the U.S. economic umbrella was an immense boon to Japanese capitalism.[13]

The Japanese economy also flourished within the San Francisco System in two additional unanticipated ways. Both the Korean War and the Vietnam War brought great profits and market breakthroughs to Japan. U.S. offshore procurements stimulated by the Korean War and thereafter routinized as "new special procurements" (*shin tokuju*) held Japan's balance of payments in line through the critical years of the 1950s. The Vietnam War boom, in turn, brought an estimated $1 billion a year to Japanese firms between 1966 and 1971—the period now identified as marking the opening stage of economic "maturity" for Japan and the beginning of the end of America's role as hegemon of the global capitalist system.[14]

At the same time, the constraints on Japanese remilitarization that stemmed from the early period of demilitarization and democratization and remained embodied in the constitution did more than merely buttress a general policy of go-slow rearmament. They also thwarted the emergence of a powerful defense lobby comparable to that in the United States. In the absence of a bona fide ministry of defense, the Ministry of Finance remained the major actor in shaping the postwar military budget. There was no Japanese counterpart to the Pentagon. And despite a handful of large military contractors such as Mitsubishi Heavy Industries, there emerged no civilian defense sector remotely comparable to the military-industrial complex in the United States. Thus, contrary to the situation in America, the best scientists and engineers in postwar Japan turned their talents to the production of commodities for the civilian marketplace, rather than weapons of war. All this was critical to the economic takeoff Japan experienced beginning in the late 1950s and the country's extraordinary competitiveness in ensuing decades. And all this also must be reckoned an integral part of the San Francisco System.

THE 1955 SYSTEM

Like the San Francisco System, the conservative hegemony later known as the 1955 System had its genesis in the occupation-period reverse course, when U.S. policymakers began to jettison many of their more radical democratic ideals and reforms. A general strike planned for February 1, 1947, was banned by General Douglas MacArthur. Prolabor legislation was watered down beginning in 1948. The immense power of the bureaucracy—augmented by a decade and a half of mobilization for "total war"—was never curtailed by the occupation reformers (beyond abolition of the prewar Home Ministry), and the financial structure remained largely untouched despite initial proposals to democratize it. Fairly ambitious plans to promote economic democratization through industrial deconcentration were abandoned by 1949. Individuals purged from public life "for all time" because of their wartime activities or affiliations began to be depurged in 1950, and by the end of the occupation only a few hundred persons remained under the original purge designation. At the same time, between late 1949 and the end of 1950 U.S. authorities and the Japanese government collaborated in a "Red purge" in the public sector, and then the private sector, that eventually led to the firing of some twenty-two thousand individuals, mostly left-wing union activists. In July 1950, in the midst of this conspicuous turn to the right, the rearmament of Japan began.[15]

The San Francisco settlement thus took place in a setting of domestic turmoil, when both of the early ideals of "demilitarization" and "democratization" were under attack by the conservative elites and their new American partners. To critics, rearmament and the "Red purges," military bases and the gutting of the labor laws, the separate peace and resurrection of the old economic and political elites—all were part of a single reverse course that was simultaneously international and domestic in its ramifications. Japanese partisanship in the Cold War required the resurrection of the civilian old guard, and the old guard required the Cold War to enlist U.S. support against domestic opponents.

With the exception of the brief Katayama interlude (May 1947 to March 1948), conservative leaders headed every Japanese cabinet of the postwar period, even before the reverse course was initiated.* However, it was not until the third Yoshida cabinet, formed in January 1949, that the conservative leadership enjoyed a firm majority in the Diet. For Yoshida personally this proved to be an ephemeral peak of power and stability. The general elections of October 1952 saw the return to national politics of hundreds of formerly purged politicians, and by 1954 conservative ranks were severely factionalized. When Yoshida and his Liberal Party supporters were unceremoniously ousted from power in December 1954, it was not anti-conservatives who did them in but rather a rival conservative coalition, the Democratic Party, headed by

---

* After this essay was written, the Liberal Democratic Party briefly relinquished the premiership between August 1993 and January 1996 and then, fifteen years later in 2009, suffered an electoral defeat that paved the way for cabinets under the centrist Democratic Party of Japan that was founded in 1998.

Hatoyama Ichirō. Hatoyama, who succeeded Yoshida as prime minister, was a former purgee with a record of support not only for Japanese aggression in the recent war but also for the suppression of dissent in the 1920s and 1930s. Also in the anti-Yoshida camp at this time was another future prime minister, Kishi Nobusuke, a brilliant technocrat who had been a leading economic planner in the puppet state of Manchukuo in the 1930s, a vice minister of munitions under Prime Minister Tōjō Hideki in 1943–44, and an inmate of Sugamo Prison from late 1945 to 1948, accused of "Class A" war crimes but never brought to trial. The conservatives were unquestionably in the saddle, but so great was their internal fighting that they seemed capable of throwing each other out of it.

This turmoil set the stage for consolidation of the conservative parties a year later. In November 1955 Hatoyama's Democrats and Yoshida's Liberals merged to form the Liberal Democratic Party—which, like its predecessors, was neither liberal nor democratic and thus woefully misnamed. Over the ensuing decades the LDP retained uninterrupted control of the government, and this remarkable stability naturally became a central axis of the so-called 1955 System. The capacity for long-term planning that became so distinctive a feature of the postwar political economy was made possible in considerable part by this continuity of single-party domination. However, 1955 was a signal year in other ways as well, and it was this larger conjunction of political and economic developments that seemed to constitute the systematization and clarification of power and influence in postwar Japan—just one decade, as it happened, after Japan's surrender. These related developments took place in both the anticonservative and conservative camps.

It was, in fact, the Socialists and left-wing unionists who moved first. In January 1955 Sōhyō—the General Council of Trade Unions, which was closely affiliated with the left-wing Socialists—mobilized some eight hundred thousand workers in the first demonstration of what subsequently was institutionalized as the *shuntō* "spring wage offensive." From this year on, the *shuntō* became

the basic vehicle for organizing enterprise unions in demanding industry-wide "base up" wage increases on a regular—almost
ritualized—basis. That same month the left-wing and right-wing
factions of the Socialist Party, which had formally split in 1951
over whether to support the San Francisco settlement, agreed to
reunite. Reunification was finalized in October, but well before
then, in the general elections of February 1955, the two factions
together won slightly more than one-third of the seats (156 of 453)
in the critical House of Representatives. Significantly, this parliamentary representation gave them sufficient combined strength to
block constitutional revision, which required a two-thirds vote of
approval in the Diet.

The LDP merger in November was in considerable part a
response to this specter of a reunified and purposeful left-wing
opposition. At the same time, it also constituted the open wedding
of big business with Japan's right-of-center politicians. Corporate
Japan (the *zaikai*) not only played a decisive role in promoting the
1955 conservative merger but also mobilized the business community at this time as the major ongoing source of money for the
LDP. The vehicle for assuring tight control of this political funding also was set up in those busy early months of 1955 in the form of
an Economic Reconstruction Council (Keizai Saiken Kondankai)
established in January and supported by all four major big-business
organizations: the Japan Federation of Employers' Associations
(Nikkeiren), Federation of Economic Organizations (Keidanren),
Japan Committee for Economic Development (Keizai Dōyukai),
and Japan Chamber of Commerce (Nisshō). Although some big-
business funds were made available to Socialists, the vast bulk of
contributions funneled through the Economic Reconstruction
Council (96 percent in 1960) went to the LDP. Reorganized as the
Kokumin Kyōkai in 1961, this consortium provided over 90 percent of LDP funding through the 1960s and 1970s.[16] This consolidation and rationalization of the relationship between the *zaikai*
and conservative politicians constituted two legs of the vaunted
"tripod" on which conservative power rested over the ensuing de-

cades. The third leg was the bureaucracy, which drafted most of the legislation introduced in the Diet and also provided a steady exodus of influential former officials into the LDP.

From a broader socioeconomic perspective 1955 also appeared to be, if not a watershed, at least a symbolic point at which lines of future development became clarified. Economically, the Korean War had wound down and as a consequence the previous year had been dismal for Japan, as conveyed in the catchphrase "1954 recession" (*nijūkyūnen fukyō*). Japanese missions to Washington in the waning years of Yoshida's premiership privately expressed deep and genuine pessimism about the future prospects of Japan's "shallow economy." Contrary to these gloomy prognostications, however, 1955 proved to be a turning point for the postwar economy, and the popular phrases of this year captured this turnabout as well: "postwar high" (*sengo saikō*) was one, "best year of the postwar economy" (*sengo keizai sairyō no toshi*) another. As it turned out, in 1955 the gross national product (GNP) surpassed the prewar peak for the first time, marking the symbolic end of postdefeat recovery. Indeed, the official *Economic White Paper* (Keizai Hakusho) published the next year heralded this accomplishment as signaling the end of the postwar period (*mohaya "sengo" de wa nai*). This upturn coincided, moreover, with the establishment of one of the most important of Japan's long-range industrial planning organizations, the Japan Productivity Center (Nihon Seisansei Honbu). Created on the basis of a U.S.-Japan agreement, with initial funding from both governments as well as Japanese business and financial circles, the center drew support from the ranks of labor as well as management and became the major postwar sponsor of technical missions sent abroad to study the most up-to-date methods of increasing industrial production. The formal wherewithal for exporting the products manufactured by these cutting-edge techniques also was obtained in 1955, when Japan was admitted to the General Agreement on Tariffs and Trade (GATT). It was also in 1955 that centralized planning was significantly advanced through creation of the Economic Planning Agency (in July) and the issuance (in December) of a Five-Year Plan for Economic Independence.[17]

By many reckonings the advent of mass consumer culture also dates from essentially this same moment in the mid-1950s. It was in 1955, for example, that MITI announced the inauguration of a "citizen's car project"; heretofore, the vehicle industry had concentrated on producing trucks (especially for U.S. use in the Korean War) and buses and taxis (including many for export to Southeast Asia). With MITI's plan as a springboard the "age of the citizen's car" (*kokumin jidōsha no jidai*) commenced with the appearance of the Datsun Bluebird four years later. The "age of the electrified household" (*katei denka no jidai*) is said to have materialized in 1955, when housewives dreamed of owning the "three divine appliances" (*sanshu no jingi*)—electric washing machines, refrigerators, and television—and magazines spoke of the seven ascending stages of household electrification: (7) electric lights, (6) radio and iron, (5) toaster and electric heater, (4) mixer, fan, and telephone, (3) washing machine, (2) refrigerator, and (1) television and vacuum cleaner. For whatever one may make of the fact, Godzilla made his debut in November 1954 and thus stepped into (or on) the popular consciousness in 1955. It was also at this time that book publishers began to cater more explicitly to mass tastes. Nicely befitting the advent of a new age of mass culture, another popular slogan of 1955 was "the age of neurosis" (*noirōse jidai*), a phrase sparked by several well-publicized suicides in midyear. As a popular weekly put it, claiming one was neurotic had now become an "accessory" (they used the English word) of modern people.[18]

That the consolidation of conservative power coincided with full recovery from the war and the onset of commercialized mass culture may help explain the staying power of the new conservative hegemony. This durability was not immediately apparent, however, and the decade and a half that followed witnessed a series of intense confrontations over basic issues of peace and democracy. The fundamental lines of political cleavage within the 1955 System have been summarized as pitting a conservative camp committed to revising the constitution and protecting the U.S.-Japan Security Treaty against a progressive (*kakushin*) opposition committed to doing just the opposite: defending the constitution and opposing the Security Treaty.[19] This summary is concise and clever, although it oversimplifies positions on both sides. The initial platform of the LDP did call for constitutional revision, and one of the first steps the new party took was to establish a Constitution Investigation Committee (Kempō Chōsakai) to prepare the ground for revision. At the same time, under Hatoyama and his successors the party also undertook to continue undoing "excesses" of the early democratic postsurrender reforms that lay outside the purview of the constitution—such as revision of the electoral system, abolition of elected school boards, imposition of restraints on political activity by teachers, promotion of "moral" and patriotic education, and strengthening of the police.

Concerning remilitarization, Hatoyama was more zealous than his predecessor Yoshida had been in supporting rearmament under the security treaty, but his reasons for doing so were by no means unambiguously pro-American. Rather, Hatoyama and his supporters desired accelerated rearmament of a more "autonomous" sort that in the long run would hasten Japan's escape from the American embrace. Just as the Security Treaty was a double-edged sword from the American perspective—simultaneously enlisting Japan as a Cold War ally and instituting U.S. controls over Japan—so also was advocacy of accelerated rearmament double-edged to the more ardent Japanese nationalists. On the surface, this policy accorded with U.S. demands for rapid Japanese rearmament, and the conservatives were indeed ideologically receptive to aligning with the Americans in their anti-Communist crusade. At the same time, however, nationalists in the Hatoyama and Kishi line also endorsed accelerated remilitarization to reduce military subordination to their Pacific partner as quickly as possible. Here, in any case, their aspirations were frustrated, for popular support could not be marshaled in support of such a policy. The general public proved willing to accept slow rearmament in the mode established by Yoshida, with little concern about the sophistries of constitutional reinterpretation that this program required of the government's legal experts. As Hatoyama learned, however, just as other conservative leaders learned after him, to the very end of the Shōwa period the public was not receptive to either rapid rearmament or frontal attacks on the constitution.

In attacking the conservatives the opposition essentially appropriated the slogan "peace and democracy" as its own, but exactly what this phrase meant was often contested among these critics themselves. As the intellectuals associated with the influential Peace Problems Symposium developed their "peace thesis" (*heiwaron*) in the late 1940s and early 1950s, it was argued that mobilization for peace must proceed through three levels: from the "human" (*ningen*) level, through the "system" (*seido*), and only on this basis to engagement in broad "international" (*kokusai*) peace issues. In the Japanese context this emphasis meant immersion in the "human" suffering of World War II (and, in actual practice, an outpouring of writings focusing on *Japanese* suffering in the battlefields abroad and under the air raids and atomic bombs at home). The Japanese "system" of overriding importance was to be found in the interlocking basic values enshrined in the new constitution, namely, people's rights, democracy, and pacifism. Finally, rooted in appreciation of these human and systemic values, the Japanese peace movement could move on to pursue basic goals conducive to the creation and maintenance of international peace. By the time the 1955 System was created, these goals usually were expressed as unarmed neutrality, backed by guarantees of support from the United Nations. In addition, inspired by two related events in 1954—the Bikini Incident, in which Japanese fishermen suffered radiation poisoning from the fallout of a U.S. hydrogen bomb test in the Pacific, and a spectacular grassroots petition drive against nuclear testing that was initiated by Japanese housewives and collected an astonishing 30 million signatures—by 1955 the Japanese peace movement also had come to focus especially keenly on the global abolition of nuclear weapons.[20]

Maintaining the constitution was of course the bridge that linked defense of peace and pacifist ideals to defense of democracy, but the latter cause extended beyond constitutional issues per se. Phrased softly, the opposition also was committed to protecting the livelihood (*seikatsu yōgo*) of the working class, which undeniably was being squeezed in the concerted quest for rapid industrial growth. In more doctrinaire terms, the overtly Marxist opposition wished to destroy monopoly capitalism and bring about a socialist revolution in Japan. The latter agenda predictably was endorsed by only a portion of the anticonservative opposition; and, predictably again, it caused the left to splinter in self-destructive ways that did not happen on the right, where factionalism was less ideological and more personally oriented. Thus, while the 1955 System began with a Socialist merger and the anticipation, by some, that in time a genuinely two-party system might evolve in Japan, in actuality the left failed to hold together or grow. As early as 1958 the political scientist Oka Yoshitake already had characterized the new political structure as a "one and one-half party system." Two years later a portion of the Socialist Party permanently hived off to form the less doctrinaire Democratic Socialist Party. By the end of the 1960s, after the quasi-religious Clean Government Party (Kōmeitō) also had emerged on the scene, it was common to speak of the political system as consisting of "one strong, four weak" (*ikkyō shijaku*) political parties.[21]

Before the opposition congealed as a permanent minority, however, it succeeded in mobilizing popular support in a series of massive protest movements that—like the earlier struggle against the occupation-period reverse course—dramatized the relationship between international and domestic politics. The first and most spectacular of these protests wedded opposition to revision and renewal of the Security Treaty (scheduled for 1960) to Kishi's assumption of the premiership in 1957. That Kishi, Tōjō's former vice minister of munitions, could assume the highest office in the country just twelve years after the war ended—and become, simultaneously, the symbol in Japan of the U.S.-Japan military relationship—graphically exemplified how far, and fast, Japan had moved away from the early ideals of demilitarization and democratization. In the end, the opposition drew millions of demonstrators into the streets and both lost and won its protest: the Security Treaty was retained and revised, but Kishi was forced to resign. In the process, a variety of concerned citizens were baptized in the theory and practice of extraparliamentary democratic expression.

This tumultuous campaign against the Cold War treaty and old-war politician overlapped, moreover, with the last great labor strike in modern Japanese history, which pitted workers at the Miike coal mine against an archetypical old-guard employer, the Mitsui Mining Company. The Miike struggle began in the spring of 1959 and in January 1960 turned into a lockout and strike that lasted 282 days and eventually involved hundreds of thousands of people. At Miike, the radical wing of organized labor confronted a broad united front of big business and the government, which correctly perceived the struggle as a decisive test for the future of state-led industrial "rationalization." And at Miike, labor lost. The defeat of the miners in late 1960 smoothed the path for the heralded "income doubling" policy of the new Ikeda Hayato cabinet, which assumed power when Kishi was forced to resign in July.

The interplay of domestic and international politics resurfaced dramatically in the late 1960s, when massive protests against Japan's complicity in the Vietnam War intersected with a wide range of domestic grievances. Indeed, in this struggle the linkage of peace and democracy was recast in stunningly new ways. Under the influence of the New Left the anti–Vietnam War movement introduced a more radical anti-imperialist critique to the discourse on peace and democracy. Essentially, the late-1960s radicals argued that under the Cold War alliance Japan not only profited materially from the misery of other Asians but also contributed to the support of corrupt and authoritarian regimes outside Japan. Peace and prosperity for Japan, in short, were being purchased at the cost of war and the repression of democracy elsewhere. Vietnam and Korea were the great examples of this repressive profiteering for the protestors of the mid- and late 1960s, especially after Japan normalized relations with the authoritarian South Korean government in 1965, under strong U.S. prodding—thereby contributing measurably to the ability of the Seoul regime to send troops to Vietnam in support of U.S. forces there. The radicalism of this critique lay in its attempt to think of democracy as well as peace in truly international and nonparochial terms, while situating the vaunted "income-doubling" policies of the 1960s in the specific context of the imbrication of Japanese bourgeois capitalism and U.S. imperialism. In the New Left critique, "peace and democracy" as the Old Left and liberals and ruling groups all imagined it was self-centered, self-serving, quintessentially bourgeois.

At the same time, the anti–Vietnam War movement intersected with highly charged domestic protests against the social and environmental costs of growth, the grasping hand of the state, and the autocratic governance of the universities. The latter, as the critics framed it, were turning into mere service organizations for the bureaucracy and big business. Antipollution movements centering on the mercury-poisoned community of Minamata and other tragic examples of environmental destruction peaked in the period between 1967 and the early 1970s. With them came a renewed appreciation of grassroots democracy, exemplified in an impressive variety of "citizens' movements" (*shimin undō*), "residents' movements" (*jūmin undō*), and "victims' movements" (*higaisha undō*)—all legacies, each in its own way, of the 1959–60 street demonstrations and community protests against the Security Treaty and Kishi and in support of the Miike workers. The Sanrizuka struggle opposing forced sale of farmland to build the new Narita international airport was initiated by the farmers themselves in 1968. And the student struggles, which began with a five-month strike at Waseda University in 1965–66, reached a crescendo in 1968–69. At the peak of the student demonstrations more than 40 percent of the nation's 377 universities were affected by strikes, and most of these campuses were under occupation. Although many of the grievances voiced by student protesters were directed at university affairs, the student radicals—like many other citizens in the late 1960s, in Japan and in Europe and America as well—immersed themselves in the broad gamut of domestic and international issues. And at their ironic best they cleverly captured the interlock of internal and external developments. One of the slogans of student radicals at the University of Tokyo, for example, was "Dismantle the Tokyo Imperialistic University"—neatly meshing the notion of a revival of prewar autocracy (when the elite University of Tokyo had been named Tokyo Imperial University) with the argument that higher education in postwar Japan once again was serving primarily the purposes of an expansionist state.[22]

It is estimated that between 1967 and 1970 alone, more than 18 million Japanese took to the streets to protest the war in Vietnam and demand the reversion of Okinawa to Japan. Uncounted others were involved in the university struggles and citizens' movements against the ravages of the growth-oriented state. As elsewhere, "people's power" entered the Japanese lexicon at this time as a legitimate and essential alternative to bourgeois parliamentary politics; and, as elsewhere, the theory and practice of "people's power" ranged from peaceful protest to wanton violence. By the mid-1970s the nationwide people's movement was moribund, but it left as legacies the memory and experience of grassroots mobilization that could be evoked in more particularistic causes thereafter.

CONFLICT AND ACCOMMODATION TO THE EARLY 1970S

At the most conspicuous level the major controversies concerning military and international policy in postwar Japan involved left-wing criticism of the government's acquiescence in the San Francisco System. Almost all of the contentious issues of later years were encoded in the peace settlement and separate peace, the Security Treaty and U.S. military bases in Japan, commitment to Japanese rearmament, detachment and semicolonization of Okinawa, entanglement in U.S. nuclear policy, and collusion in U.S. support of right-wing client regimes in the divided countries of Asia (China, Korea, and Vietnam). Inevitably, criticism of such government policies was inseparable from criticism of the United States. True to the early vision of the Peace Problems Symposium, the opposition position generally espoused an essentially non-aligned international role for Japan, although pro-Soviet and pro-Chinese allegiances also were conspicuous on the left. At critical moments in the postwar debates opinion polls indicated that a large number of Japanese also supported the option of neutrality. Fifty percent of respondents to a survey in 1959 endorsed this option, for example, and at the height of the peace movement a decade later as many as 66 percent of Japanese questioned in one poll favored neutrality.[23]

It is misleading, however, to see the conservative and opposition positions on these issues as completely antithetical. Both sides were crisscrossed with schisms. At the same time, on many critical issues the two sides shared, if not common ground, at least comparable skepticism concerning the wisdom of U.S. policies. Beyond the usual factionalism endemic to the left, the unity of the opposition was undercut by all the familiar postwar traumas of the international Communist and socialist movements—the repression in Hungary and critique of Stalin in 1956, the Sino-Soviet split that followed soon after, the Cultural Revolution in China and Soviet invasion of Czechoslovakia, the Communist concerns with "Trotskyist" deviations that accompanied the rise of the New Left in the 1960s, and the acrimonious debates over "capitalist and imperialist" nuclear weapons as opposed to "socialist and defensive" ones (which came to a head in Japan in 1963, when the left split on whether to support the Partial Nuclear Test-Ban Treaty). The conservatives, too, although relatively cohesive in their anti-Communism, nonetheless bifurcated into so-called Asianist and pro-American camps. This split was openly signaled in December 1964 and January 1965, when LDP members coalesced around either the staunchly pro-American Asian Problems Study Association (Ajia Mondai Kenkyūkai) or the more Asia-oriented Afro-Asian Problems Study Association (Ajia-Afurika Mondai Kenkyūkai).[24]

Even the most obsequious supporters of the pro-American position, however—such as Satō Eisaku, who succeeded Ikeda in 1964 and held the premiership until 1972—never planted both feet entirely in the American camp. From the earliest moments of the San Francisco System a fault line of disagreement and mistrust ran between Tokyo and Washington. While the conservative hegemony disagreed internally on a variety of critical policy issues beyond the appropriate speed and scope of remilitarization—including what policy to adopt toward China, Korea, Vietnam, and a nuclearized Okinawa—from the time of the Yoshida cabinets there was general conservative agreement that the U.S. vision of a bipolar world was inflexible and obsessively militaristic. As a consequence, in tactical if not fundamental ways there often occurred a convergence in the positions of the political left and right vis-à-vis the United States. One of the more amusing early examples of this convergence occurred in the very midst of the creation of the San Francisco System, when Yoshida—the great Red-baiter and bête noire of the left—secretly encouraged the Socialists to organize antirearmament demonstrations while John Foster Dulles was in Tokyo. For Yoshida and his conservative successors as well, the specter of popular opposition to U.S. policies was an effective, and indeed desired, bargaining chip.[25]

As a general rule, Japanese of every political persuasion desired greater autonomy and more genuine sovereignty for their country. They differed on whether this goal was better attained within the Security Treaty or outside it; and thus, in great confrontations such as the 1959–60 crisis over whether to revise the mutual security pact, there was indeed no common ground where policy was concerned. Both sides felt humiliation at the unequal nature of the original treaty. Whereas the conservative mainstream focused on the removal of inequality, however, the opposition argued that a more equitable treaty simply meant that Japan was committing itself to a larger military role. Nevertheless, the nationalist sentiments shared by participants on both sides of this struggle help explain the disintegration of the opposition over the ensuing years.

Nationalism was a bridge on which leftists could sooner or later cross to join the LDP or even the extreme right-wing advocates of an independent Japanese military capability. The well-known critic Shimizu Ikutarō, who moved from being one of the most prominent intellectuals in the Peace Problems Symposium and 1960 protests to being an advocate of a nuclear-armed autonomous Japanese state a decade later, was but the most conspicuous example of this exodus of former radicals into the conservative camp. Even where dissidents of the 1950s and 1960s did not cross over to the other side, moreover, in later years many turned their focus of opposition further inward to concentrate on essentially domestic concerns.[26]

On a wide range of other contested issues the partial convergence in viewpoint of the conservative leaders and their critics was more straightforward. Despite their anti-Communism, for example, many conservatives desired closer relations with the two Communist giants, or at least with China. Similarly, the large number of U.S. troops and military bases that remained in Japan after the occupation, and after the Korean armistice in 1953, aggravated almost everyone. On a related issue, although the conservatives and their critics were in fundamental disagreement over whether Japan should rearm, conservative politicians, bureaucrats, and businessmen as a whole (with the exception of certain vigorous defense industry lobbies) gave relatively low priority to defense spending into the 1980s. As a percentage of the total general accounts budget, military spending peaked in 1954. As a percentage of the gross national product, defense spending as commonly calculated was less than 1 percent for a full decade before Prime Minister Miki Takeo grandly proclaimed a "One Percent of GNP" guideline in 1976.[27]

Such points of partial convergence in the outlook of the conservatives and opposition are easily extended. There was no fundamental disagreement on the desirability of the reversion of Okinawa to full Japanese sovereignty, for example, and eventually little open disagreement on an early basic issue of contention: that Okinawa should be returned nuclear free. Neither the government nor opposition welcomed U.S. nuclear weapons on Japanese soil, and apart from a few conservative advocates of a Gaullist-style nuclear *force de frappe*, there was general agreement that Japan itself should remain nuclear free. In December 1967, in response to a question in the Diet, Prime Minister Satō clarified this position as the famous "Three Nonnuclear Principles," which held that Japan would not manufacture nuclear weapons, possess them, or permit them to enter the country. Also, although U.S. policy at the time of the peace settlement secretly had anticipated Japan emerging as a major supplier of war-related matériel to the anti-Communist camp, weapons production was not emphasized in subsequent years. Earlier in 1967, when public criticism arose concerning military-related exports to Vietnam, the Satō government responded with the "Three Principles of Arms Exports" prohibiting weapons sales to Communist countries, countries under arms embargo by the United Nations, and countries in or on the verge of armed conflict. Under the Miki cabinet (1974–76) the ban was extended to include all countries and cover parts used in military equipment.[28]

Although left and right remained in fundamental disagreement on the Security Treaty in general, until the end of the Shōwa period successive conservative governments took care to reiterate that Japanese self-defense forces were constitutionally prohibited from engaging in overseas missions or entering into collective security pacts. The latter position was explicitly meant to scotch any prospect of a NATO-type Northeast Asia treaty organization coupling Japan with the Republic of Korea and Republic of China. In addition, although LDP policy consistently called for constitutional revision, in actuality the conservative thrust in this direction tended to wither away beginning in the mid-1960s, after the Constitution Investigation Committee that had been created after the LDP was formed failed to come up with clear recommendations to revise the national charter. Although a majority of committee members did favor revision, it had become clear by 1964, when the group issued its report, that the public opposed this.[29]

These points of tactical convergence help clarify the low-posture external policies followed by conservative cabinets ever since Yoshida's time, as well as the sources of friction that always characterized relations between the Japanese and American managers of the San Francisco System. At the same time, they also help explain how, over the course of the 1950s and 1960s, the ruling groups succeeded in taking away much of the fire of the opposition. By the beginning of the 1970s many of the most contentious issues of external policy had been defused by a combination of policy changes and the effective use of symbolic rhetoric that associated the conservatives with restraint on issues of remilitarization. Complementary accommodations took place on the domestic front. The massive protests of the late 1960s against the environmental destruction caused by growth-at-all-costs economic policies, for example, were so successful that the 1970 Diet became known as the "Pollution Diet" because of the large number of environmental protection laws it passed. More generally, these developments coincided with Japan's emergence as a mature bourgeois society, increasingly preoccupied with consumerism within and great-power status abroad.

The key moments at which hitherto inflammatory peace issues began to be detached from the agenda of public debate are fairly easy to identify. The aggravating presence of U.S. bases and troops in Japan was dramatically diminished between 1955 and 1960, when the so-called New Look (or Radford Doctrine) of U.S. strategic planners dictated that reliance on nuclear weapons made many overseas bases obsolete. Between 1955 and 1957 U.S. forces in Japan were reduced from 210,000 to 77,000 men, and by 1960 the number had dropped to 48,000. Simultaneously, the United States retreated from its extraordinary proposals to create a huge Japanese army immediately and began instead to direct military aid to creation of less conspicuous but more technologically sophisticated Japanese naval and air forces.[30] Where the mutual security treaty itself was concerned, the failure of the mass protests of 1959–60 to block treaty renewal essentially marked the end of this as a meaningful issue. Attempts to remobilize protests against the next round of treaty renewal in 1970 were ineffective. After 1960 the Security Treaty remained a convenient target of rhetoric, but a practical fait accompli.

The antinuclear movement in Japan began not in 1945 but in 1954. Until the latter part of the occupation, reportage and public remembrance of Hiroshima and Nagasaki were forbidden. It was the irradiation of Japanese fishermen by an American nuclear test in the Bikini Incident of 1954, and the death of one of the crew, that precipitated the postwar movement against nuclear weapons—and, on the left, against nuclear energy. Even while resting comfortably under the U.S. nuclear umbrella, the conservative government did not hesitate to associate itself with antinuclear policies. Thus, the Japan Council Against Atomic and Hydrogen Bombs (Gensuikyō), founded in 1955, initially was supported by the LDP as well as parties and organizations on the left and fell under Communist Party control only in the 1960s. In 1961 the LDP aligned itself with a new antinuclear federation, the national Council for Peace and Against Nuclear Weapons (Kakkin Kaigi). And in December 1967 Prime Minister Satō's "Three Nonnuclear Principles" were effectively introduced to suggest that the government shared the ideals of the popular antinuclear movement. Along with Article 9, the prohibition on arms exports first announced in 1967, and the "One Percent of GNP" ceiling on defense expenditures proclaimed in 1976, the Three Nonnuclear Principles became popularly identified as one of the four "symbolic constraints" on Japanese remilitarization. The government's ability to partially co-opt the antinuclear movement was further enhanced by an insular strain in the movement itself. To many Japanese, Hiroshima and Nagasaki became emblematic of World War II and thus symbolic of the unique suffering of the Japanese in that conflict. They became, that is, a way of remembering Japanese suffering while forgetting the suffering that the Japanese caused others. Such "victim consciousness"—already noted in the earliest statements of the peace movement—meshed well with the emerging neo-nationalism of the ruling groups.

Okinawa and China, two of the most blatant symbols of subordinate independence, were detached from the peace agenda between 1969 and 1972. By the end of the 1960s the United States had become persuaded that reversion of the Ryukyus to Japan was both feasible and wise. The development of intercontinental missiles reduced Okinawa's importance as a forward nuclear base. Pressure for reversion within Okinawa and throughout all Japan was becoming irresistible. Perhaps most interesting, the discrepancy in living standards between Japan proper and semicolonized Okinawa was becoming so conspicuous as to pose a potential serious embarrassment for the United States.[31] Thus, in the Satō-Nixon communiqué of November 1969 the United States defused this issue by agreeing to return Okinawa to full Japanese sovereignty by 1972.

Where China was concerned, Washington's unexpected rapprochement with the People's Republic in 1971 embarrassed the Japanese government, which had long adhered reluctantly to the containment policy. Nonetheless, it paved the way for Japan's own restoration of relations with Beijing, thereby removing one of the most galling features of the San Francisco System. China, obsessed by its tensions with the Soviet Union, accompanied its embrace of the United States and Japan by renouncing its previous expressions of concern about Japanese rearmament and the U.S.-Japan military alliance. This Chinese volte-face was also a severe blow to the Japanese peace movement, which hitherto had argued that Japanese remilitarization under the Security Treaty was a destabilizing factor in Asia. Moreover, the agony and madness of China's Cultural Revolution, which became apparent to the world a few years later, by indirection further discredited the left.

By 1972 the left thus had lost hold of many of its most evocative peace issues: U.S. bases in Japan, the Security Treaty, nuclear weapons, arms production, Okinawa, and China. A year later, with the armistice in Vietnam, the last great cause that had provided a modicum of common purpose among the opposition was removed. The average citizen turned inward, to bask in Japan's new international influence as an economic power and become consumed by material pursuits, exemplified in such mass-media slogans as "My Home–ism" and "My Car–ism." Concerned citizens redirected their "citizens' movements" or "residents' movements" toward particular grievances. The violent wing of the New left turned its fury as well as its tactics of armed confrontation (the so-called *geba*, from *gebaruto*, the Japanese rendering of the German word *Gewalt*, "force") inward to engage in theoretical disputes and self-destructive factional violence (*uchigeba*). Beheiren, the broad-based and charismatic People's Organization for Peace in Vietnam, which had effectively reconciled many of the Marxist and non-Marxist protest groups between 1965 and 1973, disbanded in January 1974. No comparable coalition—eclectic, populist, both humanitarian and radical, nonviolent, genuinely internationalistic and individualistic in outlook—ever took its place.

THE UNCERTAIN SUPERSTATE

In retrospect it is apparent that the early 1970s marked a major turning point in Japan's position within the international political economy. It is from this point that we can date Japan's emergence as a truly global power—and the corollary and irreversible decline of U.S. hegemony. At the time, however, this transformation of power was by no means clear. On the contrary, the 1970s were a traumatic decade for Japan's elites, marked by a succession of crises. Twenty years of slavish adherence to the U.S. containment policy were rudely rewarded by the "Nixon shock" of July 1971, when the American president unexpectedly announced U.S. rapprochement with China. One month later the Nixon shock was recharged with the "dollar shock," as two decades of low-posture Japanese neomercantilism seemed thrown into jeopardy by the unilateral U.S. decision to reevaluate the yen-dollar exchange rate. Already in the late 1960s the United States had begun to withdraw the economic umbrella that sheltered Japanese protectionism at home and economic expansion abroad. The 1971 dollar shock accelerated

this process, and in 1973 the yen was allowed to float. This floating exchange rate coincided with the "oil shock" of October 1973,
which brought an end to Japan's remarkable period of high growth
rates and dropped the country into its most prolonged postwar recession. Production levels did not return to the 1973 level until
1978—just in time to be confronted with the "second oil shock"
of January 1979. The scale of the 1979 shock was registered in a
$25 billion shift in Japan's balance of payments from a $16 billion
surplus in 1978 to an $8.6 billion deficit in 1979. Whereas the an-
nual growth rate had been an extraordinary 10 to 11 percent between 1955 and 1970, in the 1970s it dropped to somewhat less than
5 percent. Concurrent with all these traumas, the country's quiet
penetration of U.S. and European markets suddenly crackled into
controversy, like a string of firecrackers that stretched through the
1970s and 1980s as well: over textiles in 1969–71; steel, television
sets, and electronics beginning around 1977; automobiles from the
turn of the decade; semiconductor chips and computers from the
mid-1980s; purchase of U.S. properties from the late 1980s.[32]

Despite the stronger floating yen (which made Japanese manufactures more expensive abroad), Japan's penetration of foreign
markets continued inexorably. And despite the end of abnormally
high annual growth rates, the now-massive economy still grew
enormously each year under the more normal rates. Still, it was
only in 1979 that the exaggerated phrase "Japan as Number One"
appeared on the scene, shocking Japanese and non-Japanese alike,
albeit in very different ways. Japan was not number one. It was still
a distant second to the United States in overall economic capacity,
but every conventional index indicated the gap was closing rapidly. By the mid-1980s the United States had become the world's
largest debtor country and Japan the world's great creditor. It was
now a financial, not just "economic," superpower. In the closing
years of the Shōwa period the "spin-on" military applications of
Japan's advanced civilian technologies made it clear that, even
without a military-industrial complex, Japan's technological accomplishments had made it a potentially significant military actor

worldwide.[33] Neither structurally nor psychologically were the Japanese or anyone else in the world fully prepared to cope with such rapid, fundamental, and almost entirely unpredicted changes.

In this milieu, conflict over international issues was drastically transformed. Whereas controversy through the 1960s had focused primarily on military and peace issues, economic competition now dominated the scene, and nation-state tensions became far more engrossing than domestic confrontations. Neither in the 1970s nor in the 1980s, however, did the rise of Japan, growing economic strength of Europe, disintegration of Soviet power, and relative decline of a stumbling but still powerful America result in a clearly defined new global order. What existed, on the contrary, was closer to global disorder—and in this situation the most intense conflicts took place within the rickety old San Francisco System. The major disputes occurred, that is, among the capitalist powers and especially between Japan and the United States. Within Japan itself, policy-related conflict became increasingly detached from the public arena and more concentrated among the conservative elites, where expanding international involvement was accompanied by a proliferation of competing interests in both the corporate and bureaucratic sectors.[34] As internal conflict shifted to and expanded among these vested interests, it became less visible. The highly technical nature of international trade and finance—and, indeed, of many new military developments as well—also inhibited wide-ranging public debate. Specialists and insiders now controlled the terms of public discourse.

Isolated individuals and groups continued during this period to try to offer alternative visions beyond unbridled capitalist competition and (a new term for the 1980s) "technonationalism." They emphasized such global issues as the north-south problem of growing disparity between rich and have-not nations, the social exploitation and distortions caused by multinational corporations in less developed countries, the depletion of global resources by economic powerhouses such as Japan and the other advanced industrialized countries, and the continuing intensification of the nuclear arms race. Where Japan itself was concerned, they pointed out that remilitarization was accelerating amidst all the hubbub about economics, which was entirely true. During the last decades of Shōwa the often-mentioned "symbolic restraints" on Japanese militarization all were violated in one way or another. Prime Minister Satō's famous Three Nonnuclear Principles, for example, were misleading from the start. Contrary to what they proclaimed, nuclear weapons apparently were brought in and out of Japan by the U.S. military as a matter of routine. Furthermore, the LDP coupled the Three Nonnuclear Principles with a less-publicized "Four Nuclear Principles," which included dependence on the U.S. nuclear "umbrella" and promotion of nuclear energy for peaceful use.

The critics also pointed out that the heralded "One Percent of GNP" restraint on defense spending was deceptive. In the first place, by NATO-style calculations, which include military retirement benefits and the like, Japanese military spending generally exceeded 1 percent of GNP. More important by far, 1 percent of a huge and constantly expanding economy was itself huge and constantly expanding. Thus, for most of the postwar period the rate of annual increase in Japan's *real* military expenditures was the highest in the world.[35] Moreover, in 1987 Prime Minister Nakasone Yasuhiro, an astute player with symbols, deliberately breached the one percent guideline. Four years earlier, at the urging of the U.S. government, Nakasone also had terminated another of the vaunted symbolic restraints on Japanese remilitarization by jettisoning the embargo on export of weapons and military-related manufactures. The United States desired to gain access to advanced Japanese technology in developing its "Star Wars" (Strategic Defense Initiative) dreams, and Nakasone's compliance opened the door to an absolutely uncertain future for Japanese activity in advanced weapons systems. Criticism of such developments by the remnants of serious opposition, however, made scarcely a ripple in popular consciousness.[36]

The decline of intense public debate on such issues reflected an erosion of democratic ideals and practices at a time when Japan was, in fact, being called on internationally to offer a new vision of national goals and responsibilities commensurate with its new power. Indeed, there almost appeared to be a correlation between the rise to global eminence and decline of political idealism. Japan had become a prosperous superstate by mobilizing its population and resources resolutely behind productivity and economic nationalism, and its accomplishments drew understandable admiration and envy from throughout the world. The line between mobilization and regimentation is a fine one, however, and the Japanese state of the 1970s and 1980s also appeared to many observers, especially abroad, to have stepped over that line. In part, this perception reflected the partial success of the conservative hegemony in perpetuating the occupation-period "reverse course" and steadily undermining what were called the "excesses" of early postwar political idealism. Once "democratization" was replaced by economic development as the overriding objective, most Japanese had little choice but to become socialized to corporate and national goals. As time passed, such regimentation was sweetened by the material rewards of prosperity and hardened by nationalistic appeals. The emergence of a mass consumer society created an ethos of "middle-class" homogeneity and contributed immeasurably to depoliticization (or preoccupation with personal and local matters). Global eminence, in turn, nurtured not only legitimate feelings of national pride but also more ominous attitudes of exceptionalism and racial and cultural superiority.

In theory both Japan's emergence as a global power and the rapid growth of consumerism and middle-class ideologies should have stimulated an increasingly cosmopolitan outlook at all levels of society. In many respects, a broader supranational attitude did materialize: internationalization (*kokusaika*) was perhaps the most overworked catchword of the 1980s. The opposite, however, occurred as well. Insular, nationalistic fixations became stronger side by side with the intensification of international contacts. This apparent paradox is not difficult to account for, for the pride that

Japanese felt at being called "number one" was compounded by fear and anger at the negative response of other countries to Japan's suddenly awesome competitive power. As foreign criticism of Japan's economic expansion mounted—emerging in accusations that the Japanese practiced "adversarial trade" or "neomercantilism" or "beggar-thy-neighbor" capture of markets, for example, or that domestic "nontariff barriers" and "structural impediments" made the Japanese market unfairly difficult for outsiders to penetrate— a defensiveness bordering on siege mentality developed in many circles. Mistrust and tension that had been latent within the old San Francisco System erupted openly. Strains of "victim consciousness" that had always existed across the political spectrum were drawn to the surface. War imagery became fashionable on all sides, albeit now in the post–Cold War context of "economic war" among the capitalist powers, especially the United States and Japan.[37]

In these circumstances, pride-inspiring and fear-inspiring at once, many Japanese began to turn inward and argue that the differences between the Japanese and other nations, races, and cultures were greater than the similarities and that Japan's contemporary accomplishments derived primarily from these unique characteristics—more so, that is, than from more general factors such as unanticipated historical opportunities (like war booms), global circumstances (such as the decline of the United States for reasons fundamentally having little to do with Japan), external patronage (notably the U.S. economic and military umbrella), transnational market mechanisms, rational (rather than cultural) policy structures and decisions, and, indeed, the consolidation of power in the hands of a competitive and diversified but still remarkably close-knit hegemony of business leaders, bureaucrats, and conservative politicians. Eventually this insular and usually narcissistic preoccupation with so-called traditional values took on a life of its own in the mass media—primarily in the runaway genre of writings and discussions devoted to the uniqueness of "being Japanese" (*Nihonjinron*)—but from the outset such introversion was promoted as a clearcut ideology by the conservative leadership.[38] In

1968, for example, the LDP showed its hand clearly in this regard when it attempted to turn centennial celebrations of the Meiji Restoration into an occasion for repudiating the most liberal ideals of the early postwar period. "We have forfeited the inherent form of the Japanese people," the party lamented in an important statement, and to rectify this loss it was desirable to reaffirm the great values of the Meiji era and bring about "the elevation of racial spirit and morality" (*minzoku seishin to dōgi no kōyō*).[39]

The conservatives never lost sight of this goal, and the closing decades of the postwar era saw them advance steadily toward it. They proved themselves masters of symbolic politics, and most of the controversial neonationalist developments of late Shōwa reflected this ideological fixation on re-creating a traditionalistic "racial spirit" that would counterbalance the purportedly corrupting influences of excessive internationalization. In numerous ways the government assumed an increasingly active role in romanticizing the patriotic and public-spirited nature of Japan's prewar imperial and imperialistic history. The corporate sector, on its part, made brilliant use of group pressures and "family" ideologies to reassert not merely the primacy of the group over the individual, but also the primacy of the family writ large (the corporation and the state) over the real nuclear family. Collectivist and consensual values were promoted as the antidote to individualistic democracy and the ideals of principled dissent.

The postwar period ended on this discordant clamor, with fanfare about "internationalization" mingling with paeans to "racial spirit" and "being Japanese." The juxtaposition of external and domestic concerns was familiar, but the contradictions between opening outward and turning inward, cosmopolitanism and exceptionalism, were unusually blatant. What this contradiction boded for the future was unpredictable. In every way, however, it seemed a far cry from the earlier and more visionary era when large notions of "peace" and "democracy" had defined the parameters of political consciousness.

9

MOCKING MISERY: GRASSROOTS SATIRE IN DEFEATED JAPAN

In 1999 I published a book titled Embracing Defeat: Japan in the Wake of World War II *that focuses on the period between August 1945 and April 1952, when Japan lacked sovereignty and was under the rule of U.S.-led Allied occupation authorities. The book's title and subtitle eschew reference to "the U.S. Occupation of Japan," for although the great majority of studies of this period approach the subject from the conqueror's perspective and through the voluminous English-language documentary record, this is not what most interested me. Rather, I wished to explore the early postwar years as a* Japanese *experience. Without in any way denying the inordinate influence of the Americans, I saw the Japanese people themselves, at every level of society, as the paramount agents in determining how they would rebuild their lives and society.*

The working title of the manuscript during the years it was being written was not Embracing Defeat, *but* Starting Over. *The latter title was vetoed by the publisher's publicity department, on grounds that it would mislead readers into assuming the book was a manual for divorcées; and in retrospect I regret that I did not hold my ground more firmly and adjust my title more adroitly. What the book is about—what a better title would have been—is "Starting Over in a Shattered Land." Almost all of the many chapters focus primarily on the Japanese and their extraordinarily diverse, resilient, and creative—as well as cynical, corrupt, divisive, and decadent—responses to disaster and defeat.*

*Despite its length, the book as published required substantial cuts, including a projected chapter on Japanese comic strips and cartoons in the years following surrender. The essay that follows here involved retrieving and elaborating on a case study from this jettisoned chapter: cartoon panels based on a traditional "syllable cards" (*iroha karuta*) game that ever since late feudal times had been a vehicle for social commentary combining pictures and pithy sayings. My major case-study ephemera was published just a few months after the surrender, when daily life was very difficult indeed, in the New Year 1946 issues of some small publications. Droll, barbed, colloquial, full of puns and insider allusions, these witty "new syllable cards" were but one of countless modes of popular expression, and venting, that existed beyond the conquerors' ken.*

The essay appeared in an edited Festschrift published in 2005.

* * *

On January 17, 1947, a clever letter published in the *Asahi Shimbun* under the title "What's Fashionable in the Capital Now" offered a snapshot of life in Tokyo less than a year and a half after Japan's defeat. The vignette was simultaneously lively and bleak—a nice mirror, in every way, to the ambience of the time.

Those who peopled this cityscape bore little resemblance to the "hundred million" whose hearts had supposedly beat as one a few years earlier, when the militarists controlled the scene and the emperor's soldiers and sailors were engaged in a mad campaign to create a new "Greater East Asia" imperium. *Ichioku isshin* (one hundred million, one heart) was surely the most overworked slogan of the war years. The *Asahi*'s letter writer, by contrast, portrayed a society in which a myriad hearts seemed to be working at cross-purposes. Japan's vaunted social harmony was nowhere to be seen.

Pistol-wielding robbers, gangs of thieves, pickpockets, swindlers, runaway prisoners, kidnappers, murderers, and "fake police detectives" prowled these streets, alongside prostitutes, black mar-

ket operatives, purged ex-officials, and a horde of functionaries who
had totally reversed their expressed views about right and wrong.
Dark deeds took place in bright daylight. Prices were rising so fast
that postcards with the postage printed on them quickly became
out of date. (What to do? Buy a sheet of supplemental stamps, cut
them with scissors, paste them on with glue.) Disruptive strikes
and demonstrations were erupting everywhere. People played the
lottery, looking like cheerful Ebisu, the god of good luck, when
they won—and like Enma, the scowling guardian at hell's gate,
when they lost.

The transportation system was a horror. Robbers worked the
railways as they worked the streets. The trains ran late or were canceled entirely, largely because of the shortage of coal. They broke
down and had dreadful accidents. ("Don't let your beloved child
travel," the writer warned.) Deliveries did not arrive on time. Fake
edibles—pickled garnishes with misleading labels, "imitation cakes
without sugar, saké and soy sauce diluted with water"—were being sold. Consumers were confronted with "light bulbs with short
lives, pencils that break when sharpened, knives that don't cut even
when sharpened, screws that bend when turned." This was but a
fraction of what could be told. Japanese society, alas, threatened to
"go on descending, descending, into a bottomless pit."[1]

What made this satire particularly droll was that it was a takeoff on a famous fourteenth-century parody of the same title—
an anonymous lampoon that ridiculed the sorry state into which
the capital city of Kyoto had fallen during the so-called Kenmu
Restoration, when civil war plagued the land. Times changed and
did not change, and the possibility of ransacking the past for language and precedents usable in the present made the sting of defeat
more bearable. Past, present, and future were inextricably linked
in defeated Japan.

"What's Fashionable in the Capital Now" is a small example of
what I have characterized elsewhere as the "bridges of language"
that enabled many Japanese to navigate the transition from war
to peace with a certain sense of continuity—even, indeed, with a

sardonic sense of humor.[2] Wartime Japan tolerated homespun jokes alongside satire of the enemy, and periodicals such as the monthly magazine *Manga* (Cartoon) kept a substantial cadre of housebroken humorists and cartoonists employed right up to (and through) the surrender. In the crushing sanctimony of the holy war, however, it was taboo—and seriously hazardous to one's health—to openly mock such targets as the state and "national polity," or the ruling groups, or the vaunted "Yamato spirit" that purportedly made every Japanese an obedient subject tingling with patriotism, loyalty, and filial piety. The fragile but venerable tradition of public satire and self-mockery that had taken root in late feudal Japan and carried over to the early twentieth century was one of the more minor casualties of the war. It was also one of the first "traditions" to recover.

At an elemental level, this recovery involved little more than the inventive reapplication of proverbs and catchphrases. "Thanks to our fighting men" (*heitaisan no okage desu*), one of the most pious expressions of the war years, for example, became almost overnight a caustic allusion to how the country had fallen into such miserable circumstances. Other well-known sayings proved similarly adaptable to explaining the national disaster. "The frog in the well doesn't know the ocean" (*i no naka no kawazu taikai o shirazu*), a hoary old saw, now was evoked to belittle the militarists and nationalists and their fatuous wartime proclamations about "spiritual strength" and "certain victory." Merchants, politicians, and other opportunists who quickly swallowed the bitterness of defeat and began catering to the U.S. occupation forces confirmed the old saying that "the burning sensation is forgotten once things pass your throat" (*nodomoto sugureba atsusa o wasureru*).

"Proof surpasses theory" (*ron yori shōko*, a rough equivalent to "the proof of the pudding is in the eating") found ubiquitous application amid the rubble. One magazine, for instance, used this as a caption for a photograph of burned-out buildings. In its New Year issue of 1946, the pictorial weekly *Asahi gurafu* (Asahi graphic) made grim use of another familiar expression by printing a photo of the mushroom cloud over Hiroshima with the caption "truth that emerged out of lies" (*uso kara deta makoto*). "Sailing with the wind" (*ete ni ho o ageru*), a phrase with counterparts in every culture, was used to characterize everything from a commitment to democracy to the most crass opportunism.[3]

Even the rapacious black market, which constituted much of the "real" economy from the time of surrender until around 1949, contributed to the humorous redirection of pious set phrases. While Emperor Hirohito spent an inordinate amount of time agonizing over the sanctity and preservation of the regalia associated with his dynastic line (the sequestered mirror, sword, and jewel), black-market toughs made a stab at charisma by flaunting their own "three sacred regalia": aloha shirts, nylon belts, and rubber-soled shoes. This was a witty, irreverent appropriation of imperial pretensions indeed—an irreverence that indirectly said something about the throne's waning mystique.[4]

The black market also inspired a suggestive revision of the lyrics of one of the country's most popular and sentimental children's songs, "Big Sunset, Little Sunset" ("Yūyake koyake"). In this instance, moreover, we can see the seeds of postdefeat cynicism in the war years themselves, for "Yūyake koyake" had also inspired at least one subterranean presurrender parody. The original song (dating from 1923) opens as follows:

Yūyake koyake de	Big sunset, little sunset—
hi ga kurete	the day draws to a close.
Yama no otera no	From the mountain temple
kane ga naru	sounds the bell
Otete tsunaide	Hand in hand,
mina kaero	let's all head home.
Karasu mo issho ni	Let's go home together
Kaerimashō	with the crows.

During the war, however, as Japan's leaders continued to spout the rhetoric of ultimate victory while the country's plight became more and more palpably desperate, even children gave voice to

disillusion. Apparently inspired by the fact that many temple bells
had been melted down to feed the war machine and thus were no
longer to be heard, the lyrics to "Big Sunset, Little Sunset" underwent such mocking revision as this:

Yūyake koyake de	Big sunset, little sunset—
hi ga kurenai	the day doesn't come to a close.
Yama no otera no	From the mountain temple
kane naranai	no bell sounds.
Sensō naka naka	The war doesn't seem
owaranai	to ever end.
Karasu mo ouchi e	Even the crows
kaerenai	cannot go home.[5]

A third stage in this lyrical metempsychosis appeared in
the form of a letter to the *Asahi* in 1947, a week before "What's
Fashionable in the Capital Now," under the title "Big Black Market,
Little Black Market" ("Ōyami koyami"). The new lyrics, a pithy
mix of cynicism and idealism perfectly in tune with the times, ran
as follows:

Big black market, little black market—
the day draws to a close,
and honest men are made out to be fools.
Skimpy dinner, out of firewood,
trembling in a house where rain leaks in.

The small black marketeer is chastised
and finds himself in jail,
while out in a mansion, drinking and eating,
the big black marketeer is laughing.

When I become a grown-up,
Mister Big Round Moon,

let's make a really bright country
where honest men aren't made out to be fools.[6]

One of the more popular and ritualized forms of mocking misery in defeated Japan derived from the annual New Year's practice of playing "syllable card" (*iroha karuta*) games. Dating from around 1800 as a children's game, this originally involved associating the elements of the cursive hiragana syllabary with the opening syllable of well-known proverbs or sayings. This quickly evolved into a game in which a set of 96 cards—half with the sayings written on them (each beginning with a different syllable), the other half decorated with illustrations of each particular saying (with the opening kana syllable itself appearing in one corner)—was scattered on the floor. The textual cards were picked up at random and read aloud, and participants competed to find and pick up the illustrated card that corresponded to what had been read. This was a literate and frequently raucous amusement, and it encouraged many variations. Since there was no fixed collection of proverbs or sayings that had to be used, the makers of *iroha* sets were free to introduce their own associations, and even to create their own catchy phrases.

The game apparently originated in the Kansai area (Kyoto and Osaka) and was quickly adopted (and adapted) in Edo, where the feudal lords congregated in homage to the shogun. It reflected the culture and inventiveness of the townspeople rather than the samurai, however, and, among other things, revealed how widely and *vertically* literacy had spread during the long era of warrior domination. Many proverbs used on the cards were Chinese in origin, and introducing them to children's play obviously served a certain didactic or hortatory educational purpose. As a product of commoner culture, however, the early card sets often revealed a certain detachment from the pious platitudes and moral injunctions of the ruling groups. Contrary to what one might expect, the virtues of loyalty and filial piety (*chū* and *kō*) that so obsessed the chattering ruling classes were most conspicuous by their absence from Edo-period *karuta* sets.[7]

By and large, the early nineteenth-century *iroha* cards produced in the Kansai area appear to have featured short and sweet aphorisms about wasting time and energy. Typical examples are "driving a nail into rice bran," "putting a clamp on bean curd (*tofu*)," "shooting a gun in the dark," "giving a gold coin to a cat," "looking over a fence when blind," "putting in eye drops from the second floor" (a Kansai gem indeed!). *Iroha* cards in Edo, by contrast, were apparently strongest on exhortations to be sharp and wary—such as "inattentiveness is the great enemy" and "look around three times before having a smoke." Confucian pieties—or, more precisely, the pieties of Confucianists—sometimes received decidedly oblique acknowledgment. For example, "reading the *Analects* but not knowing the *Analects*" ("*Rongo*" *yomi no* "*Rongo*" *shirazu*)—one way of referring to "a learned fool"—was the saying chosen for the syllable *ro* in one late-feudal set of syllable cards. While commoner children in the waning decades of warrior rule apparently were spared indoctrination about filial piety in their little card game, they did on the other hand learn about "old people who ought to know better" (*toshiyori no hiyamizu*).

What did these youngsters learn about the venerable samurai from their *iroha karuta*? Not a great deal, it seems, although they did encounter the well-known observation that "the samurai uses a toothpick even though he hasn't eaten" (*bushi wa kuwanedo takayōji*). This does not exactly seem to have been designed to promote awe of the ruling class. Similarly, it is doubtful that card-playing greatly enhanced religious piety among youngsters. On the contrary, their New Year's Day play reminded them that "even a sardine's head seems precious if you believe in it" (*iwashi no atama mo, shinjin kara*) and that Buddhist priests were inclined to give "inept and long-winded sermons" (*heta no nagadangi*). At the same time, however, under *ko* they might encounter the harsh Buddhist injunction that "a child is an encumbrance in all three stages of existence" (*ko wa sangai no kubikase*). Other aphorisms offered these young people a very hard-nosed and pragmatic mixture of the sacred and profane. Under the syllable *chi* (here read *ji*), for example, the card game might remind them that "money can affect your fate even in hell" (*jigoku no sata mo kane shidai*).

Inherent ambiguity sometimes sharpened the potential double edge of these "educational" games. This is suggested by the famous saying that (since it begins with the syllable *i*) opens many of the earliest sets: *inu mo arukeba bō ni ataru*, or "if even a dog moves around, it will encounter a stick." What exactly did this mean? Apparently, one thing at one time, another and quite contrary thing at another time. Originally, the saying seems to have been intended as a warning that anyone who got out of line would find trouble (that is, be hit with a stick). The sanguine spin came in thinking of the dog happily finding a stick by wandering around. In this case, going out of bounds might bring good fortune.[8] When cartoonists picked up the *iroha karuta* as a vehicle for satire in defeated Japan a century later, they obviously had an established but extremely flexible "tradition" to play with. As we shall see, they even reintroduced their own version of the wandering dog.

In the modern era that followed the Meiji Restoration, the *iroha karuta* spread throughout the country. Sometimes they were even popularly called "dog-stick cards" (*inubō karuta*) from that best-known of opening sayings. In the Meiji and Taishō periods, card sets were sometimes attached to children's books as a merchandising bonus. Pithy phrases were cleaned up and rendered more "wholesome." By the 1930s, when the cards became vehicles for patriotic exhortation, soldiers (*heitai*) marched in where an earlier generation might have found farts (*he*) more entertaining as an opening syllable. In a typical card set from 1940, for example, the association for *he* was "Playing soldier, don't cry even if you fall" (*heitaigokko korondemo nakuna*).[9]

The convention of associating *kana* syllables with illustrated graphics had obvious attractions for cartoonists addressing adult audiences. It was natural and easy, that is, to transfer the multiple "card" format to the printed pages of periodicals as an extended sequence of single-panel illustrations with witty *iroha* captions.

Among other things, this provided a clever format through which to kick off each new year with a wry, impressionistic commentary—sometimes by turning old phrases to new uses, sometimes by bending or cleverly altering an old proverb, sometimes by coining a sharp new aphorism or wedding a barbed graphic to a pithy and newly fashionable phrase. For several years following the defeat, such cartoons in the form of "new edition syllable cards" (*shinpan iroha karuta*) provided an ironic magazine commentary on the contemporary scene.

Although these graphic little jokes certainly constitute one of the most modest and ephemeral forms of social commentary and cultural expression imaginable, in retrospect they capture the flavor of the times with remarkable pungency. At the same time, they also convey a sense of grassroots cynicism and iconoclasm that (in one way or another) tells us quite a bit about the transition to "democracy" in postwar Japan. There is even, perhaps, a small sense of coming full circle—in that public discourse was regaining the more detached, ironic, even sacrilegious tone that had been present in earlier times. In a wonderful little example of this reinvented tradition, one of the first postdefeat cartoon adaptions of the syllable card motif opened (almost) with that hoary dog-and-stick proverb. The illustration portrayed a trembling dog

staring at a boiling pot of stew. This was a commentary on the acute food shortage that Japanese in all walks of life confronted in the wake of defeat, and the accompanying revised caption read: "If a dog walks around, it may well become soup" (*inu mo arukeba nabe ni sareru*).[10]

Until 1949, the Japanese media were subjected to formal censorship by the American-led occupation authorities. All media expression thus took place in a box. Although the parameters of permissible expression were much greater than had been the case under the presurrender Japanese regimes, certain logical targets of satire were formally taboo. The victors and their entire early agenda of "demilitarization and democratization" were by and large off-limits to criticism—hardly an elegant or admirable model of democracy in action. As a consequence, the postsurrender cartoonists, like everyone else in the media, practiced self-censorship as a matter of course. During the war years, they had ridiculed and demonized the "devilish Anglo-Americans." Now they mocked themselves and the sorry plight into which their "holy war" had led them.[11]

Such mockery tended to zero in on several targets. The most immediately striking were the folly of the recent war and the deservedly humiliating fall from grace of the country's erstwhile leaders. Yesterday's holy war was now more than just profane. It was a joke, an act of profound stupidity, a stain on the nation's honor. And yesterday's heroes, both military and civilian (but almost always excluding the emperor), had become today's goats. An incisive early example of this new cynicism and ridicule—and, indeed, of the *iroha karuta* as a vehicle for postwar political commentary—is an exuberant sequence of 47 "New Edition Syllable Cards" by Saji Takashi and Terao Yoshitake (see Fig. 9.1) that appeared in the 1946 New Year issue of a labor-oriented periodical named *Kyōryoku shimbun* (Cooperative press). What follows here is a close-up selection of Saji and Terao's vignettes of the new Japan (their *i-ro-ha* panels run top to bottom, right to left):[12]

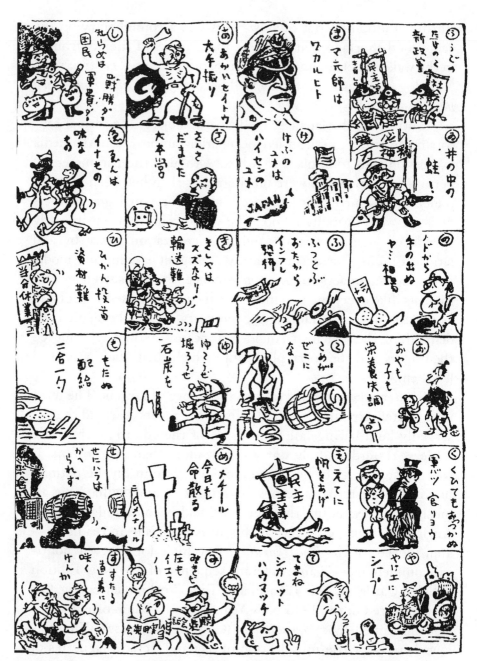

Fig. 9-1. "New Edition Syllable Cards for 1946" (Saji Takashi and Terao Yoshitaka, "Shinpan iroha karuta," *Kyōryoku shimbun*, New Year issue, 1946).

This cartoon version of the traditional syllable-cards sequence begins at the top right, reads top to bottom, and thus proceeds to the left in vertical rows.

NI
"Despised fellow being kicked out"
(*nikumarekko yo o hijikaru*)
Graphic: foot stomping a uniformed officer

HO
"Much pain for a lost war"
(*hone ori zon no makeikusa*)
Graphic: white flag of surrender above a stack
of rifles

HE
"Thanks to our fighting men"
(*heitaisan no okage desu*)
Graphic: distressed faces of a mother, father,
and child

TO
"Even old men are breaking out in cold sweat"
(*toshiyori mo hiyaase*)
Graphic: three trembling men, one in military
cap, with one of them thinking "war crimes"[13]

CHI
"Vowing to build a new Japan"
(*chikatte kinzuku shin Nippon*)
Graphic: repatriated soldier holding hands
with a smiling woman

RI
"Army general in a cage"
(*rikugun taishō ori no naka*)
Graphic: former General and Prime Minister Tōjō
Hideki behind bars

O
"Women entering the election wars"
(*onna noridasu senkyosen*)
Graphic: newly enfranchised woman campaigning
for office

WA
"Me too, me too—black market dealings"
(*ware mo ware mo no yami shōbai*)
Graphic: man with black-market goods

KA
"The Divine Wind didn't blow"
(*kamikaze mo fukisokone*)
Graphic: crowded houses in flames, with bombs
falling on them[14]

YO
"Thanks for quitting [the war]"
(*yoku koso yamete kudasatta*)
Graphic: seven smiling faces of ordinary people

TA [DA]
"Even cabinet ministers do the black market"
(*daijin mo yami*)
Graphic: elderly official with black-market fish

RE
"Great Asia War that stained history"
(*rekishi o kegasu Dai Tōa Sen*)
Graphic: military boot stomping on the pages of an
open book

SO
"The sky is blue, the ground in ruins"
(*sora wa aozora chi haikyo*)
Graphic: bombed-out building against the sky

NE
"No bedding or house to sleep in"
(*neru ni ie nashi futon nashi*)
Graphic: shivering mother, father, and child

MU
"Making trouble and losing rationality"
(*muri o tōshite dōri ni maketa*)
Graphic: man holding a bamboo spear being hit on
the helmet with a sledgehammer labeled "reason"

KU
"Militarists and bureaucrats—too late for regrets"
(*kuitemo ottsukanu gunbatsu kanryō*)
Graphic: officer and top-hatted bureaucrat in
handcuffs

SA
"Imperial Headquarters, which deceived all the
way"
(*sanza damashita Daihon'ei*)
Graphic: wartime military officer broadcasting a
speech

Probably because its 1946 New Year special appeared so soon after the defeat, at a time when the occupation's censorship operation was still cranking up, the *Kyōryoku shimbun* also included several direct references to the conquerors and, in some instances, transgressed the subsequent bounds of permissible expression. The conquerors entered the *iroha* tradition thusly:

MA
"General MacArthur, an understanding man"
(*Ma gensui wa wakaru hito*)
Graphic: the general's face, wearing his familiaar cap and sunglasses

KE [KYŌ]
"The capital's dreams are defeat dreams"
(*kyō no yume wa haisen no yume*)
Graphic: the Stars and Stripes flying over a Japanese building, and a small map of the archipelago with JAPAN written in English[15]

YA
"Jeep on burned land"
(*yaketsuchi ni jiipu*)
Graphic: the ubiquitous American jeep driving through ruins

TE
"Hand signal—cigarette, how much?"
(*temane—shigaretto hau maachi*)
Graphic: Japanese man communicating with a GI

E
"The ties that bind are strange and wonderful"
(*en wa ina mono aji na mono*)
Graphic: a black GI and Japanese woman walking arm in arm[16]

While the *Kyōryoku shimbun* was ushering in the first new year of the era of defeat with these indelicate observations, readers of another publication were offered a different but complementary set of *kana* associations in a "new edition syllable cards" cartoon sequence by Ogawa Takeshi titled "Voice of the People" (Fig. 9-2). Here, for example, the graphic for *me* depicted a Tōjō-esque figure wearing dark glasses, with the simple caption "blind leader." The holy war was trashed in the rendering for *se*, which depicted a military sword discarded in a garbage bin, accompanied by the caption "fed up with war." A splendid little evocation of popular sentiment was conveyed in the rendering for *mo*, which portrayed a determined-looking peasant leaning on a hoe in a field. The caption read: "Not going to be deceived any more."

ME
"Blind leader"
(*mekura shidōsha*)
Graphic: Prime Minister Tōjō as blind man giving a speech

SE
"Fed up with war"
(*sensō wa korikori*)
Graphic: military sword in a trash bin

MO
"Not going to be deceived any more"
(*mō damasarenu*)
Graphic: determined farmer leaning on a hoe

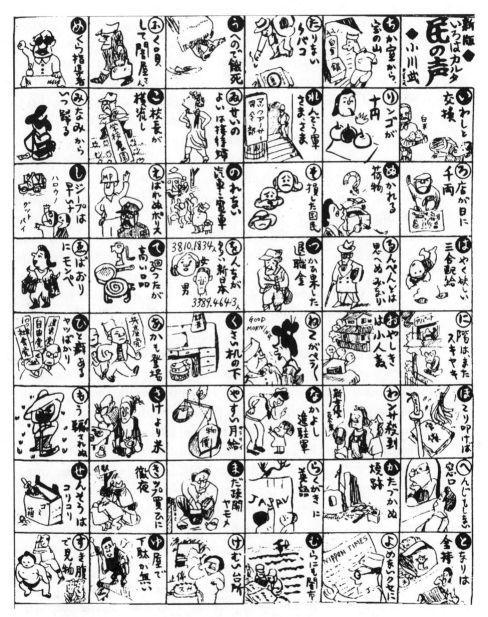

Fig. 9-2. "Voice of the People: New Edition Syllable Cards" (Ogawa Takeshi, "Tami no koe: shinpan iroha karuta," *Manga to yomimono*, New Year issue, 1946).

The attraction of this last entry for the cultural and political historian is that it captured in a few swift strokes what was surely the most popular of all explanations among Japanese as to how they had become embroiled in such a disastrous war. They had, it was said time and again, "been deceived" (*damasareta*). From this, it followed that the people as a whole had to take care never again to be misled by their leaders. And from this observation, in turn, it was but a natural step to argue that the best way to do away with irresponsible leaders was to create a genuinely open, rational, "democratic" society. Seen from this perspective, the scowling cartoon farmer was saying a great deal indeed. He represented (whether he fully realized it or not) a potentially solid "grassroots" basis of support for a drastically liberalized national polity.

The "Voice of the People" sequence also included a few wryly obsequious genuflections to the occupation force. Thus, the drawing for *re* depicted the entry to General MacArthur's headquarters, with the sidebar "Doubly Honorable Allied Force." For *na*, readers were offered an American sailor engaged in conversation with a little Japanese girl. The caption literally read "Friendly Advancing Force"—picking up a familiar euphemism for the occupation force that, in itself, could be used as a point of departure for a disquisition on the Japanese penchant for weasel words. During the war, for example, it had been military gospel that the imperial army and navy always advanced and never retreated. Thus, when they *did* withdraw from a confrontation, this was rarely acknowledged by plainly speaking of "retreat" (*taikyaku*). Rather, the emperor's soldiers and sailors were said to be engaged in *tenshin*, literally "turning around and advancing." In a similar manner, the country's defeat (*haisen*) was most often referred to in official pronouncements (much less so in popular discourse) as the "termination of the war" (*shūsen*), a far more gentle construction. Much the same linguistic aversion was involved in denaturing the occupation force (*senryōgun*) by referring to it as the "advancing force" (*shinchūgun*).

RE
"Doubly Honorable Allied Force"
(*rengōgun samasama*)
Graphic: entrance to "MacArthur General
Headquarters"

NA
"Friendly Occupation Force"
(*nakayoshi Shinchūgun*)
Graphic: American sailor with Japanese child

The cartoon *karuta*, in any case, went far beyond these rendi-
tions of conquered and conqueror. They were also, in their way, a
more literally graphic counterpart to the word pictures of chaos
and confusion conveyed in parodies such as "What's Fashionable
in the Capital Now" and "Big Black Market, Little Black Market."
From 1946 to 1949, a good many of these graphics focused on an
aspect of the defeat that virtually every Japanese encountered on
a daily basis: the black market. Rampant egoism prevailed here, as
already seen in some of the mocking entries in *Kyōryoku shinbun*.
Ogawa's cartoon *karuta* for *fu* observed that many of the millions
of servicemen and civilians who had been overseas when the war
ended made ends meet as black market operatives after they were
repatriated.[17]

FU
"Repatriated and now in the black market"
(*fukuin shite yamiyasan*)
Graphic: Ex-serviceman, still wearing his military cap

Over two years after the surrender, a humor magazine ush-
ered in 1948 by inviting well-known cartoonists to contribute
karuta-style graphics and found many of them still obsessed with

the centrality of the black market in everyday life. For *chi*, for example, Katō Etsurō pointed out the relationship between the dynamism of the illegal market and the incompetence of the government with a drawing of a sturdy man in gaiters, carrying a huge bundle on his back. The caption read, "delay in rations makes the black marketeer fat" (*chihai de futoru yami shōnin*). Ogawa Tatsuo satirized the lucrative gains farmers made by diverting their produce from the official distribution system to the black market. His graphic for the syllable *wa* (involving a subtle wordplay) depicted a gloating farmer seated in his house with foodstuff behind him and paper currency spread all over the floor in front of him. Tanaka Hisao used the syllable *ya* to belittle the big operatives who were "getting fat on the black market, forgetting one's place" (*yamibutori mi no hodo shirazu*). His drawing depicted an obese man in a suit picking up paper money with chopsticks. Katō Etsurō then reentered this collaborative card set with an unusually scathing riff on *fu*. His drawing offered a woman in a kimono giving a speech, while a fat, grinning man in dark glasses stood behind her. What was this slice of life all about? Simple: "Wife is Diet member, husband is black marketeer" (*fujin wa daigishi teishu wa yamiya*).[18]

Beyond these conquered/conqueror vignettes, and beyond the black humor of the market, the *iroha* satires captured the sheer chaos of everyday life as well as any other mode of popular expression in these years. Saji and Terao captured this most vividly in their rendering of a shivering family with "no bedding or house to sleep in." Ogawa's "Voice of the People" went further. His grim offering for *u*, for example, depicted the feet of a corpse sticking out from under a blanket, a common scene in railway stations and other underground public facilities where the homeless congregated for several years after the surrender. The wives, parents, and children who waited, often for years, for word of whether their overseas loved ones were still alive provided the subject for *mi*, a woman brushing away tears. In a "syllable card" for *o*, Ogawa offered a woman's face with the figure 38,101,834 and a man's face by the number 33,894,643—picking up statistics that revealed the demographic imbalance caused by the war deaths of young men, a loss that meant many Japanese women of marriage age were deprived of potential spouses.

U
"Starved to death in Ueno Station"
(*Ueno de gashi*)
Graphic: feet of a corpse protruding from a covering

MI
"When will he return from the south?"
(*minami kara itsu kaeru*)
Graphic: woman weeping over the failure of a loved one to return

O
"More women in New Japan"
(*onna ga ōi shin Nippon*)
Graphic: Numbers indicating how Japanese women now greatly outnumbered men due to heavy fatalities in the war

In a lighter vein, the prevalence of petty theft became a man leaving a public bath house and discovering someone had stolen one of his wooden clogs. Shortage of decent clothing emerged in "Voice of the People" as a woman wearing the *haori* coat worn with kimono along with the decidedly unglamorous *monpe* pantaloons common during the war and, for many poor women, for many years after. Another vignette of daily vexations offered a white-collar worker picking a cigarette butt off the ground. "Not enough tobacco" was the concise legend.

Other illustrators and wordsmiths used the syllable-card format in comparably pointed ways. Thus, the *desirability* of being sent to prison (where one was at least guaranteed food and

YU
"Clog missing at the public bath"
(*yuya de geta ga nai*)
Graphic: Man leaving a bathhouse and staring at a
single wooden clog

E
"Formal coat and pantaloons"
(*ebaori ni monpe*)
Graphic: Woman wearing a formal overgarment for
kimono along with the unglamorous cotton pants worn
during the war and often for several years after

TA
"Not enough tobacco"
(*tarinai tabako*)
Graphic: picking up a discarded cigarette butt

lodging) inspired, for the syllable *tsu*, a prisoner singing happily
as a policeman led him off to the slammer. The accompanying
text read "volunteering to go to prison by committing a crime"
(*tsumi o okashite keimusho shigan*). Another card set picked up on the
postsurrender efflorescence of messianic new religions, several of
which were founded by women who claimed to have had ecstatic
visions. The graphic here offered a cross-eyed woman kneeling in
front of a Shinto pendant with her hands clasped in prayer and
tiny figures prostrating themselves before her. Playing on the syllable *ki*, the caption called less than reverential attention to "new
religions where an insane person becomes a deity" (*kichigai ga ka-
misama ni naru shinshūkyō*).[19]

Such barbed observations went on and on. The once prized
virtue of frugality was ridiculed with aphorisms (here for the 1947
New Year) to the effect that, in the midst of runaway inflation,
it was "foolish to make a plan for the year" (*ichinen no hakarigoto
suru dake yabo*). The best one could do was "steal when poor, spend
madly when prosperous" (*kasshite wa dorobō, uruoeba ranpi*). It was

a rare cartoonist who could resist a grim (or sick) reference to the prevalence of blindness caused by drinking the cheap methyl alcohol popular among the down-and-out. "Stoned and blind" (*yoi shirete me ga tsubure*) was the blunt association for the syllable *yo* that accompanied a cartoon of a disoriented man with a bottle labeled "methyl" before him. A drawing of a man in the berth of a railway sleeper car was turned into a joke by contrasting his comfortable accommodation with the "fourth class" status to which—in General MacArthur's own humiliating words—Japan had fallen as a nation. A first-class sleeper in a fourth-class country (*yontō koku ni ittō shindai*) was the caption here. Although Emperor Hirohito generally escaped the barbs of the humorists just as he evaded almost every other sort of substantive criticism, his unprecedented post-defeat decision to tour the country and mingle with common people prompted one publication to enlarge a famous old saying. "A crane in the dump" became "crane in the dump, emperor in the crowd" (*hakidame ni tsuru, hitonami ni tennō*).[20]

The postwar spread of commercialized sex drew attention with renderings of nude shows and old men reading pornography. "Showing thighs is a business" (*momo o miseru ga shōbai*) was one dignified new association for *mo*. The difficulties of true romance during the acute food shortage that lasted for three or four years after the defeat was conveyed in a 1948 graphic of a couple on a park bench trying to have a "rendezvous while carrying sweet potatoes" (*imo motte rendezvous*). The postwar phenomenon of seeking a marriage partner at public meetings devised solely for that purpose was captured in the notion that "the ties that bind come from a group marriage meeting" (*en wa shūdan miai*).

Struggling to survive day to day by selling personal possessions such as clothing piece by piece, just as one peeled and ate the edible bamboo shoot, inspired one of the most famous coinages of the postsurrender period—"bamboo-shoot existence." From this came, in 1948, a predictable cartoon *karuta* depicting a woman standing before an empty bureau, with the caption "already three years of bamboo-shoot existence" (*takenoko gurashi mo sannen*). In another syllable-card sequence for 1948, hunger for a touch of glamour prompted the observation that "women can be caught by a dress" (*onna wa ishō de tsurareru*). The accompanying illustration clearly slipped by the occupation's American censors: it depicted a young woman reaching for a dress dangled by a male figure with a gigantic nose in silhouette—a decidedly uncomplimentary rendering of the Caucasian conquerors who exchanged luxury gifts for sexual favors.

What the new freedoms associated with "democracy" might mean for old virtues such as filial piety inspired the talented cartoonist Ono Saseo to offer, also in 1948, a drawing of a little boy giving a speech to his trembling father. "Child humbles parent" (*ko wa oya o hekomasu*) was Ono's association for *ko*. In the same issue in which this cartoon appeared, however, Miya Shigeo offered hope that some old customs were still being preserved. His rendering for *re* introduced "a cultured person who knows manners" (*reisetsu o shiru bunkajin*)—but it was not, in fact, intended to put traditionalists' hearts at rest. Miya's "cultured person," depicted bowing before a Shinto shrine, was a young American GI.

And how did young Japanese emerge in these *iroha* sallies (when not engaged in the black market or in personal and family relationships)? University students worked part-time jobs instead of attending classes or spent their time waving red flags in front of their old professors. Workers celebrated May Day under hammer-and-sickle flags. A young woman with high and "westernized" aspirations was sure to end up an old maid because "her ideals are too high" (this particular graphic offered a kimono-clad woman brushing off men with her elbow while holding a book with the English title "Love Is Best"). Alternatively, young people could enjoy another of democracy's great attractions, the boogie-woogie—or attend auditions held by movie studios looking for "new talent" (here the unkind graphic portrayed a young would-be female star with a nose like a potato).

* * *

Much of this was frivolous, of course. While the satirists were poking fun at the postwar confusion, a great many other Japanese were seriously searching for "bridges of language" that would provide them with usable traditions for the present and future. The Shōwa emperor, guided by advisers like the career diplomat Shigemitsu Mamoru (soon to be indicted as a war criminal) and ever intent on preserving the sanctity of his dynasty, rediscovered the 1868 Charter Oath of the Meiji founding fathers. His mission, like that of his grandfather, the Meiji emperor, he declared on New Year's Day 1946, had always been to throw off the evil customs of the past and seek knowledge throughout the world. (He did not explain how this cosmopolitan search had led to Nazi Germany.)[21] Less rhetorically but more dramatically, the emperor's postwar decision to become a "crane in the dump" and mingle with the hoi polloi had its most obvious precedent in the imperial tours his grandfather, the Meiji emperor, had carried out in various parts of the country in the 1880s. On both occasions, these carefully choreographed royal excursions were undertaken to stabilize popular support for the throne at a time of political agitation and uncertainty.

Within days after the emperor announced Japan's capitulation, millennial rhetoric about "changing the world" (*yonaoshi*) that had been popular in the late feudal period was resurrected as an appropriate way of thinking about the challenges now posed by defeat. Closer in time, liberals rediscovered "Taishō democracy." Progressives and leftists called attention to the aborted ideals of the "freedom and people's rights movement" (*jiyū minken undō*) of the early Meiji period and to the proletarian and labor movements that had emerged (and been crushed) after the turn of the century. The celebration of "May Day" resumed in 1946, after having been suppressed for ten years—the seventeenth such celebration in Japan. Popular protests against the government's woefully inept rationing system, which culminated in a tumultuous "Food May Day" a few weeks later, were in certain ways a striking replication of the most dynamic occasion of popular protest in prewar Japan— the 1918 "rice riots." In both instances, the impetus to nationwide demonstrations derived from spontaneous local protests by house-wives. The birth of a radical postwar university student movement (beginning with Student May Day in 1946) was explicitly linked to the anniversary of a notorious prewar incident involving suppression of academic freedom (the Takigawa incident of 1933).

Marxists quickly revived the acrimonious but intellectually stimulating *Rōnō-kōza* theoretical debates suppressed in the 1930s. Libertines, hedonists, and exhausted escapists resurrected the *ero-guro-nansensu* vogue that had embraced the "erotic, grotesque, and nonsensical" in the early 1930s in a thinly sublimated expression of protest against the rising tide of militarism. Scientists talked about returning to "our peaceful research." Conservative philosophers like Kōsaka Masaaki criticized the absence of Western-style "objectivity" in Japanese culture but saw hope for the future in the "sacred power" and estimable state-centered and family-centered "morality" that supposedly characterized Japanese culture. Writers as diverse as the austere "Kyoto School" philosopher Tanabe Hajime and the enormously popular writer of historical epics Yoshikawa Eiji turned to the thirteenth-century evangelist Shinran for wisdom concerning both repentance (*zange*) and ecstatic conversion (*ōsō*). Outcast thinkers of "dangerous thoughts" from the war years, such as Kawakami Hajime, Miki Kiyoshi, Ozaki Hotsumi, and Miyamoto Yuriko became postwar (and, for Miki and Ozaki, posthumous) heroes and heroines.

Industrialists and other leaders of big business quickly called attention to the many usable "pasts" on which postwar economic reconstruction could and should be built. Predictably, these included the rehabilitation of a *zaibatsu*-dominated capitalist system and the restoration of intimate commercial and personal ties with the United States and Great Britain. At the same time, business leaders and economic planners also called attention to the dramatic advances in applied science and technology that the long war itself had stimulated. This, they argued—coupled with continued strong state input into economic planning—would provide the foundation for the country's future development as an advanced economic power. Indeed, in technocratic as well as technological ways, the very mobilization for "total war" that had led to miserable defeat soon proved to be an unexpectedly dynamic and adaptable "past" on which to construct a more democratic and peacefully oriented Japan.[22]

Even the Japanese post office took part in the business of re-inventing tradition and building bridges from the old to the "new" Japan. There was no place for a Meiji-era hero like General Nogi Maresuke on postage stamps anymore, but who could take his place? From early on, it was clear that the country's new indig-enous heroes had to be modern "cultural" figures, but it took a long time to decide who these should be. It was not until 1949 that the postal service inaugurated its Cultural Leaders Series with a stamp honoring the medical researcher Noguchi Hideyo. Between 1950 and 1952, sixteen eminent prewar men and one distinguished woman (the writer Higuchi Ichiyō) were similarly commemorated as prewar models for the new postwar era.[23]

The bridges that linked past, present, and future were many and various indeed.

10

LESSONS FROM JAPAN
ABOUT WAR'S AFTERMATH

This short article, like the one that follows, returns to the "uses of history"—more particularly, the uses and misuses of modern Japanese history—that I first wrestled with in bringing the writings of E.H. Norman back into print in the 1970s. Both were written in conjunction with the U.S. "war on terror" and invasion of Iraq following Al Qaeda's attacks on the World Trade Center and Pentagon on September 11, 2001.

The article appeared as an op-ed essay in the New York Times *at the end of October 2002, when the machinery for war against Iraq was moving into high gear. This is when administration officials began evoking the occupations of Japan and Germany after World War II as models or mirrors—or even talismans of a sort—for the liberalization and pro-American reorientation that could be expected in Iraq once Saddam Hussein was overthrown. Japan quickly emerged as a more seductive putative lodestar than Germany, for obvious reasons: like Iraq, it was non-Western, nonwhite, and non-Christian.*

This was spin and propaganda, like so much else in the run-up to the invasion. At the same time, however, it also reflected the astounding level of wishful thinking that saturated the highest levels of policymaking in the Bush administration. Anyone knowledgeable about Iraq and early postwar Japan recognized that all the key indigenous factors to which we attribute the successful elimination of authoritarianism and militarism in Japan were absent in Iraq. Occupied Japan should have been a red light, rather than the green light the war-makers chose to see.

The op-ed fell like water on stone, of course. What is most interesting in retrospect is that there was nothing original about it. We now know that the same arguments against invasion were being made in much greater detail at lower levels throughout the U.S. civilian and military bureaucracy. That these warnings had no impact on top leaders in the White House is a sobering commentary on the real workings of "democracy" under an imperial presidency. That they were not picked up or pursued in any serious or sustained way by the mainstream media that jumped onboard the invasion is no less disturbing.*

*   *   *

In their immediate response to the shock of September 11, journalists and pundits across America evoked, almost as one, Japan's attack on Pearl Harbor sixty years earlier. Headlines proclaimed a new "day of infamy." Feature stories dwelled on similarities (and differences) between the holy-war fanaticism of the Islamic terrorists and that of the Japanese—and, of course, on the dismal failure of American intelligence to anticipate either attack.

Now, with the Bush administration itself promoting the virtue of preemptive strikes, Japan has emerged as possibly offering a very different sort of historical precedent. Does America's successful occupation of Japan after World War II provide a model for a constructive American role in a post–Saddam Hussein Iraq?

The short answer is no.

By almost all standards, the occupation of defeated Japan was a remarkable success. A repressive and militaristic society emerged from defeat and occupation to become a viable democracy that

---

* The preinvasion warnings in the civilian and military bureaucracies are discussed in Dower, *Cultures of War: Pearl Harbor / Hiroshima / 9-11 / Iraq* (New York: W.W. Norton and The New Press, 2010), which also includes an extended comparison of occupied Japan and occupied Iraq.

has posed no threat to its neighbors for half a century. Naysayers who declared the Japanese people to be culturally incapable of self-government—and their numbers were great in 1945—were proved impressively wrong.

Contrary to what self-anointed "realists" seem to be suggesting today, however, most of the factors that contributed to the success of nation-building in occupied Japan would be absent in an Iraq militarily defeated by the United States.

When war ended in 1945, the United States–dominated occupation of Japan had enormous moral as well as legal legitimacy in the eyes of the rest of the world. This was certainly true throughout Asia, so recently savaged by the Japanese war machine. It was true among America's European allies as well. There was a level of unequivocal regional and global support that a projected U.S. war against Saddam Hussein does not enjoy.

The occupation also had legitimacy in the eyes of almost all Japanese. The Japanese government formally accepted this when it surrendered. Emperor Hirohito, great weather vane that he was, gave his significant personal endorsement to the conquerors. And Japanese at all levels of society quickly blamed their own militaristic leaders for having initiated a miserable, unwinnable war. Saddam Hussein will never morph into a Hirohito figure, and a preemptive war will surely alienate great numbers of Iraqis, even many who might otherwise welcome Mr. Hussein's removal.

In defeat, the Japanese proved to be anything but homogeneous. Political allegiances ran the spectrum from conservatives to Communists. Nonetheless, Japan was spared the religious, ethnic, regional and tribal animosities that are likely to erupt in a postwar Iraq. By the same token, the suicidal fanaticism that characterized Japanese behavior on the battlefield did not survive the war. In an occupation that lasted from 1945 to 1952, there was not one instance of Japanese terror against the occupation forces. Does anyone really imagine this would be the case in an occupied Iraq?

Much of the success of the Japanese occupation derived from the fact that Japan surrendered "unconditionally," thereby ceding absolute and nonnegotiable authority to the victors. The exercise of this authority, moreover, was vested in an unusually charismatic supreme commander, General Douglas MacArthur, who, in effect, was authorized to rule by fiat. It is not conceivable to think of the United States military or any single American commander wielding comparable civil authority in a foreign land today.

Planning for the occupation of Japan actually began in the immediate aftermath of Pearl Harbor, and the general objectives of demilitarization and democratization of the vanquished foe were spelled out in the Potsdam Proclamation of July 1945, weeks before the Japanese government finally capitulated. MacArthur's staff had considerable leeway for creative interpretation of their orders, but those orders reflected long interdepartmental deliberation in Washington, in contrast to today's hasty policymaking.

The great legal and institutional reforms that continue to define Japanese democracy today reflected liberal New Deal policies that now seem testimony to a bygone age: land reform that eliminated widespread rural tenancy at a stroke; serious encouragement of organized labor; the drafting of a new constitution that not only outlawed belligerence by the state, but also guaranteed an extremely progressive range of civil rights to all citizens; restructuring of schools and rewriting of textbooks; revision of both the civil and penal codes, and so on. It is hard to imagine today's "realists" making this sort of lasting, progressive agenda their primary concern.

Ideology aside, the simple logistics of such serious nation-building would seem prohibitive. The key military and civilian personnel who carried out civil-affairs policy under MacArthur numbered around 5,000 to 6,000 individuals at any given time, stationed mostly in Tokyo but also in grassroots offices throughout the country. Many tens of thousands of bilingual Japanese support staff were hired. And for most of the occupation, American military forces—whose mission quickly turned to Cold War objectives rather than the prevention of domestic unrest—numbered more than 100,000 men.

What ultimately enabled the Americans to institutionalize democracy in defeated Japan was not only the existence of strong prewar democratic traditions, but also the survival and cooperation of the existing bureaucracy. The administrative structure remained essentially intact from the central ministries and agencies down to the level of town and village governments, and administrators at all levels often proved genuinely receptive to the vision of a new and better society. Again, it is difficult to imagine a postwar Iraq in which structures of the old regime will provide so ready a vehicle for carrying out far-reaching reforms.

One could easily go on with examples of the unique nature of Japan's occupation. As an island, Japan was physically isolated from neighbors (like China) that soon became hostile to its incorporation in America's Cold War strategy. By contrast, Iraq shares borders with apprehensive and potentially intrusive neighbors.

Of even greater importance, MacArthur and his staff had the period of relative quiet from 1945 to 1947 to concentrate on promoting democratization, while policymakers in Washington were preoccupied with developments in Europe. In the cauldron of Middle East politics, there will be no such period of calm after a war with Iraq.

Defeated Japan also had the blessing of being poor in natural resources and of virtually no economic interest to outsiders. It was spared the presence of carpetbaggers who might have tried to manipulate occupation policy to serve their private interests. In oil-rich Iraq, foreign capital is poised to play a major political as well as economic role.

While occupied Japan provides no model for a postwar Iraq, it does provide a clear warning: Even under circumstances that turned out to be favorable, demilitarization and democratization were awesome challenges. To rush to war without seriously imagining all its consequences, including its aftermath, is not realism but a terrible hubris.

11

THE OTHER JAPANESE OCCUPATION

Any Westerner who spends a career engaged with a non-Western nation or society knows that when it comes to modern or contemporary times, the practice of comparison is a one-way street. "The West" is the model; "the Rest" are evaluated in terms of the degree to which they succeed or fail in approaching the advanced accomplishments of that model. The "modernization theory" paradigm that mesmerized academe when I entered the field in the 1960s was very explicit about this: the measure of "modernity" was how closely other countries converged *with the great accomplishments of the West in science, industry, international contacts, pluralism, "rationality," what have you. It was irrational to suggest that an advanced Western power like the United States might be scrutinized critically against a template of anyone who had the misfortune to belong to "the Rest."*

Prior to March 2003, I had written in several places that occupied Japan was a terribly misleading example to hold up as an indication of what might be expected in a post-invasion Iraq. After the invasion, as the heavy-handed U.S. military occupation unfolded, I was struck by a different, thoroughly heretical, model for what was taking place: the Japanese invasion of Manchuria in 1931, followed by the creation of the puppet state Manchukuo one year later. Of course the parallels were not exact. In critical areas, the differences were immense: the United States was a democracy of sorts, for example, whereas imperial Japan was not.

*But both countries were militaristic; high rhetoric and low deeds charac-
terized both invasions and both occupations; in each case, enormous public
and private resources were poured into what we now call nation-building;
and once one began pulling at this thread, various other sorts of resonance
between 1930s Japan and early twenty-first-century America began to
emerge. This little essay suggesting a range of places where comparison of
the undertakings in Manchuria and Iraq can be illuminating appeared
in* The Nation *in June 2003, three months after the invasion.*

*Almost no one bought this argument, so far as I am aware; but I
still am not ready to discard it. The essence of what patriots speak of as
"American exceptionalism" is that the United States is superlative in
virtue and, in this and most everything else in the moral and material
worlds, beyond compare. Much of the chatter about "the West and the
Rest" rests on a similar presumption—and so does the popular vogue of
"clash of civilizations" thinking as most Westerners embrace this. Serious
historical comparisons, however, crosscut time and place.*

* * *

As we enter a dramatically altered world, both internationally
and domestically, it is only natural that we look to history for
bearings, points of comparison, glimmerings of the familiar. In
these predictable uses of the past, "Japan" has emerged as a small
trope for both horror and hope. Thus, September 11 became our
generation's Pearl Harbor (headline writers across America turned,
almost instinctively, to "Day of Infamy!"). Our new enemies have
been declared an "axis of evil" (with North Korea presumably re-
placing the Japan of the 1930s). And now we have the sanguine scenario of the democratization of "occupied Japan" after World War
II as a model for post-hostilities Iraq.

None of those analogies withstand serious scrutiny, and looking back at occupied Japan should really remind us both how fundamentally different Iraq is from the Japan of 1945 and also how
far the United States itself has departed from the ideals of a half-
century ago. Liberalism, internationalism, serious commitment to

human rights, a vision of economic democratization in which the state is assigned an important role—these were watchwords of the Americans who formulated initial policy for occupied Japan. In the Bush administration, they are objects of derision.

There are, in any case, several other mid-century Asian occupations that may deserve close analysis when evaluating U.S. policy today. Two of these—in Okinawa and South Korea—were conducted under the same American "supreme command" that presided over the occupation of Japan proper. A third, surely most suggestive and provocative, is the Japanese occupation of Manchuria, which began in 1931 and soon extended to China south of the Great Wall and eventually to Southeast Asia.

Okinawa and South Korea are instructive as reminders that where security concerns were paramount from the start, the United States turned its back on serious "democratization" of the sort initially introduced to the greater part of Japan. Coveted by military strategists as a great stationary aircraft carrier off the coast of Asia, Okinawa, Japan's southernmost prefecture, was immediately turned into a huge U.S. military installation. Although the occupation of Japan formally ended in April 1952, Okinawa remained a U.S. colony until the early 1970s, when sovereignty was returned to Japan. The sprawling, grotesque complex of U.S. bases remains.

In South Korea, as in the northern half of that tragically divided country, autocratic rule followed ostensible liberation from Japanese colonialism in 1945. Stability and anti-Communism were the bedrock of U.S. occupation and post-occupation policy, and it took decades before the people of South Korea themselves succeeded in throwing off America's client regimes and establishing a more democratic society.

It is the almost forgotten interlude of Japan as an occupying power in Manchuria and later China, however, that poses the most intriguing analogy to the creation of a new American imperium today. Obviously, there are enormous differences between the two cases. Imperial Japan was not a hyperpower when it launched its campaign of accelerated empire-building in 1931. Its propagandists did not spout the rhetoric of democratization, privatization and free markets that fills the air today. Domestically, Japan operated under the aegis of a real emperor, rather than behind the shield of an imperial presidency.

Still, the points of resonance between the abortive Japanese empire and the burgeoning American one are striking. In both instances, we confront empire-building embedded in a larger agenda of right-wing radicalism. And in each, we find aggressive and essentially unilateral international policies wedded to a sweeping transformation of domestic priorities and practices.

Scholars are only now beginning to appreciate fully how perversely "modern" imperial Japan's mobilization for war and accelerated expansion actually was. Self-styled patriotic renovationists not only seized the initiative in calling for a "new order" abroad and "new structure" at home but also made it clear that these goals were inseparable. Their exhortations were bold and articulate.

They did not hesitate to employ subterfuge, intimidation, and fait accompli to achieve their ends. They forged potent alliances of corporate, bureaucratic, and political interests while vesting unprecedented power in the military. And they mobilized popular support domestically through masterful manipulation of a newly emergent mass media.

In retrospect, we tend to dwell on the hubris and madness of these men. Their short-lived empire is dismissed as little more than a "dream within a dream," to borrow a Japanese phrase, but this is too simple. In their passing moment of devastating triumph, these right-wing radicals not only changed the face of Asia in unanticipated ways but also permanently transformed Japan. And their great concerns, aspirations and accomplishments find eerie echo in much of what we behold in U.S. policy today. Regime change, nation-building, creation of client states, control of strategic resources, defiance of international criticism, mobilization for "total war," clash-of-civilizations rhetoric, winning hearts and minds, combating terror at home as well as abroad—all these were part and parcel of Japan's vainglorious attempt to create a new order of "coexistence and co-prosperity" in Asia.

It is testimony to the peculiar power of the silver screen that Bernardo Bertolucci's 1987 epic *The Last Emperor*, winner of an impressive nine Academy Awards, managed to fascinate movie-goers without restoring the Japanese quest for hegemony on the Asian continent to popular memory. The new stage of empire in Asia began in 1931 when Japan, which had long exercised neocolonial control over Manchuria in collaboration with local warlords, seized the region in the wake of a bogus casus belli. (Elements in Japan's Kwantung Army blew up railway tracks controlled by the Japanese near Mukden and blamed indigenous forces.) The following year, the puppet state of "Manchukuo" was established under the regency of Pu Yi, the "last emperor" of the Manchu dynasty, which ruled China from 1643 until 1911. In 1933 Japan withdrew from the League of Nations in response to condemnation of its defiant unilateralism.

This exercise in what we now euphemistically refer to as regime change was subsequently extended to China south of the Great Wall, where the eruption of all-out war in 1937 left Japan in control of the entire eastern seaboard and a population of some 200 million Chinese. In 1941, bogged down in China and desperate for additional strategic resources, the imperial war machine advanced into the colonial enclaves of Southeast Asia (French Indochina; the Dutch East Indies; America's Philippines colony; and Great Britain's Hong Kong, Malaya, and Burma). The attack on Pearl Harbor was in today's terminology a preemptive strike aimed at delaying America's response to this so-called liberation of Asia.

"Liberation" was the consistent byword of Japan's advances—liberation from warlords, guerrillas, "bandits," and generalized chaos in Manchuria and China proper; liberation from the uncertainty and rapacity of the global capitalist system in the wake of the Great Depression; liberation from the "Red Peril" of Soviet-led international Communism and the "White Peril" of European and American colonialism. In the grandest of ideological formulations, Japanese propagandists evoked the image of a decisive clash between "East" and "West"—manichean hooey as seductive then as it is today.

While the takeover of Manchuria initially produced deep anxiety in Japan, this was soon dispelled by a great wave of patriotic solidarity. ("A hundred million hearts beating as one" was the analogue to today's "united we stand.") Propagandists evoked the same rhetoric of mission and Manifest Destiny that had animated European and U.S. expansionists. They even appropriated the language of America's Monroe Doctrine by defending the seizure of Manchuria as part of creating a new "Monroe sphere in Asia." It was acknowledged that control of Manchuria would guarantee access to strategic raw materials (notably iron and coal), but the greater objective was, of course, peace and prosperity. The establishment of Manchukuo, it was declared, would bring about an unprecedented "harmony of the five races" (Japanese, Chinese, Manchus, Mongolians, and Koreans). Beyond this, and of far greater significance, Manchukuo was envisioned as a perfect pilot project for establishing a political economy consistent with the most basic ideals of the radical right-wing agenda.

The evocative catchphrase of those heady days was "Manchuria as ideology," and the ideology embraced was on the surface very different from that trumpeted by the hard-core ideologues of a new American empire today. In the wake of the Depression, which had savaged Japan as it had the rest of the world, the very notion of "free markets" and unrestrained capitalism was, to put it mildly, unpalatable. In this milieu, Manchukuo was seized upon as an ideal opportunity to introduce a new model of "state capitalism" or "national socialism."

Even this great difference, however, does not diminish the many points of similarity between the Japanese and the American cases. As always, the devil is in the details, and the most interesting details concern the manner in which adoption of a positive policy abroad was accompanied by a sweeping reordering of the domestic political economy. As in the United States today, governing circles in imperial Japan were riddled with factionalism. Out of these internecine struggles, elements associated with the military emerged as dominant, led by the "Control Faction" (*Tōsei-ha*), associated with General and later Prime Minister Tōjō Hideki.

The Control Faction's name had a dual origin. It implied controlling other factions, including more hotheaded rightists. More important, it signaled a dedication to harnessing the economy, and society as a whole, to the ultimate objective of creating a capacity to wage "total war." The "total war" concept had captured the imagination of military planners since World War I. The "Manchurian incident" of 1931 made it possible to put these plans into effect.

Politically, mobilization for total war entailed military domination of domestic as well as international policy. The Ministry of Foreign Affairs—Japan's counterpart to our State Department—was shouldered aside. Economic ministries and agencies became handmaidens to military demands. The Home Ministry—roughly comparable to the Justice Department and the Department of Homeland Security—intensified its role in domestic policing and the suppression of "dangerous thoughts." (The 1930s also witnessed a number of home-grown terrorist incidents in Japan, involving assassinations of prominent figures and, in 1936, a major attempted coup d'état.) The elective Diet or parliament became a rubber stamp. Communists and leftists in great numbers publicly recanted their criticism of the imperial state and declared themselves to be devoted to bringing about "revolution under the brocade banner" of the emperor. The mass media, hamstrung by formal censorship, also practiced self-censorship. Once the war machine had been put in motion, and a "blood debt" to the war dead established, it was inconceivable not to support the emperor's loyal troops.

* * *

Economically, mobilization for total war was particularly striking in its modernity—a notion that overturns the once-fashionable argument that backwardness and "feudal legacies" precipitated Japan's drive for control of Asia. The national budget was tilted overwhelmingly toward military-related expenditures. The decade after the seizure of Manchuria witnessed what academics now refer to as Japan's "second industrial revolution," marked by the takeoff of heavy and chemical industries. A massive wave of mergers took place, not only in the industrial and financial sectors but in the mass media as well.

Before the 1930s, the modern Japanese economy was dominated by four huge *zaibatsu*, or conglomerate-type business combines (Mitsui, Mitsubishi, Sumitomo, and Yasuda). After the takeover of Manchuria, the "big four" became major suppliers of the military, major beneficiaries of development projects in occupied areas, major actors in the suppression of a nascent labor union movement, and major contributors to the consolidation of a domestic "dual structure" characterized by increasing disparities of wealth and power.

At the same time, the 1930s also witnessed the emergence of a technologically innovative corporate sector known as the "new zaibatsu" (*shinko zaibatsu*), which was primarily devoted to military contracting and empire-building. Like the big four—and like the cutting-edge U.S. corporations clamoring to get in on the gravy train of today's "war on terror"—these new zaibatsu worked hand in glove with the military and cultivated what we now call crony capitalism. By war's end, the six largest new zaibatsu (Asano, Furukawa, Nissan, Okura, Nomura, and Nakajima) accounted for more than 16 percent of paid-in capital in mining, chemical, and heavy industries, while the share of the big four had increased to more than 32 percent. When all was said and done, "national socialism" proved very hospitable to aggressive privatization.

Within the civilian ministries, the counterpart to the military hawks and innovative new zaibatsu was a loosely linked cadre known as the "new bureaucrats" (*shin kanryō*) or "renovationist bureaucrats" (*kakushin kanryō*)—accomplished technocrats devoted to wedding the new order abroad to new institutional structures at home. Adversaries and factional opponents may have denounced these men as rogue bureaucrats—or rogue capitalists, or rogue military—but the rogues were in the saddle.

Although we speak of a military takeover of Japan in the 1930s, electoral politics and most functions of civil society continued through war into the postwar era. Tōjō himself was eased from power, in proper parliamentary manner, in 1944. No one could stop the machine he and his fellow right-wing radicals had set in motion, however, until the war came home, culminating in Hiroshima and Nagasaki. Japan's was a short ride as empires go, but the devastation left in its wake was enormous.

Despite the deepening quagmire of occupation and empire, Japanese leaders and followers alike soldiered on—driven by patriotic ardor and a pitiful fatalism. It was only afterward, in the wake of defeat, that pundits and politicians and ordinary people stepped back to ask: How could we have been so deceived?

We are in a better position to answer this now.

SOURCES

1. "E.H. Norman and the Uses of History" is excerpted from the introduction to John W. Dower, ed., *Origins of the Modern Japanese State: Selected Writings of E. H. Norman* (Pantheon Books, 1975), 3–5, 80–93. The full introduction in the original printing runs from pages 3 to 101.

2. This illustrated version of "Race, Language, and War in Two Cultures: World War II in Asia" appeared in Lewis A. Erenberg and Susan E. Hirsch, eds., *The War in American Culture: Society and Consciousness During World War II* (University of Chicago Press, 1996), 169–201. [For copyright reasons, Figure 2-3 replaces an American newspaper cartoon that is no longer accessible.] An earlier version of this essay, without illustrations, appeared in Dower, *Japan in War and Peace* (The New Press, 1993).

3. "Japan's Beautiful Modern War" appeared in a lavishly illustrated exhibition catalog edited by Jacqueline M. Atkins under the title *Wearing Propaganda: Textiles on the Home Front in Japan, Britain, and the United States, 1931–1945* (Yale University Press, for The Bard Graduate Center for Studies in the Decorative Arts, Design, and Culture, 2005), 93–113.

4. "'An Aptitude for Being Unloved': War and Memory in Japan" appeared in Omer Bartov, Atina Grossmann, and Mary Nolan, eds., *Crimes of War: Guilt and Denial in the Twentieth Century* (The New Press, 2002), 217–41, 313–21.

5. "The Bombed: Hiroshimas and Nagasakis in Japanese Memory" originally appeared in a symposium published in *Diplomatic History* 19, no. 2 (Spring 1995): 275–95. The symposium was subsequently reprinted as a book edited by Michael J. Hogan under the title *Hiroshima in History and Memory* (Cambridge University Press, 1996), 116–42.

6. "A Doctor's Diary of Hiroshima, Fifty Years Later" was written as a foreword to the fiftieth anniversary edition of Michihiko Hachiya, *Hiroshima Diary: The Journal of a Japanese Physician, August 6–September 30, 1945: Fifty Years Later* (University of North Carolina Press, 1995), v–xvii.

7. "How a Genuine Democracy Should Celebrate Its Past" appeared as an op-ed in the *Chronicle of Higher Education*, June 16, 1995.

8. "Peace and Democracy in Two Systems: External Policy and Internal Conflict" appeared in Andrew Gordon, ed., *Postwar Japan as History* (University of California Press, 1993), 3–33.

9. "Mocking Misery: Grassroots Satire in Defeated Japan" appeared in Gail Lee Bernstein, Andrew Gordon, and Kate Wildman Nakai, eds., *Public Spheres, Private Lives in Modern Japan, 1600–1950* (Harvard University Asia Center, 2005), 345–74. This volume was a Festschrift in honor of Professor Albert M. Craig.

10. "Lessons from Japan about War's Aftermath" appeared as an op-ed in the *New York Times*, October 27, 2002.

11. "The Other Japanese Occupation" was published in *The Nation*, July 7, 2003. A revised excerpt from this, focusing on imperial Japan's grand policy in China including Manchuria, was published in Stephen R. MacKinnon, Diana Lary, and Ezra F. Vogel, eds., *China at War: Regions of China, 1937–1945* (Stanford University Press, 2007), 17–21.

NOTES

1. E.H. NORMAN, JAPAN, AND THE USES OF HISTORY

1. James Morley, "Introduction," in James Morley, ed., *Dilemmas of Growth in Prewar Japan* (Princeton University Press, 1972).

2. Shlomo Avineri, *Social and Political Thought of Karl Marx* (Cambridge University Press, 1971), 65.

3. Cf. Morley, *Dilemmas of Growth in Prewar Japan*, 12.

2. RACE, LANGUAGE, AND WAR IN TWO CULTURES: WORLD WAR II IN ASIA

This chapter summarizes some of the themes developed at length in my *War Without Mercy: Race and Power in the Pacific War* (Pantheon Books, 1986), where extensive annotations can be found. Here I have focused in particular on racial language in comparative perspective.

1. "Answer to Japan," 20. This report appears in several archival collections at the Hoover Institution, Stanford University. Cf. "Bonner Frank Fellers Collection," boxes 1 and 15; also "U.S. Army Forces in the Pacific, Psychological Warfare Branch," box l.

2. From Hino's 1942 book *Bātān Hantō Kōjōki*, as quoted in Haruko Taya Cook, "Voices from the Front: Japanese War Literature, 1937–1945" (M.A. thesis in Asian Studies, University of California, Berkeley, 1984), 59–60.

3. I have addressed these themes in contemporary U.S.-Japan relations in greater detail in *Japan in War and Peace* (The New Press, 1993), 279–335.

3. JAPAN'S BEAUTIFUL MODERN WAR

1. Some of the themes concerning Japanese, American and British attitudes during the war that are touched on in this essay were introduced in John W. Dower, *War Without Mercy: Race and Power in the Pacific War* (Pantheon Books, 1986), and are reprised in chapter 2 in this present volume. Academic and polemical writings on the Rape of Nanking have proliferated in recent years. For a balanced overview of Chinese, Japanese, and English-language writings, see Daqing Yang, "Convergence or Divergence? Recent Historical Writings on the Rape of Nanjing," *American Historical Review* (June 1999): 842–65. See also Joshua A. Fogel, ed., *The Nanking Massacre in History and Historiography* (University of California Press, 2000), which also includes an essay by Yang.

2. For general fatality estimates, see Dower, *War Without Mercy*, 293–300. The Japanese figures would include more than 100,000 killed in successive air raids on Tokyo, beginning with the great attack of March 9–10, 1945; another 200,000 to 300,000 killed in the conventional firebombing of over 63 other Japanese cities that followed the first Tokyo air raid; more than 200,000 killed by the atomic bombing of Hiroshima (an estimated 140,000 dead) and Nagasaki (an estimated 75,000 dead); some 100,000 to 150,000 civilians killed in the Battle of Okinawa that ended in June 1945; and perhaps 100,000 civilians who perished attempting to return from Manchuria in the wake of Japan's defeat.

3. For an extended analysis of the cherry-blossom imagery, see Emiko Ohnuki-Tierney, *Kamikaze, Cherry Blossoms, and Nationalism: The Militarization of Aesthetics in Japanese History* (University of Chicago Press, 2002). The following song, popular among naval cadets and titled "Cherry Blossoms of the Same Class," is quoted in ibid., 141: "You and I are two cherry blossoms. We bloom in the shadow of a pile of sand bags; / Since we are flowers, we are doomed to fall. Let us fall magnificently for the country. . . . / You and I are two cherry blossoms. Even if we fall separately, / the capital of flowers is Yasukuni Shrine. We meet each other in the treetops in the spring."

4. The full imperial rescripts announcing both the initiation and end of the war are reprinted in numerous sources. See, for example, the appendices in Edwin P. Hoyt, *Japan's War: The Great Pacific Conflict, 1853–1952* (Da Capo Press, 1986). Hoyt notes that the 1941 rescript was reprinted every month.

5. For the full 1937 tract, see Japan Ministry of Education, *"Kokutai no Hongi": Cardinal Principles of the National Entity of Japan*, trans. John O. Gauntlett and ed. Robert K. Hall (Harvard University Press, 1949). The 1940 "Way of the Subject" appears as an appendix in Otto D. Tolischus, *Tokyo Record* (Reynal & Hitchcock, 1943), 405–27. Also of interest in this regard is Robert K. Hall, *Shūshin: The Ethics of a Defeated Nation* (Columbia University Press, 1949). The Japanese cartoon is reproduced in Dower, *War Without Mercy*, 191.

6. For a very explicit expression of this, see Nyozekan Hasegawa, "Beautifying War," in the English-language magazine *Nippon* 16 (1938): 18ff. Hasegawa was a well-known Japanese cultural commentator.

7. The Kyoto School of philosophers, which took its name from Kyoto Imperial University and was associated with the particularly influential ideas of Nishida Kitarō, has attracted close scrutiny (and considerable controversy) in recent years concerning its intellectual contributions to the rise of nationalism and militarism in Japan. See James W. Heisig and John C. Maraldo, eds., *Rude Awakenings: Zen, the Kyoto School, and the Question of Nationalism* (University of Hawai'i Press, 1994).

8. See Tetsuo Najita and H.D. Harootunian, "Japanese Revolt against the West: Political and Cultural Criticism in the Twentieth Century," in Peter Duus, ed., *The Cambridge History of Japan: Volume 6—The Twentieth Century* (Cambridge University Press, 1988), 711–74. This volume includes survey articles by leading Japanese and non-Japanese scholars.

9. On the modernity of Manchuria and Japan's accelerated overseas expansion in the 1930s, see Louise Young, *Japan's Total Empire: Manchuria and the Culture of Wartime Imperialism* (University of California Press, 1998); also Bill Sewell, "Reconsidering the Modern in Japanese History: Modernity in the Service of the Prewar Japanese Empire," *Japan Review* 16 (2004): 213–58; this "Journal of the International Research Center for Japanese Studies" is published by Nichibunken (Kyoto).

10. For a standard periodization of Japan's modern economic growth that calls attention to the "second industrial revolution,"

see Kazushi Ohkawa and Henry Rosovsky, "A Century of Japanese Economic Growth," in William W. Lockwood, ed., *The State and Economic Enterprise in Japan* (Princeton University Press, 1965), 47–92.

11. For concise general discussions of Japan at war, see Ronald H. Spector, *Eagle Against the Sun: The American War with Japan* (New York: Vintage Books, 1985), especially chapter 2 on Japanese states of mind prior to Pearl Harbor; also Gordon W. Prange, with Donald M. Goldstein and Katherine V. Dillon, *Pearl Harbor: The Verdict of History* (McGraw Hill, 1986), especially chaps. 29–31. The most accessible critical work by a Japanese scholar, drawing on voluminous Japanese-language resources is Saburō Ienaga, *The Pacific War, 1931–1945* (New York: Pantheon, 1978; originally published in Japanese in 1968).

12. The modern girl persona emerges vividly in Tanizaki Jun'ichirō's novel *Chijin no Ai* (A Fool's Love) serialized in 1924–25 and translated by Anthony Chambers as *Naomi* (Vintage, 2001). For a recent scholarly study, see Barbara Sato, *The New Japanese Woman: Modernity, Media and Women in Interwar Japan* (Duke University Press, 2003). In the late 1920s and early 1930s, the modern girl and modern boy vogue morphed into a more twisted popular trend identified as *ero-guro-nan-sensu*—borrowed English for the erotic, grotesque, and nonsensical. Here, the rise of militarism and intensification of domestic repression were accompanied by decadent, perverted, and manic behavior and expression comparable to that taking place in Germany at the same time.

13. The sumptuously illustrated magazine *Taiyō* has devoted a number of special issues (*Bessatsu Taiyō*) to late nineteenth- and early twentieth-century children's culture in Japan. See, for example, *Kodomo Asobishō* (Spring 1985, on toys, games, and the like); *Kodomo no Shōwa shi, 1935–1945* (August 1986); and *Ehon* and *Ehon II* (Spring 1984 and Autumn 1984, on illustrated books).

14. For an outstanding collection of poster art from 1860 to 1956, see Japan Art Directors Group, ed., *Nihon no kōkoku bijutsu—Meiji, Taishō, Shōwa* (Bijutsu Shuppansha, 1967).

15. The classic Japanese survey of prewar Japanese photography is Nihon Shashinka Kyōkai (Japan Photographers Association), ed., *Nihon shashin shi, 1840–1945* (Heibonsha, 1971); for an English adaptation with an introduction and bibliography on the visual history of modern Japan by John W. Dower, see *A Century of Japanese Photography* (Pantheon, 1980). For a broad recent survey, see Anne Wilkes Tucker et al., *A History of Japanese Photography*, the catalogue for a major exhibition at the

Houston Museum of Fine Arts (Yale University Press, 2003). Iwanami's *Nihon no shashinka* (Photographers of Japan) series consists of forty slim, elegant volumes, the first of which appeared in 1998.

16. Modern Japanese art is reproduced in numerous Japanese publications. For an excellent exhibition catalogue in English, focusing on Western-influenced oil painting, see Shūji Takashina and J. Thomas Rimer, with Gerald D. Bolas, *Paris in Japan: The Japanese Encounter with European Painting* (The Japan Foundation and Washington University, 1987).

17. On the "war responsibility" debates in Japan, see Laura Hein and Mark Selden, eds., *Censoring History: Citizenship and Memory in Japan, Germany, and the United States* (M.E. Sharpe, 2000), especially the contribution by Gavan McCormack; also John W. Dower, "'An Aptitude for Being Unloved': War and Memory in Japan," reprinted in chapter 4 in this present volume.

18. The more intriguing wartime propaganda campaign in China, still largely withheld from scholarly or popular scrutiny, would be the films, posters, and general sloganeering the Japanese directed, with Chinese collaboration, at the Chinese audience.

19. Capra is quoted in "Japan at War: Rare Films from World War II," the informative program that accompanied a 1987 presentation by the Japan Society of New York of twenty-seven Japanese films made between 1937 and 1947. The films, all subtitled for this retrospective, were subsequently returned to the National Archives (most of them had been seized at the outset of World War II)—a treasure trove essentially rendered inaccessible again to the general English-speaking public. An analysis of Japanese war films based on this series is given in "Japanese Cinema Goes to War," in Dower, *Japan in War and Peace*, 33–54.

20. See, for example, the Hollywood formulas delineated in Jeanine Basinger, *The World War II Combat Film: Anatomy of a Genre* (Columbia University Press, 1986), and "The Beast in the Jungle," chapter 9 in Clayton R. Koopes and Gregory D. Black, *Hollywood Goes to War: How Politics, Profits and Propaganda Shaped World War II Movies* (The Free Press, 1987).

21. Although Kurosawa recalls *The Most Beautiful* with affection in his memoirs, as of 2004 it had fallen under the tacit censorship that still governs propagandistic treatments from Japan's war years. Unlike his many other films, it still had not been made commercially available with English subtitles.

The contrast between Japanese and Hollywood films extends to animated cartoons. The American cartoons involved slapstick mayhem against generic short, buck-toothed, slant-eyed figures who wore horn-rim glasses and kept saying things like "So solly." The "Popeye" cartoons were a perfect expression of this, as their titles alone suggest ("Scrap the Japs," "You're a Sap, Mister Jap"). Looney Tunes propagated the stereotype of buck-toothed idiots in a series titled *Tokio Jokio*. The wittiest rendering of these cartoon clichés was *Bugs Bunny Nips the Nips*. By contrast, the major Japanese animation—which did not appear until near the end of the war—was a long, innovative treatment that wedded Japanese folklore and children's culture (the story of "Momotarō," the Peach Boy) to long-ago history (inserted as a shadow-play account of the European conquest of a peaceful Southeast Asian kingdom). The film placed all this in the imagined rendering of Japanese paratroopers capturing a British stronghold in the South Seas and forcing its absurd and craven officers (who had demonic horns on their heads) to agree to unconditional surrender. The enemy officers actually spoke British English—with subtitles in Japanese that made it clear that adults were a major part of the intended audience. Titled *Momotarō to Umi no Shinpei* (Momotarō and the Divine Troops of the Ocean), this was propaganda with a vengeance—but also with levels of artistic finesse and conceptual complexity very different from the poke-in-the-eye jocularity of Popeye and Bugs Bunny. The "Momotarō paradigm" is discussed in Dower, *War Without Mercy*, 251–57.

22. Before the confiscated Japanese paintings were returned to Japan, they were copied for reproduction in an elaborate but little-known U.S. government publication: see *Reports of General MacArthur: Japanese Operations in the Southwest Pacific Area, vol. 2, pts. I and II* (1966); these two volumes include scores of glossy reproductions. The major compilation of these paintings appeared shortly after their return to Japan in *Taiheiyō sensō meigashū* (Nobelsha, 1967). This carries the English title *The Pacific War Art Collection* and romanizes artists' names and translates picture titles in the captions. There are one hundred plates in this large-format volume, which remains the major source for accessing this remarkable artwork.

4. "AN APTITUDE FOR BEING UNLOVED": WAR AND MEMORY IN JAPAN

1. Watanabe Kazuo, *Haisen Nikki* (Diary of defeat), ed. Kushida Magoichi and Ninomiya Atsushi (Hakubunkan Shinsha, 1995), 36–38,

56–58, 77. The passage in question appeared in Romain Rolland's *Au-dessus de la melée,* and the original German phrase that Rolland quoted and Watanabe rendered as "aptitude for being unloved" (*aisarenu nōryoku; aisarenai nōryoku*) was *Unbeliebtheit.* The 1946 essay is reprinted in ibid., 43–48. In 1970, Watanabe added a very brief "postscript" to this essay expressing concern that Japanese pride in emerging as an industrial power was but one more reflection of the superficiality that caused his compatriots to be so unloved.

2. By "Germany," I refer primarily to the former "West Germany" here.

3. High Japanese government officials have in fact made numerous public statements of "regret" and "apology" concerning imperial Japan's acts of colonialism (especially in Korea) and belligerency and atrocity in World War II. Some of these statements have been quite forthright, but few have attracted widespread media attention outside of Japan. None has been praised for being a statesman-like, *emblematic* utterance comparable to the famous speech delivered by Germany's former president Richard von Weizsacker on May 8, 1985, the fortieth anniversary of Germany's surrender. It is noteworthy, and hardly a coincidence, that the two most unequivocal statements acknowledging Japan's war responsibility were delivered by prime ministers who headed short-lived coalition cabinets and were not affiliated with the Liberal Democratic Party: Hosokawa Morihiro in 1993 and Murayama Tomiichi on the occasion of the fiftieth anniversary of the end of the war in 1995. For a detailed critical summary of official Japanese statements on the war, see Wakamiya Yoshibumi, *The Postwar Conservative View of Asia: How the Political Right Has Delayed Japan's Coming to Terms with Its History of Aggression in Asia* (LICB International Library Foundation, 1998). Wakamiya is an editor at the *Asahi Shimbun* newspaper, and this volume is a translation of his 1995 book *Sengo Hoshu no Ajia Kan.* Ian Buruma offers a comparative study of German and Japanese recollections of the war in *The Wages of Guilt: Memories of War in Germany and Japan* (Farrar, Straus and Giroux, 1994). See also Thomas U. Berger, *Cultures of Antimilitarism: National Security in Germany and Japan* (The Johns Hopkins University Press, 1998). For a comparative study focusing on textbooks, see Laura Hein and Mark Selden, eds., *Censoring History: Citizenship and Memory in Japan, Germany, and the United States* (M.E. Sharpe, 2000). The issue of massaging official statements of apology for the war so as not to besmirch

the memory of Japan's own war dead emerged vividly in 1995, when the Diet debated (and watered down) a formal statement on the fiftieth anniversary of the end of the war. For a selection of translated documents from this debate, see John W. Dower, "Japan Addresses Its War Responsibility," *ii: The Journal of the International Institute* (newsletter of the International Institute, University of Michigan) 3, no. 1 (Autumn 1995): 8–11.

4. Mori was forced to step down as party head and prime minister in April 2001, after merely a year in office. The manner in which his "land of the gods" comment triggered a critical public debate on national identity is exemplified by a series of guest essays initiated in August 2000 in the influential daily newspaper *Asahi Shimbun* under the topical title "Land of the Gods, Land of the People" (*Kami no Kuni, Hito no Kuni*). The general thrust of the series was to demonstrate in detail how reactionary and anachronistic Mori's rhetoric was. At the same time, however, non-Japanese—and Americans in particular—should keep in mind how *typical* Mori's rhetoric is of conservative nationalism in general. To give but one recent example, in the U.S. presidential campaign of 2000, the Democratic vice-presidential candidate called the United States "the most religious country in the world" and spoke of all Americans as being "children of the same awesome God," while the Republican presidential candidate was proclaiming that "Our nation is chosen by God and commissioned by history to be a model to the world of justice and inclusion and diversity without division" (*New York Times*, August 29, 2000).

5. The *Yomiuri* poll, based on a random sample of 3,000 individuals, was published on October 5, 1993, and is reproduced in the October 1993 issue of the Japanese government publication *Japan Views* (10). The full poll results are as follows:

WAS JAPAN AN "AGGRESSOR"?

	Agree (%)	Disagree (%)	No Response (%)
TOTAL	53.1	24.8	22.1
Age over 70	41.1	39.5	19.5
60s	49.1	33.6	17.3
50s	48.4	27.6	24.0
40s	56.0	21.5	22.5
30s	57.4	15.4	27.3
20s	61.7	17.1	21.2

6. The "Carthage" quote appears in an essay by Namikawa Eita in Japanese Society for History Textbook Reform, *The Restoration of a National History: Why Was the Japanese Society for History Textbook Reform Established, and What Are Its Goals?* (Tokyo, 1998), 15. This pamphlet, published in English, was widely distributed among English-speaking Japan specialists. The society (whose slightly differently named Japanese parent group is the Atarashii Rekishi Kyōkasho o Tsukuru Kai) is one of two influential organizations founded in the mid-1990s by Fujioka Nobukatsu, a professor of education at the University of Tokyo. The other organization is the misleadingly named Liberal View of History Study Group (Jiyūshugi Shikan Kenkyūkai). Numerous books and countless articles have been promoted by these organizations, including a huge (775 pages) new "History of the Japanese People" (*Kokumin no Rekishi*) written by Professor Nishio Kanji (a specialist in German literature at Electro-Communications University), and published in 1999 by Sankei Shimbunsha (publisher of the conservative national newspaper *Sankei*, a major mouthpiece for the revisionist position). Nishio's book became an immediate bestseller. For an incisive introduction to these groups and activities, see Gavan McCormack's essay on "The Japanese Movement to 'Correct' History," in Hein and Selden, *Censoring History*.

7. These "typologies" are, of course, open-ended. Space permitting, it would have been fruitful to explore at least two other "kinds of memory" here. One is the manner in which "national memory" is *doubly* mediated and manipulated by others (how Chinese and Americans, for example, tend to set simplistic negative renderings of the situation in Japan against equally selective positive constructions of their own history and contemporary collective mind-set). The other might be called, in the Japanese case, "legally suffocated memory" (referring specifically to the manner in which official fears of costly lawsuits have prompted the Japanese government to dismiss current individual claims for redress and reparations). For a recent study of war memory sensitive to the approaches of contemporary critical theory, see Yoshiyuki Igarashi, *Bodies of Memory: Narratives of War in Postwar Japanese Culture, 1945–1970* (Princeton University Press, 2000). I address the multiple memories associated with just the atomic-bomb experience in chapter 5 in this present volume.

8. A high point in the revisionist campaign to promote a "correct" view of history occurred in early 2001, when the conservative activists succeeded in gaining certification of a middle-school history textbook

reflecting their position. To gain such certification, the publisher and authors agreed to some 137 large and small changes. Among the more revealing of these was a passage in the epilogue that originally read as follows: "After the war (in which as many as 700,000 civilians were killed in indiscriminate bombing, culminating in the atomic bombs), the direction the country should take was determined by the Occupation force, and Japan has remained under this influence to the present day. . . . Regrettably, the scars of defeat have not healed after more than fifty years. Because of this, the Japanese are on the verge of losing their independent spirit." In the version approved by the central government, this was revised as follows: "As many as 700,000 civilians were killed in indiscriminate bombing, culminating in the atomic bombs. After the war, the Japanese people, through great effort, achieved economic recovery and attained a position among the world leaders, but in spite of this they still lack self-confidence. . . . Regrettably, the scars of defeat have not healed." The controversy concerning this textbook (and a companion "civics" volume) is covered in considerable detail in *Asahi Shimbun*, April 4, 2001.

9. I have discussed the problems of the Tokyo trial at length in chapter 15 of my *Embracing Defeat: Japan in the Wake of World War II* (W.W. Norton and The New Press, 1999). The most dramatic recent use of Pal's dissenting opinion by the conservative revisionists took the form of a slick 1998 feature film titled *Pride: The Fatal Moment* (*Puraidu: Unmei no Toki*). Conceived and promoted by prominent conservatives, and funded by a nationalistic entrepreneur, this was a courtroom drama that re-created the physical setting and *defense* arguments of the Tokyo trial with considerable skill. Although former general and prime minister Tōjō Hideki, the trial's best-known defendant, emerges as a flawed leader but humane and sincere victim of "victor's justice," the elegant and irreproachable hero of the film is Justice Pal himself. *Pride* is a dishonest film (its treatment of atrocities such as the Rape of Nanking, for example, is reprehensible), but its presentation of half-stories and half-truths is exceedingly clever.

10. "The Forgotten Holocaust of World War II" is the subtitle of Iris Chang's phenomenal international best-seller, *The Rape of Nanking* (Basic Books, 1997). In Japan, such rhetoric and the broader flawed analogies that lie behind it (compounded by a number of petty factual errors in this particular case) has turned what could have been a persuasive indictment of Japanese war behavior into a perfect straw man for those who argue that Japan's critics have no interest in even getting the

facts straight. Substantial right-wing money has been poured into attempts to counter Chang's indictment in English-language publications distributed gratis outside Japan. See, for example, Takemoto Tadao and Ohara Yasuo, *The Alleged 'Nanking Massacre': Japan's Rebuttal to China's Forged Claims* (Meiseisha, 2000); Tanaka Masaaki, *What Really Happened in Nanking: The Refutation of a Common Myth* (Sekai Shuppan, 2000); and Hata Ikuhiko, "Nanking: Setting the Record Straight," *Japan Echo 25*, no. 4 (August 1998).

11. At the Tokyo tribunal, the prosecution calculated that a total of 9,348 U.S. and U.K. servicemen died at the hands of the Germans and Italians, out of a total of 235,473 prisoners. The corresponding figures given for the Pacific theater were 35,756 deaths out of 132,134 prisoners taken by the Japanese; see Dower, *Embracing Defeat*, 625n4. The official estimate of the number of Japanese prisoners who died in the hands of the Soviet Union is 55,000. Soviet sources, however, suggest that as many as 113,000 POWs may well have perished in the gulags between 1945 and 1956; see Philip West, Steven I. Levine, and Jackie Hiltz, eds., *America's Wars in Asia: A Cultural Approach to History and Memory* (M.E. Sharpe, 1998), 232. The Soviet Union was one of the eleven Allied nations represented on the bench at the Tokyo trial, having entered the war in Asia at the last moment, in violation of its neutrality pact with Japan. This (a perfect example of the "double standards" argument, since the Tokyo tribunal found Japan's leaders guilty of violating international agreements), *plus* atrocities committed by the Soviet military against Japanese civilians and soldiers in Manchuria at the end of the war, *plus* the abusive years-long imprisonment of over half a million prisoners in Siberia, has understandably drawn particularly outraged attention from Japanese conservatives. The tactic of arguing that "nothing we may have done was as bad as the horrors perpetuated by the Soviets and Communists" is to be found, of course, among German conservatives as well.

12. It is impossible to give exact figures for Japanese fatalities in World War II (or, by the same token, for any other peoples or nations). The confusion of the times made precise enumeration difficult if not impossible. Beyond this, however, whole categories of deaths sometimes are excluded from conventional calculations. Estimates of the number of Japanese killed in the air raids and by the atomic bombs vary, for example, while figures for the number of civilians slaughtered in ferocious battles such as Saipan and, most devastatingly, Okinawa often are ne-

glected. Little attention has been given to civilian deaths attributable to the collapse of the home front (such as more numerous deaths of mothers and infants in childbirth, as well as rising mortality from malnutrition, infectious diseases such as tuberculosis, etc.). War-related deaths that occurred after Japan's surrender are also difficult to tally. These would include prisoners who died in the hands of their captors (especially, but not exclusively, the Soviets), as well as those who died of war-related wounds or illness in the immediate or longer-term wake of the defeat. It would also include a truly forgotten category of Japanese war victims: the many tens of thousands of civilian men, women, and children who perished attempting to make their way home from Manchuria and other parts of China.

I attempted to examine the confusing available numbers in a 1986 publication; see Dower, *War Without Mercy*: *Race and Power in the Pacific War* (Pantheon Books, 1986), 293–301. The most recent "official" estimate given by the Japanese is a total of 3.1 million war dead (2.3 million servicemen and 800,000 civilians); see *Asahi Shimbun*, August 16, 2000. The total number of U.S. fatalities from all theaters of World War II was roughly 400,000. The number of Chinese war dead was at least four or five times that of the Japanese, possibly more. The point to keep in mind where Japanese war memories are concerned, in any case, is not the precise number of deaths but rather the intimate impact of these large numbers in strengthening the "victim consciousness" of virtually all who survived.

13. At a very particular level of comparison, the "context-less" nature of the Vietnam War Memorial invites comparison to the atomic-bomb memorials in Hiroshima and Nagasaki. Until recently, visitors to the latter sites could be excused for emerging with the impression that the war began in August 1945 and consisted primarily of innocent Japanese being slaughtered with nuclear weapons. Non-Japanese commentators routinely dwell on this as a typical example of Japan's peculiar "historical amnesia," when in fact it is better understood as being typical not of Japan but of victim consciousness more generally.

14. On the exclusion of Emperor Hirohito from war responsibility, see Dower, *Embracing Defeat*, chap. 9–11; also Herbert P. Bix, *Hirohito and the Making of Modern Japan* (HarperCollins, 2000), especially chap. 15. The deplorable cover-up of the activities of Unit 731 is addressed in depth in Peter Williams and David Wallace, *Unit 731: Japan's Secret Biological Warfare in World War II* (The Free Press, 1989). The major

research-based critical Japanese study of the *ianfu*, by Yoshimi Yoshiaki, is now available in English under the title *Comfort Women: Sexual Slavery in the Japanese Military During World War II* (Columbia University Press, 2000). On chemical warfare, see Yuki Tanaka, "Poison Gas: The Story Japan Would Like to Forget," *Bulletin of the Atomic Scientists*, October 1988, 10–19.

15. The extraordinary American-Japanese collusion not only to keep the emperor out of the Tokyo trial, but also to ensure that no imputation whatsoever of his possible war responsibility be introduced into the proceedings, emerges vividly in the 1961 testimony given by Shiohara Tokisaburō, a former defense attorney at the trial, to representatives of Yasukuni Jinja, the shrine dedicated to the memory of those who died for the emperor. (The archival citation is "Kyokutō Kokusai Gunji Saiban Kankei Chōshu Shiryō," in Shozō Inoue Tadao Shiryō, Yasukuni Kaikō Bunko, July 4, 1961. I am indebted to Professor Yoshida Yutaka for sharing a copy of this document, which was unknown to me when I wrote *Embracing Defeat*.)

The neo-nationalist "revisionists" who have so vigorously attacked "the Tokyo War Crimes Trial view of history" have been surprisingly reticent, to date, on the emperor issue—in sharp contrast to the more thuggish element in the right. In some cases (such as the feature film mentioned in note 9), they have even used the emperor's exemption from the trials to *reinforce* their argument that defendants like Tōjō were not ultimately responsible for the crimes with which they were charged.

16. The transcript of the press conference appears in Takahashi Hiroshi, *Heika, Otazune Mōshiagemasu: Kisha Kaiken Zenkiroku to Ningen Tennō no Kiseki* (Bunshun Bunko, 1988), 226–27. The *nengo* system, by which the years are measured in accordance with the reign of the emperor (1945 was thus "Shōwa 20"), is a modern practice, dating back only to the nineteenth century. Its political and ideological ramifications are particularly pernicious in the case of Hirohito's "Shōwa" era. Not only does this highlight Japan's emperor-centered "uniqueness" as the key to postwar and contemporary national identity; simultaneously, it dilutes popular consciousness of the horrors of the 1930s and 1940s by essentially pouring these years into a larger brew of postwar peace and prosperity. The "Shōwa Day" proposal was shelved following the adverse public reaction to Prime Minister Mori's definition of Japan as an "emperor-centered land of the gods." The Imperial

Household Agency controls all private materials pertaining to Emperor Hirohito (and his predecessors), and vigilantly guards these against outside scrutiny. The general taboo on serious discussion of the emperor as a political actor while he was still living extended to withholding from publication personal accounts by persons who had been close to him.

17. For an overview of the claims for "individual" reparations from Japan that have proliferated since the mid-1990s, see Laura Hein, "Claiming Humanity and Legal Standing: Contemporary Demands for Redress from Japan for Its World War II Policies," in John Torpey, ed., *Politics and the Past: On Repairing Historical Injustices* (Rowman & Littlefield, 2001).

18. If the phenomenon of "binational sanitizing of Japanese war crimes" were pursued in more detail, it undoubtedly would be found that Americans in general, at both official and media levels, became more critical of Japan's failure to address its "war responsibility" beginning in the early 1970s. The explanation for this seems obvious. This is when the exaggerated perception of Japan as an "economic superpower" threatening U.S. hegemony became voguish—and, with this, the resurrection of martial rhetoric and imagery (Japanese "treachery," "economic war," "a financial Pearl Harbor," etc.). Coincident with this, the reopening of U.S. relations with China—and the rather heady and uncritical Sinophilism that accompanied this—made it politically acceptable and even fashionable for Americans to once again think sympathetically about China and its "suffering."

19. For the constitutional debates at the start of the new century, see Glen D. Hook and Gavan McCormack, eds., *Japan's Contested Constitution* (Routledge, 2001). I have tried to sketch out the broader milieu of postwar political and ideological contention—a topic that runs against the grain of popular stereotypes of Japan as a peculiarly harmonious and "consensual" society—in chapter 8 in this present volume.

20. The famous "Ienaga textbook case," involving a legal challenge to the Ministry of Education's certification process, was initiated in 1965 and dragged through the courts for some three decades. The case attracted a strong cadre of activist supporters, and the media publicity that accompanied the protracted process of appeal and reappeal made Ienaga's position far more widely known than would have been the case if his textbook had just been allowed to pass into the system of approved texts. For a recent intimate account, see Ienaga Saburō, *Japan's*

Past, Japan's Future: One Historian's Odyssey, translated and introduced by Richard H. Minear (Rowman & Littlefield, 2001).

21. The best English source on the security treaty struggle is George R. Packard III, *Protest in Tokyo: The Security Treaty Crisis of 1960* (Princeton University Press, 1966).

22. These "New Left" protests are well treated in Thomas R.H. Havens, *Fire Across the Sea: The Vietnam War and Japan, 1965–1975* (Princeton University Press, 1987).

23. For a belated English-language sample of popular writings on war crimes in China beginning in the early 1970s, see Honda Katsuichi, *The Nanjing Massacre: A Japanese Journalist Confronts Japan's National Shame* (M.E. Sharpe, 1999). Historians affiliated with Marxist-oriented research organizations such as the large and influential Rekishigaku Kenkyūkai turned attention to these issues soon after the defeat, and have consistently played an important role in uncovering basic archival materials. In 1993, these research activities were elevated to a new level with the establishment of Japan's War Responsibility Data Center (Nihon no Sensō Sekinin Shiryō Sentā), publisher of an invaluable quarterly titled *Sensō Sekinin Kenkyū* (The report on Japan's war responsibility).

24. Bix's study of Hirohito, cited in note 14, draws extensively on primary as well as secondary materials that became available after the emperor's death. It is perhaps a sign of changing times that the Japanese translation of his prize-winning study was picked up by Kodansha, one of Japan's largest mainstream publishing houses.

25. *New York Times*, March 6, 1995; cited in Mark Osiel, *Mass Atrocity, Collective Memory, and the Law* (Transaction, 1997), 183, 189.

5. THE BOMBED: HIROSHIMAS AND NAGASAKIS IN JAPANESE MEMORY

1. Hara Mieko, untitled memoir in *Children of Hiroshima*, ed. Publishing Committee for "Children of Hiroshima" (Tokyo, 1980), 244–46, quoted in John Whittier Treat, *Writing Ground Zero: Japanese Literature and the Atomic Bomb* (University of Chicago Press, 1995).

2. The first occupation forces did not arrive in Japan until the very end of August; the formal surrender ceremony took place on September 2; and the occupation headquarters in Tokyo did not become effectively operational until mid-September. Formal occupation

censorship generally is dated from September 19, 1945, when a press code was announced. Beginning on October 5, prepublication censorship was imposed on major newspapers and periodicals. For general accounts concerning nuclear-related censorship see Matsuura Sōzō, *Senryōka no Genron Danatsu* (Suppression of speech under the occupation) (Tokyo, 1969), esp. 167–212; Committee for the Compilation of Materials on Damage Caused by the Atomic Bombs in Hiroshima and Nagasaki, comp., *Hiroshima and Nagasaki: The Physical, Medical, and Social Effects of the Atomic Bombings*, trans. Eisei Ishikawa and David L. Swain (Basic Books, 1981), 5, 503–13, 564, 585 (hereafter this basic source, originally published in Japanese in 1979, is cited as *Hiroshima and Nagasaki*); Monica Braw, *The Atomic Bomb Suppressed: American Censorship in Occupied Japan* (M.E. Sharpe, 1991); and Glen D. Hook, "Censorship and Reportage of Atomic Damage and Casualties in Hiroshima and Nagasaki," *Bulletin of Concerned Asian Scholars* 23 (January–March 1991): 13–25.

3. Hatoyama's statement appeared in *Asahi Shimbun*, September 15, 1945. His account of this incident and enduring contempt of the "recklessness" and hypocrisy exemplified in the U.S. use of the atomic bombs and punishment of him for criticizing this emerges clearly in his memoirs: *Hatoyama Ichirō Kaikoroku* [Hatoyama Ichirō memoirs] (Tokyo, 1957), 49–51.

4. On American POWs in Hiroshima, see "Nijūsannin no Beihei Horyo mo Bakushi Shite Ita" (Twenty-three American POWs also killed by bombing), *Shūkan Yomiuri*, August 13, 1978, 28–31; Barton J. Bernstein, "Unraveling a Mystery: American POWs Killed at Hiroshima," *Foreign Service Journal* 56 (October 1979): 17ff; and Robert Karl Manoff, "American Victims of Hiroshima," *New York Times Magazine*, December 2, 1984, 67ff. This became the theme of a 1971 mural by the painters Iri and Toshi Maruki, who are discussed below. See John W. Dower and John Junkerman, eds., *The Hiroshima Murals: The Art of Iri Maruki and Toshi Maruki* (Tokyo, 1985), 21, 78–81.

5. *Asahi Shimbun*, September 7, 1945; Grant Goodman, *Amerika no Nihon—Gannen, 1945–1946* (America's Japan—the first year, 1945–1946) (Tokyo, 1986), 120–23.

6. Japan's research on the possibility of making a nuclear weapon is described in "'NI' and 'F': Japan's Wartime Atomic Bomb Research," in John W. Dower, *Japan in War and Peace: Selected Essays* (The New Press, 1993), 55–100.

7. *Hiroshima and Nagasaki*, 496.

8. Katō Etsurō, *Okurareta Kakumei* (The revolution that was given to us) (Tokyo, 1946). A copy of this fascinating booklet, which is now almost impossible to find in Japan, is in the Gordon Prange Collection of McKeldin Library, University of Maryland, College Park.

9. The great majority of Japanese at the time exonerated the emperor from such criticism. Postsurrender propaganda by the Japanese elites, parroted by U.S. occupation authorities, strongly emphasized that the emperor too had been misled by the military.

10. From the historian's perspective, we now can identify many ways in which Japan's fifteen-year mobilization for war created positive technological, technocratic, and institutional legacies for the postwar state, but these certainly were not apparent in the immediate postsurrender years. See "The Useful War" in Dower, *Japan in War and Peace*, 9–32.

11. The quotations come from the *Asahi Shimbun* in the period immediately following capitulation, but such sentiments were ubiquitous.

12. The social stigma attached to weapons-related research was reinforced by institutional constraints. In the early reformist phase of the occupation, the imperial military establishment was eliminated. Although constitutional prohibition of the maintenance of military forces under the new "no war" charter was violated after the Korean War broke out and Japan began to rearm (beginning in July 1950), the constitutional restraint did remain strong enough to prevent the creation of an institutionalized militarism comparable to the Pentagon and military-academic-industrial complex in the United States. Preservation of bureaucratic turf helped to perpetuate this situation over the decades, for primary responsibility for budgetary allotments resided in the hands of the Ministry of Finance, which remained largely committed to civilian-oriented policies. There was no defense ministry per se in Japan until 2007. At the same time, public opinion, while tolerating incremental remilitarization, remained opposed to constitutional revision and the more blatant sort of all-out militarization this might permit. There is no question that the "no war" constitution is an anomaly in the 1990s, when Japan does in fact have a large military budget, has become a major producer of "dual use" technologies, and has sent "peace keeping forces" abroad under UN auspices in response to immense U.S. pressure. Nonetheless, the persistence of popular opposition to constitutional revision for almost half a century to date has conspicuously influenced the nature and balance of Japan's economic and political policies in non-

military directions; and the most effective arguments against such revision consistently have played upon memories of Japan's "victimization" in World War II, of which Hiroshima always will remain the prime symbol. Contemporary political struggles over who will control the memory of the war (as seen in the Ministry of Education's notorious efforts to produce sanitized textbook coverage of this topic) are intimately tied to these issues of constitutional revision and whether or not Japan should become a more "normal" state with a bona-fide military. In this context, Japanese liberals and leftists commonly are able to make more effective neo-nationalistic use of the bombs than their conservative and right-wing opponents. To encourage popular support for constitutional revision and more "normal" militarization, the latter must perforce downplay the horrors of the old war—not only the suffering the imperial forces caused to others but also the horror brought home.

13. For good early examples of this political logic equating "science" with a more "rational" democratic society generally, see *Asahi Shimbun*, August 22, 1945; and Toyoshima Yoshio's comments in the September–October 1945 issue of *Bungei*, quoted in Honda Shūgo, *Monogatari: Sengo Bungaku Shi* (The story of postwar literary history) (1966; reprint, Tokyo, 1992), 1:13.

14. See Wilfred Burchett, *Shadows of Hiroshima* (Verso, 1981), esp. chaps. 1–3. Burchett's story, essentially as published in the *Daily Express*, is reproduced on 34–37. The counterpart scoop from Nagasaki, squelched by occupation headquarters, was by George Weller of the *Chicago Daily News* and totaled some 25,000 words. Ibid., 44–45. Laurence's special relationship with the Department of War, kept secret at the time, is discussed in my 2010 book *Cultures of War*.

15. Iwasaki Akira, *Nihon Gendai Taikei: Eiga Shi* (Outline of contemporary Japan: Film history) (Tokyo, 1961), 226–27; Matsuura, *Senryōka no Genron Danatsu*, 192–95. Iwasaki was part of the project filming the aftermath of the bombs in Hiroshima and Nagasaki, which was conducted by the Nichiei studio.

16. The United States Strategic Bombing Survey, *The Effects of Atomic Bombs on Hiroshima and Nagasaki* (GPO, 1946), 3–5. Accurate estimates of atomic bomb–related deaths are made problematic by many factors: the demographic turmoil that prevailed in Japan at war's end, especially in urban areas; the extraordinary destructiveness of the bomb, which obliterated whole neighborhoods, along with the records pertaining to their residents; the chaos prevailing after the bombs were

dropped, including hasty mass cremations of victims to prevent disease; and the absence of clear, coordinated, publicly accessible records
of subsequent *hibakusha* illnesses and deaths. Useful data on fatalities,
and the difficulty of calculating them, appears in the voluminous 1970
Japanese report translated into English as *Hiroshima and Nagasaki* (note 2
above); see 113–15, 367, 369, 406. Although conflicting figures are given
here, the general conclusion is that total long-term *hibakusha* deaths
were approximately double the 1946 figures for each city. In 1994, when
the Japanese parliament belatedly debated legislation concerning death-
benefits compensation to *hibakusha* families (see note 18 below), Ministry
of Health and Welfare statistics that seem implausibly high commonly
were cited indicating that between 300,000 and 350,000 *hibakusha* had
died prior to 1969, with all but 50 to 70,000 of these deaths occurring
prior to 1958; see *Asahi Shimbun*, October 27 and November 3, 1994.
Persistent replication of the outdated initial low estimates of fatalities
has contributed to perpetuation of one of the enduring misleading statements in standard accounts of the war—namely, that many more people
were killed in the Tokyo air raid of March 9 and 10, 1945, than by the
atomic bombs in each city. Official Japanese estimates for fatalities in
the first Tokyo raid are slightly less than one hundred thousand. Indeed,
the Ministry of Health and Welfare estimates that *total* Japanese deaths
from the conventional U.S. bombing of some sixty-four Japanese cities apart from the two nuclear targets was in the neighborhood of three
hundred thousand persons—that is, equal to or less than its own (high)
estimate of the fatalities associated with Hiroshima and Nagasaki.

17. On the ABCC, see John Beatty, "Genetics in the Atomic
Age: The Atomic Bomb Casualty Commission, 1947–1956" in *The
Expansion of American Biology*, ed. Keith R. Benson, Jane Maienschein,
and Ronald Rainger (Rutgers University Press, 1991), 284–324; and M.
Susan Lindee, *Suffering Made Real: American Science and the Survivors at
Hiroshima* (University of Chicago Press, 1995).

18. Passage of a comprehensive "*hibakusha* relief law" remained
a subject of parliamentary debate in the final months of 1994 and was
widely covered in the Japanese press. For a concise critical commentary
on the national government's relative neglect of the *hibakusha*, see Shiina
Masae, *Hibakusha Engohō* (Hibakusha relief law) (Tokyo, 1992).

19. The general U.S. policy of media censorship in occupied Japan
began to be eased in late 1948 and was formally terminated in mid-1949.
It was not until the February 1952 meeting of the Hiroshima Association

of Medical Sciences, however, that academic societies were allowed to engage freely in investigation and discussion of the medical effects of the bombs. See *Hiroshima and Nagasaki*, 513. In 1994, some Americans, including several Nisei who had been involved in censorship at the local level, argued that they were sensitive to these matters and would have been lenient if the Japanese had submitted noninflammatory writings on their bomb experiences. Such writings, the ex-censors said, simply were not submitted; see *Asahi Shimbun*, May 16, 1994. Such claims are unpersuasive, however, given the clear top-level opposition to such writings, plus concrete examples of local suppression of such materials, plus the deplorable ban on scientific writings until the very end of the occupation (which apparently involved bureaucratic complications in Washington, and not just Tokyo). In the three years from 1946 through 1948, a total of seven published books or articles, plus twenty-seven written testimonies, were recorded in Hiroshima, most of them appearing in 1946; *Hiroshima and Nagasaki*, 586. U.S. restrictions on scientific findings concerning the effects of the bombs were so severe that, even in the closing years of occupation, American medical investigators working with Japanese *hibakusha* for the ABCC were uninformed of the existence of earlier studies pertinent to their own research. See James N. Yamazaki, M.D., with Louis B. Fleming, *Children of the Atomic Bomb: Nagasaki, Hiroshima, and the Marshall Islands* (Duke University Press, 1995).

20. *Hiroshima and Nagasaki*, 512–13.

21. Maruki Iri and Akamatsu Toshiko (Maruki Toshi), *Pika-don* (Tokyo, 1950). The Marukis' remarkable series of collaborative paintings, which eventually extended beyond the atomic bombs to deal with such subjects as the Rape of Nanking and Auschwitz, are reproduced in Dower and Junkerman, *The Hiroshima Murals*. A documentary film of the artists' work by Junkerman and Dower, entitled *Hellfire: A Journey from Hiroshima*, is available from First Run Features, New York.

22. The Marist priest Paul Glynn published a book-length homage to Nagai entitled *A Song for Nagasaki* (Hunters Hill, Australia, 1988). In Nagai's eschatology, after singling out Nagasaki, God then inspired the emperor to issue the sacred proclamation ending the war. These views emerge vividly in Glynn, esp. 115–21, but the ideological logic of the connection between the patriotic Christian visionary and erstwhile Shintoist god-emperor, who had portrayed himself as intervening to prevent the apocalypse in the surrender proclamation of August 15, 1945, is generally overlooked. Nagai's radiation sickness, incidentally, may have

been contracted from his research prior to the bombing of Nagasaki, although his suffering from the bomb is beyond dispute.

23. For an English translation of this book, see Takashi Nagai, *The Bells of Nagasaki*, trans. William Johnston (Kodansha, 1984). Prior to *Nagasaki no Kane*, Nagai had been permitted to publish a moving, senti-mental account entitled *Kono Ko o Nokoshite* (Leaving these children be-hind) (Tokyo, 1948), reflecting on the future of his soon-to-be-orphaned children. This became an immediate "top ten" bestseller in 1948 and remained on the top-ten list in 1949, where it was joined by *Nagasaki no Kane;* see Shiozawa Minobu, *Shōwa Besuto-serā Sesō Shi* (Social history of Shōwa bestsellers) (Tokyo, 1988), 108–10.

24. According to records compiled in Hiroshima, atomic-bomb writings pertaining to that city alone totaled 54 books, essays, and sto-ries plus 284 testimonials from 1949 through 1951. By 1971, the total was 500 published books and short pieces and 2,234 written testimoni-als; *Hiroshima and Nagasaki*, 586. In 1983, major literary writings on the atomic-bomb experience were collected in a fifteen-volume series entitled *Nihon no Genbaku Bungaku* (Japanese atomic-bomb literature) (Tokyo, 1989). See also the thirty-article series on atomic-bomb litera-ture during the occupation published in *Chugoku Shimbun*, the leading Hiroshima-area newspaper, between June 30 and August 12, 1986. For English translations of some of this extensive literature, see Kenzaburō Ōe, ed., *The Crazy Iris and Other Stories of the Atomic Aftermath* (Grove, 1985); Kyoko and Mark Selden, eds., *The Atomic Bomb: Voices from Hiroshima and Nagasaki* (M.E. Sharpe, 1989); and Richard H. Minear, ed. and trans., *Hiroshima: Three Witnesses* (Princeton University Press, 1990).

25. Minear, *Hiroshima*, 305. Hara's "Summer Flowers" and Tōge's "Poems of the Atomic Bomb" both are translated in full by Minear, along with another early classic of atomic-bomb literature, Ōta Yōko's 1950 narrative "City of Corpses." In his commentary, Minear calls atten-tion to the implicit anti-Americanism in many of Tōge's poems; 295–97.

26. *Asahi Shimbun*, August 23, 1945.

27. For the English version of this stunning collection, see Japan Broadcasting Corporation (NHK), comp., *Unforgettable Fire: Pictures Drawn by Atomic Bomb Survivors* (Pantheon, 1977).

28. The nonlethal consequences of the "black rain" are noted in Yamazaki with Fleming, *Children of the Atomic Bomb*, and attributed to the relatively high altitude at which the Hiroshima and Nagasaki bombs

were detonated. This is in contrast to the conspicuously lethal fallout from the 1954 U.S. hydrogen-bomb test in the Marshall Islands.

29. For a broad annotated discussion of Cold War struggles within Japan in general, see chapter 8 in this present volume. By far the most influential collection of student-conscript letters was Nihon Senbotsu Gakusei Shuki Henshū Iinkai, ed., *Kike—Wadatsumi no Koe: Nihon Senbotsu Gokusei no Shuki* (Listen—the voice of the ocean: Testimonies of conscripted Japanese students) (Tokyo, 1949). Like Nagai Takashi's *Bells of Nagasaki*, this also was quickly refashioned as a popular movie. This collection of student letters tapped not only an earlier postwar collection of wartime letters by Tokyo Imperial University conscripts but also a wartime series of such letters published in the Tokyo Imperial University student newspaper—a striking example indeed of war words becoming peace words. After Japan's defeat, such wartime writings often were reinterpreted as evidence of peaceful, idealistic, and even antiwar sentiments—as well, of course, as intimate examples of the tragic loss of talented and attractive young men in a foolhardy and misguided war.

30. The appeal is reproduced in Nihon Jyānarizumu Kenkyūkai, ed., *Shōwa 'Hatsugen' no Kiroku* (A record of Shōwa pronouncements) (Tokyo, 1989), 138–39.

31. Gensuikyō, short for Gensuibaku Kinshi Nihon Kyōgikai (Japan Council Against Atomic and Hydrogen Bombs) was founded in September 1955. Its domination by the Japan Communist Party led to the splintering off of rival organizations in the 1960s. In 1961, the centrist Democratic Socialist Party and conservative Liberal Democratic Party formed the National Council for Peace and Against Nuclear Weapons (Kakukin Kaigi, short for Kakuheiki Kinshi Heiwa Kansetsu Kokumin Kaigi), and in 1965 the Japan Socialist Party formed the Japan Congress Against Atomic and Hydrogen Bombs (Gensuikin, short for Gensuibaku Kinshi Nihon Kokumin Kaigi). Factionalism on the left has continually plagued the antinuclear movement.

32. For an English translation of Ōe's early essays, which originally appeared in the monthly *Sekai*, see his *Hiroshima Notes*, trans. Toshi Yonezawa and ed. David L. Swain (YMCA Press, 1981).

33. For an English translation, see Masuji Ibuse, *Black Rain*, trans. John Bester (Kodansha, 1969). This is without question the classic Japanese literary reconstruction of the atomic-bomb experience. The Japanese film version of *Black Rain*, directed by Imamura Shōhei, did not appear until 1988.

34. Three volumes from the *Barefoot Gen* series (originally published in Japanese by Shōbunsha, Tokyo) are available in English translation from New Society Publishers, Philadelphia.

35. See note 27 above for an English rendering of NHK's edited collection of *hibakusha* drawings.

36. These later developments in demographic, medical, and linguistic understandings are scattered throughout the chaotic but invaluable *Hiroshima and Nagasaki* (note 2 above).

37. Sodei Rinjirō, *Watakushitachi wa Teki Datta no ka: Zaibei Hibakusha no Mokushiroku* (Were we the enemy?—A record of *hibakusha* in the United States) (Tokyo, 1978).

38. *Hiroshima and Nagasaki*, 471, 474. Korean groups place the figures of Korean casualties much higher; see ibid., 468. See also Kurt W. Tong, "Korea's Forgotten Atomic Bomb Victims," *Bulletin of Concerned Asian Scholars* 23 (January–March 1991): 31–37. Apart from the previously mentioned American POWs killed in Hiroshima, the atomic bombs also killed small numbers of Chinese, Southeast Asian, and European individuals.

39. This reencounter with China, and with Japanese war atrocities there, began with nongovernmental contacts in the mid-1960s, before the formal restoration of relations in 1972. The key Japanese writer in bringing the Rape of Nanking to public attention was the well-known progressive journalist Honda Katsuichi, whose influential writings from China were published in newspapers and magazines in 1971 and subsequently collected in a volume entitled *Chūgoku no Tabi* (Travels in China) (Tokyo, 1972). The ensuing contentious debates on this topic in Japan are concisely summarized in Daqing Yang, "A Sino-Japanese Controversy: The Nanjing Atrocity as History," *Sino-Japanese Studies* 3 (November 1990): 14–35.

40. In 1994, in anticipation of the fiftieth anniversary of the dropping of the atomic bombs, officials associated with the memorial museum in Hiroshima announced that they would expand their exhibitions beyond depictions of Japanese victimization to include reference to Hiroshima's military role since the Meiji period, Japanese aggression and atrocities in World War II, and the presence of Korean and Chinese forced laborers in Hiroshima at the time of the bombs.

41. Convenient compilations of Nagano's statements appear in *Asahi Shimbun*, May 7 and 19, 1994. Although the government officially repudiated Nagano's comments, his remarks accurately reflect a mainline conservative view in Japan.

42. *Asahi Shimbun*, May 20, 1994. There were other arguments against the state visits as well, including the liberal and left-wing criticism that it would involve repoliticizing the role of the emperor in significant ways. The nuances of these acts of symbolic politics are subtle and convoluted.

43. In the realm of popular symbolic "equations," the most extreme expression of Japanese victimization involves pairing the Holocaust in Europe and "nuclear holocaust" of Hiroshima/Nagasaki. In the more specifically Asian context, the most familiar equation pairs the Rape of Nanking and the nuclear destruction of the two Japanese cities. Americans are most likely to conjoin Pearl Harbor and Hiroshima/Nagasaki, but this is a view that has little credence in Japan. Here again, the issue is a contentious one. Whereas the U.S.-dominated Tokyo war-crimes trials portrayed Pearl Harbor as a deep-seated "conspiracy" against peace, the more persuasive view in Japan is that the attack was an ill-conceived response to a collapsing world order—and best comprehended in the capitalistic, imperialistic, and colonial terms of the time. The Japanese also tend to place greater emphasis than Americans do on the fact that the imperial government had intended to break off formal relations with the United States at the eleventh hour, minutes prior to the Pearl Harbor attack, and only failed to do so because of a clerical breakdown in the Japanese embassy in Washington. In this construction, Pearl Harbor emerges more as a tactical and technical blunder than as a treacherous and atrocious act.

8. PEACE AND DEMOCRACY IN TWO SYSTEMS: EXTERNAL POLICY AND INTERNAL CONFLICT

1. Hirano Kenichirō, "Sengo Nihon gaikō ni okeru 'bunka,'" in Watanabe Akio, ed., *Sengo Nihon no taigai seisaku* (Yūhikaku, 1985), 343–45.

2. I have discussed the "reverse course" in some detail in *Empire and Aftermath: Yoshida Shigeru and the Japanese Experience, 1878–1954* (Cambridge: Harvard Council on East Asian Studies, 1979), 305–68, and in "Occupied Japan and the Cold War in Asia," in Michael J. Lacey, ed., *The Truman Presidency* (Woodrow Wilson International Center for Scholars and Cambridge University Press, 1989), 366–409; see also Dower, *Japan in War and Peace*, 155–207. For a criticism of the reverse-course argument by a former American participant in the occupation,

see Justin Williams Sr., "American Democratization Policy for Occupied Japan: Correcting the Revisionist Version," *Pacific Historical Review* 57, no. 2 (May 1988): 179–202, and rejoinders by John W. Dower (202–9) and Howard Schonberger (209–18).

The "1955 System" designation appears to have been introduced to intellectual circles in an article published by Masumi Junnosuke in the June 1964 issue of *Shisō*. See Masumi, *Postwar Politics in Japan, 1945–1955*, Japanese Research Monograph 6 (Institute of East Asian Studies, University of California, 1985), 329–42; see also Masumi, "The 1955 System in Japan and Its Subsequent Development," *Asian Survey* 28, no. 3 (March 1988): 286–306. The rise and fall of the 1955 System was the subject of the 1977 annual publication of the Japanese Political Science Association: Nihon Seijigakkai, ed., "Gojūgo-nen taisei no keisei to hōkai," *Seijigaku nenpō 1977* (Nihon Seijigakkai, 1979). For a broad, annotated overview of Japanese academic analysis of the 1955 System, see Miyake Ichirō, Yamaguchi Yasushi, Muramatsu Michio, and Shindō Eiichi, "Gojūgo-nen taisei' no seiritsu to tenkai," in *Nihon seiji no za-hyō: Sengo 40-nen no ayumi* (Yūhikaku, 1985), 83–116. Like any political or socioeconomic "system," the 1955 System was dynamic, and the so-called conservative hegemony from the outset was internally competitive and riven with tensions. For an analysis in English of the unraveling of the system, see T.J. Pempel, "The Unbundling of 'Japan, Inc.': The Changing Dynamics of Japanese Policy Formation," in Kenneth B. Pyle, ed., *The Trade Crisis: How Will Japan Respond?* (University of Washington Society for Japanese Studies, 1987), 117–52.

3. *Kanpō gōgai—shūgiin*, 7th Diet sess., January 28, 1950, 200; *Official Gazette Extra—House of Representatives*, 7th sess., January 28, 1950, 15. For an extended treatment of Yoshida's interpretation of Article 9, see Dower, *Empire and Aftermath*, 378–82, 397–99.

4. The basic inside source on Japanese military and strategic projections between surrender and restoration of sovereignty is Nishimura Kumao, *San Furanshisuko heiwa jōyaku*, vol. 27 of *Nihon gaikō shi*, ed. Kajima Heiwa Kenkyūjo (Kajima Kenkyūjo, 1971). The Socialists, as represented in the Katayama Tetsu cabinet of May 1947 to March 1948, shared these views.

5. Nishimura, *San Furanshisuko heiwa jōyaku*; Dower, *Empire and Aftermath*, 369–414; Frederick S. Dunn, *Peace-making and the Settlement with Japan* (Princeton University Press, 1963); Michael Yoshitsu, *Japan and the San Francisco Peace Settlement* (Columbia University Press, 1982).

6. I have summarized the official U.S. record in some detail in "Occupied Japan and the Cold War in Asia."

7. John Welfield, *An Empire in Eclipse: Japan in the Postwar American Alliance System* (Athlone Press, 1988), 250. This is the most detailed and useful source in English on Japan within the San Francisco System.

8. "Sengo heiwaron no genryū: Heiwa Mondai Danwakai o chūshin ni," *Sekai*, July 1985, 150–51. This special issue commemorating the fortieth anniversary of the end of World War II contains the basic texts of the Heiwa Mondai Danwakai. A partial translation of the December 1950 statement appears in *Journal of Social and Political Ideas in Japan* 1, no. 1 (April 1963): 13–19 (see also the critique of the progressive intellectuals by the editor, 2–13). For an overview of opinion on the original Security Treaty, see George R. Packard III, *Protest in Tokyo: The Security Treaty Crisis of 1960* (Princeton University Press, 1966), 3–32.

9. *Journal of Social and Political Ideas in Japan* 1, no. 1 (April 1963): 13.

10. Fujiyama and Reischauer are quoted in Welfield, *Empire in Eclipse*, 147, 224. The American acknowledgment of the grossly inequitable nature of the 1951 treaty emerged strongly in later congressional hearings concerning revision; see U.S. Senate, Committee on Foreign Relations, *Treaty of Mutual Cooperation and Security with Japan*, 86th Cong., 2d sess., June 7, 1960. Yoshida's comments appear in Yoshida Shigeru, *Sekai to Nihon* (Bancho Shōbō, 1962), 186–87. Japan also was "divided" by Soviet acquisition of four small and virtually unpopulated islands north of Hokkaido, an emotional issue that remained unresolved when the Shōwa period ended.

11. Statement by Assistant Secretary of State U. Alexis Johnson, *U.S. Security Agreements and Commitments Abroad: Japan and Okinawa Hearings*, 91st Cong., 2d sess., pt. 5, January 26–29, 1970, 1166; cited in Hideki Kan, "The Significance of the U.S.-Japan Security System to the United States: A Japanese Perspective," in Glenn D. Hook, ed., special Japan issue of *Peace and Change: A Journal of Peace Research* 12, nos. 3–4 (1987): 20.

12. See Michael Schaller, *The American Occupation of Japan* (Oxford University Press, 1985), 104, on "independent identity"; see Dower, *Empire and Aftermath*, 420, on Dodge; see U.S. Department of State, *Foreign Relations of the United States, 1952–1954*, vol. 14, pt. 2, pp. 1724–25 (September 12, 1954), on Dulles; cf. ibid., p. 1693 (August 6, 1954).

13. See the concise summary "Economic Relations with the United States, 1945–1973" by Gary Saxonhouse in *Kodansha Encyclopedia of Japan* (Kodansha, 1983), 8:161–64.

14. For the Korean War boom and "special procurements," see Takafusa Nakamura, *The Postwar Japanese Economy: Its Development and Structure* (University of Tokyo Press, 1981), 41–48; G.C. Allen, *Japan's Economic Recovery* (Oxford University Press, 1958), 19–22, 34–35, 166–69, 203. For the Vietnam War boom, see Thomas R.H. Havens, *Fire Across the Sea: The Vietnam War and Japan, 1965–1975* (Princeton University Press, 1987), 96. This is a useful source on this period in general. Japan's entry into economic "maturity" is commonly dated from 1964, when the country was accorded full membership in the Organization for Economic Cooperation and Development (OECD) and "advanced country" status in the International Monetary Fund (IMF).

15. See Dower, *Empire and Aftermath*, and Masumi, *Postwar Politics in Japan*, for general political developments in the first postwar decade. The evolution of U.S. policy is closely documented by Howard Schonberger in *Aftermath of War: Americans and the Remaking of Japan, 1945–1952* (Kent State University Press, 1989). I have dealt at length with the extensive presurrender legacies to the postwar state and society in "The Useful War," *Daedalus*, Summer 1990, 49–70; see also Dower, *Japan in War and Peace*, 9–32.

16. Chitoshi Yanaga, *Big Business in Japanese Politics* (Yale University Press, 1968), 83–87; Haruhiro Fukui, "Liberal Democratic Party," *Kodansha Encyclopedia of Japan* 4:385.

17. For catchphrases, cf. Takahashi Nobuo, *Shōwa sesō ryūkōgo jiten* (Ōbunsha, 1986), 142–43, 148–49. The "shallow economy" is discussed in Dower, *Empire and Aftermath*, 449–63. For the origins of the famous white paper phrase, see Nakano Yoshio, "Mohaya 'sengo' de wa nai," *Bungei shunjū*, February 1956, reprinted in Bungei shunjū, ed. *"Bungei shunjū" ni miru Shōwa shi* (Bungei shunjū, 1988), 2:349–59; cf. Kōno Yasuko, "'Sengo' no owari," in Watanabe, *Sengo Nihon no taigai seisaku*, 182. On the five-year plan, see Masumi, *Postwar Politics in Japan*, 237–39.

18. Kōnosuke Odaka, Keinosuke Ono, and Fumiko Adachi, *The Automobile Industry in Japan: A Study of Ancillary Firm Development* (Kinokuniya Company and Oxford University Press, 1988), 46, 102–5; Takahashi, *Shōwa sesō ryūkōgo jiten*, 146, 149, 151; Sakakibara Shōji, *Shōwago* (Asahi Bunko, 1986), 124. On bestsellers, cf. Ueda Yasuo, *Gendai no shuppan: Kono miryoku aru katsuri sekai* (Risō Shuppansha, 1980), 162.

19. Miyake et al., "'Gojūgo-nen taisei,'" 83, 88, citing Kamishima Jirō on the difference between the two camps.

20. Takahashi Shin and Nakamura Kyūichi, "Sengo Nihon no heiwaron," *Sekai* 391 (June 1978): 202–25, esp. 202–7.

21. Miyake et al., "'Gojūgo-nen taisei,'" 83–84, 89–90, 117. The "four weak" parties were the Communists, Socialists, Democratic Socialists, and Kōmeitō.

22. See Packard, *Protest in Tokyo*, for the 1960 struggle and Havens, *Fire Across the Sea*, for the anti–Vietnam War movement in Japan. The grassroots movements are discussed in Margaret A. McKean, *Environmental Protest and Citizen Politics in Japan* (University of California Press, 1981). On the university disturbances, see Henry D. Smith II, "University Upheavals of 1966–1969," in *Kodansha Encyclopedia of Japan* 8:171. I also have drawn on an as yet unpublished manuscript on the New Left by Mutō Ichio.

23. See Kan in Hook, *Peace and Change*, 27, for the 1959 NHK survey. Welfield, *Empire in Eclipse*, 197, cites a 1968 *Shūkan Asahi* poll showing 66 percent support for neutralism; an *Asahi Shimbun* poll in 1969 showed 56 percent support.

24. Welfield points out conservative disagreements on international policy throughout *Empire in Eclipse*; see esp. 210–14. On internal LDP debates on China policy, see Haruhiro Fukui, *Party in Power: The Japanese Liberal Democrats and Policy-making* (University of California Press, 1970), 227–62.

25. Takeshi Igarashi, "Peace-making and Party Politics: The Formation of the Domestic Foreign-Policy System in Postwar Japan," *Journal of Japanese Studies* 11, no. 2 (1985): 323–56.

26. For an extended critique of the conceptual shortcomings of the opposition as reflected in the 1960 struggle, see Takabatake Toshimichi, "'Rokujū-nen anpo' no seishin shi," in Najita Tetsuo, Maeda Ai, and Kamishima Jirō, eds., *Sengo Nihon no seishin shi* (Iwanami Shoten, 1989), 70–91.

27. Welfield, *Empire in Eclipse*, 364–68, 413; on Japan's military industries, see 434–41.

28. Kenneth B. Pyle, "Japan, the World, and the Twenty-First Century," in Takashi Inoguchi and Daniel I. Okimoto, eds., *The Political Economy of Japan*, vol. 2, *The Changing International Context* (Stanford University Press, 1988), 455–56.

29. The committee was established in 1956, met from 1957 to 1964,

and dissolved in 1965. Its final report made clear that a majority favored revision, but no recommendation was made and the cabinet did not forward the report to the Diet. The nadir of the movement to revise the constitution is commonly dated from this time. This situation changed drastically after the Gulf War of 1991, when U.S. and European criticism of Japan facilitated the conservatives in dispatching an overseas "Peacekeeping Force" under United Nations auspices and thereby invigorated the movement to revise the constitution.

30. Welfield, *Empire in Eclipse*, 109–13.

31. Kōno in Watanabe, *Sengo Nihon no taigai seisaku*, 192.

32. For a general contemporary overview of the Japanese economy in the 1970s, see Daniel Okimoto, ed., *Japan's Economy: Coping with Change in the International Environment* (Westview Press, 1982), especially the contributions by Gary Saxonhouse (123–48) and Hugh Patrick (149–96).

33. John W. Dower, "Japan's New Military Edge," *The Nation*, July 3, 1989; Steven K. Vogel, *Japanese High Technology, Politics and Power*, Research Paper No. 2, Berkeley Roundtable on the International Economy, March 1989.

34. See Pempel, "Unbundling of 'Japan, Inc.,'" for an analysis of this diversification among the ruling elites. This is generally seen as marking the end of the 1955 System. This same theme permeates many of the articles in Pyle, *Trade Crisis*.

35. In 1976, the year the "1 percent of GNP" ceiling was first singled out as a formal guideline, Japan's military spending ranked seventh in the world—after the two superpowers, China, West Germany, France, and Great Britain. Its military budget was more than triple that of South Korea, far greater than that of any of the Warsaw Pact powers, and far greater than that of neutral powers such as India, Sweden, and Switzerland. Japan's 1976 military budget was almost 14 times that of 1954. For Britain over the same period the increase was 2.5 times, for France roughly 5 times, and for West Germany a little less than 7 times. Welfield, *Empire in Eclipse*, 366–69, includes useful tables of these expenditures.

36. Publishing houses such as Iwanami, which includes the monthly *Sekai* among its periodicals, continued to address these issues with a rigor reminiscent of the earlier period, and scholars such as Sakamoto Yoshikazu remained devoted to "peace research" in the broadest sense. See Sakamoto, *Shinpan: Gunshuku no seijigaku* (Iwanami Shinsho, 1988).

For critical evaluations of the course of democracy in postwar Japan, see Rokurō Hidaka, *The Price of Affluence: Dilemmas of Contemporary Japan* (Penguin Books Australia, 1985); Gavan McCormack and Yoshio Sugimoto, eds., *Democracy in Contemporary Japan* (Hale and Iremonger, 1986); and Takeshi Ishida and Ellis S. Krauss, eds., *Democracy in Japan* (University of Pittsburgh Press, 1989).

37. Kenneth Pyle has summarized the range of opinion on Japan's world role in two useful articles: see "Japan, the World, and the Twenty-First Century," and "In Pursuit of a Grand Design: Nakasone Betwixt the Past and Present," in Pyle, *Trade Crisis*, 5–32.

38. For extended critical analyses of the *Nihonjinron* genre, see Ross E. Mouer and Yoshio Sugimoto, *Images of Japanese Society: A Study in the Structure of Social Reality* (KPI, 1986), and Peter N. Dale, *The Myth of Japanese Uniqueness* (St. Martin's, 1986).

39. The full text appears in *Asahi Shimbun*, January 17, 1968. The LDP also defined "the inherent form of the Japanese people" (*Nihon kokumin no konzen no sugata*) as consisting of "human love and public duty, love of the motherland and racial spirit, defense consciousness, etc." (*ningenai to kōtokushin, sokokuai to minzoku seishin, bōei ishiki nado*).

9. MOCKING MISERY: GRASSROOTS SATIRE IN DEFEATED JAPAN

1. Asahi Shimbunsha, ed., *Koe* (Voice) (Asahi Bunko, 1984), I: 264–65. This is a selection of letters to the editor originally published in the "Koe" section of the *Asahi Shimbun*: vol. 1 covers 1945 through 1947. See also the lengthy "Picture of Tokyo" printed in the February 20, 1947, issue of the *Asahi* and quoted in Tōkyō yakeato yamiichi o kiroku suru kai, ed., *Tōkyō yamiichi kōbō shi* (Sōfūsha, 1978), 55–57.

2. Examples of the search for a usable past appear throughout John W. Dower, *Embracing Defeat: Japan in the Wake of World War II* (W.W. Norton and The New Press, 1999). "Bridges of Language" is the title of chapter 5 in that study.

3. For a good sample of such "reapplication" of old proverbs and clichés, see the series of photographs accompanied by satirical captions in *Asahi gurafu*, January 1946. This clever graphic commentary is another early example of the *iroha* associations discussed in this essay. The captions alone are reproduced in *Iroha karuta*, a Winter 1974 special

volume (*bessatsu*) of the elegant magazine *Taiyō*, 102 (hereafter cited as *Iroha karuta*).

4. Tōkyō yakeato yamiichi o kiroku suru kai, *Tōkyō yamiichi kōbō shi*, 52.

5. Torigoe Shin, *Kodomo no kaeuta kessakushū* (Heibonsha, 1998), 109–11. This was by no means the only wartime song subjected to mockery before the defeat. The same fate, for example, befell the lyrics of the "Patriotic March" ("Aikoku kōshinkyoku"), a song that appeared shortly after the initiation of war with China in 1937 and enjoyed explicit government support. The tasty flavor of this particular parody is suggested by the metamorphosis of the march's opening line, where "Look, dawn comes to the Eastern Sea" (*Miyo Tōkai no sora akete*) became "Look, Tōjō's head is bald" (*Miyo Tōjō no hage atama*). Another patriotic song, in this instance dating from 1940 and celebrating the purported founding of the Yamato state 2,600 years previously, inspired several parodies. Entitled "Twenty-six-hundred Years Since the Founding" ("Kigen wa nisen roppyaku nen"), the song dwelled on mythical birds and glorious radiance and concluded with heartfelt evocation of "ah, the pounding heart of the hundred million" (*aa, ichioku no mune wa naru*). In the parody, the names of cigarette brands replaced the nouns in the original, and the song became a lament about inflation driving up the price of tobacco. The lyrics concluded with the sad observation that "ah, the hundred million has no money" (*aa, ichioku wa kane ga nai*)—or, in a slightly different rendition, "ah, the hundred million weep" (*aa, ichioku no tami ga naku*). Most shocking (and surely most intriguing for the practitioner of psychohistory to ponder) were the parodies of a 1930s children's song entitled "I Love Soldiers." The first verse of the original lyrics ran as follows: "I love soldiers / When I grow up / I'll put on medals and don a sword / Mount a horse and gallop off" (*Boku wa gunjin daisuki yo / Ima ni ōkiku nattaraba / Kunshō tsukete ken sagete / Ouma ni notte hai dōdō*). Children sang several variations of this, all apparently ending with essentially the same first three lines. Here is one such version: "I hate soldiers / When I become small / I'll be held by Mother and drink her milk / Get a coin and go buy candy" (*Boku wa gunjin daikirai / Ima ni chisaku nattaraba / Okūsan ni dakarete chichi nondā / Issen moratte ame kai ni*). In other versions, children sang about drinking Mother's milk, after which "I'll disappear into her stomach" (*Onaka no naka e kiechau yo*)—or "I'll sleep soundly on her lap" (*Ohiza de suyasuya nenne suru*). For these examples, see ibid., 183–94.

6. Asahi Shimbunsha, *Koe*, 1:253. This appeared in the January 9, 1947, issue of the *Asahi*.

7. The *kana* syllabary consists of 48 "syllables," but the symbol read as "n" is omitted from the game (since it never begins a word), giving a total of 47. However, the syllable *kyō* (from Kyoto, where the game may have originated) was commonly included in the old card games, thus accounting for the conventional total of 48 cards (doubled to 96). The appearance of the initial *kana* syllable on the picture cards made the game appropriate for teaching children the syllabary itself (and not just proverbs). The order in which the *kana* appear in the card set derives from the famous "*iroha* poem"(*iroha uta*) that dates from the late tenth century and is made up of the 47 syllables (again excluding *n*) of the syllabary. (This *iroha* order was the most common way of "alphabetizing" lists, entries, and the like until 1889, when the *a-i-u-e-o* order familiar today became conventional.) The term *karuta* itself comes from the Portuguese for "card" and entered the native vocabulary in the sixteenth century, when the Japanese first encountered and began to copy the foreigners' illustrated playing cards. The original name for the children's game introduced at the turn of the nineteenth century was *iroha-tatoekaruta*, with *tatoe* meaning "proverb." See *Iroha karuta*, 57–68, and for the observations and examples about commoner attitudes that follow here, 72–75.

8. Ibid., 6, 79.

9. Ibid., 79, 87. One of the unwholesome early flatulence "sayings" for *he* was "tightening the buttocks after passing a fart" (*he o hette shiri tsubomeru*). *Iroha karuta*, which contains many excellent full-color reproductions of card sets, includes a good one from the war years on 87.

10. *Kyōryoku shimbun*, January 1946. A nastier variation on this most famous of opening *karuta* proverbs was offered in the *Asahi gurafu* issue of the same date. Here virtually the identical classic saying (given as *inu ga* [rather than *mo*] *arukeba bō ni ataru*)—that is, "If a dog walks around, it will encounter a stick"—was accompanied by a photograph of three GIs accompanied by three young Japanese women. Readers were left to speculate on their own who was the dog and who the stick, but the sarcasm was unmistakable.

11. See Dower, *Embracing Defeat*, chap. 14 on "Censored Democracy."

12. *Kyōryoku shimbun*, January 1946. See also *Shōwa manga shi*, a special volume (*bessatsu*) of the engaging multivolume illustrated collection

Ichiokunin no Shōwa shi (Shōwa history of the hundred million) (Tokyo: Mainichi shinbunsha, 1977). This unpaginated volume devoted to Shōwa-era cartoons (up to 1977) includes the opening 23 entries of the *Kyōryoku shimbun* feature by Saji and Terao, plus the full reproduction (47 "cards") of another sequence discussed at length below: Ogawa Takeshi's "Voice of the People: New Edition Syllable Cards" (hereafter cited as Ogawa, "Voice of the People"). Many of the phrases or "captions" on these cards involved ironic twists on well-known clichés or catchphrases that are impossible to convey in English.

13. This is a good example of the subtle, clever, historically resonant (and thoroughly untranslatable) wordplays that were so often involved in these graphic jokes. *Toshiyori mo hiyaase* is very close to the mocking phrase that appeared in the Edo-period *iroha karuta* and was translated earlier in this chapter as "old people who ought to know better" (*toshiyori no hiyamizu*). *Hiyamizu* is literally "cold water," and the connotation of imprudent old people derives from the notion that they might carelessly imperil their health by drinking cold water. *Hiyaase*, "cold sweat"—the term used in the 1946 *iroha* cartoon—is a wonderfully vivid characterization of the old-guard leaders who were trembling in fear of being convicted of war crimes. At the same time, whether consciously or subconsciously, *hiyaase* is layered over *hiyamizu*. The "cold sweat" of these men in defeat is inseparable from their imprudence in leading Japan into hopeless war and miserable defeat.

14. This is not only a supremely ironic deflation of the wartime "divine wind" mystique but also another example of a subject—the wartime U.S. air raids—that subsequently rarely passed the censor's screening. This is also true of the associations given for the syllables *so* and *ya* that follow.

15. For reasons maddening to delineate, *kyō* is actually written *kefu* in the old writing style, and so this particular *iroha* association is given for the syllable *ke*. "Dreams of the capital" was an old phrase referring to Kyoto. Here, of course, the allusion is to "dreams in Tokyo." Since *kyō* also can mean "today," the clever pun has even further connotations.

16. See also note 10 above concerning the comparably disdainful treatment of fraternization in the *Asahi gurafu* issue of January 1946. This same "photo-*karuta*" feature in *Asahi gurafu* also used the syllable *e* to highlight the presence of blacks in the U.S. occupation force. In this instance, a photograph of an old Japanese man lighting the cigarette of a black GI was accompanied by the same proverb ("The ties that

bind are strange and wonderful"). Japanese commentators reasonably speculate that such taboo observations probably made it into the media at this early stage because the censors simply did not pick up on or pay attention to these clever, insider word games. See, e.g., *Iroha karuta*, 102. For the duration of the occupation, verbal or graphic treatment of black Americans was negligible, although Japanese racial responses to their presence were not negligible at all.

17. See the 1946 *iroha* cartoon entries reproduced in *Shōwa manga shi*.

18. This interesting "collaborative" *iroha* cartoon sequence appears in the January 1948 issue of *Nippon yūmoa* (Japan humor). A more common postsurrender mockery of the two-income couple had the husband being a black market operative and the wife a *"panpan* prostitute" (the "panpan" catered primarily to the foreign personnel affiliated with the occupation); see, e.g., the unillustrated *iroha* witticisms in *Manga*, January 1947, 23.

19. These last two examples, as well as those that follow in the text, have been selected from the various cartoon sets previously cited, plus a December 1948 sequence in *Shin Osaka* (New Osaka) that is reproduced in *Iroha karuta*, 103–4.

20. The emperor reference, regrettably, appeared as an *iroha* witticism without illustration (in *Manga*, January 1947). Ono Saseo drew the emperor removing a huge mask-like head capped with traditional Heian court headgear, and emerging as an ordinary man in a Western suit, as an association for *te*. "Even the emperor is a human being" (*tennō mo ningen*) was his caption, referring to the January 1, 1946, imperial rescript in which Emperor Hirohito more or less renounced his "divinity"; see *Nihon yūmoa*, January 1948.

21. A diary entry by Tokugawa Yoshihiro, dated April 24, 1968, and disclosed in the Japanese media in 1999, is the most recent revelation of the emperor's obsession with the regalia and preservation of his family line; see *Asahi Shimbun*, January 6, 1999. On Shigemitsu and the emperor's belated appreciation of the Charter Oath, see Dower, *Embracing Defeat*, 287–89, 313–15; examples of all other "uses of tradition" mentioned in these concluding paragraphs appear scattered throughout this same source.

22. I have summarized some of the literature on the legacies of Japan's so-called Fifteen-Year War in "The Useful War," an essay reprinted in John W. Dower, *Japan in War and Peace: Selected Essays* (The New Press, 1993), 9–32.

23. For postage stamps, see the popular annual catalogs issued by Nihon yūbin kitteshō kyōdō kumiai (Japan stamp dealers' association), *Nihon kitte katarogu*. The 1949–52 Cultural Figures Series is reproduced on p. 12 of the 1998 catalog. Individuals honored in 1950 were the educator Fukuzawa Yukichi, writer Natsume Sōseki, writer Tsubouchi Shōyō, Kabuki actor Ichikawa Danjūrō, and educator Niijima Jō. In 1951, stamps honored the painter Kanō Hōgai, theologian Uchimura Kanzō, writer Higuchi Ichiyō, writer Mori Ōgai, poet Masaoka Shiki, and painter Hishida Shunsō. The series concluded in 1952 with stamps commemorating the philosopher Nishi Amane, legal scholar Ume Kenjirō, astronomer Kimura Sakae, educator Nitobe Inazō, scientist Terada Torahiko, and artist and aesthetic critic Okakura Tenshin. Presurrender Japanese stamps did not, in fact, commemorate many "cultural heroes," apart from General Nogi.

INDEX